D1047626

THE READER'S GUIDE TO THE
BEST EVANGELICAL BOOKS

THE
Reader's Guide
TO THE
Best Evangelical Books

MARK LAU BRANSON

1817

Harper & Row, Publishers, San Francisco

Cambridge, Hagerstown, New York, Philadelphia
London, Mexico City, São Paulo, Sydney

THE READER'S GUIDE TO THE BEST EVANGELICAL BOOKS. Copyright © 1982 by Mark
Lau Branson. All rights reserved. Printed in the United States of America. No part
of this book may be used or reproduced in any manner whatsoever without written
permission except in the case of brief quotations embodied in critical articles and
reviews. For information address Harper & Row, Publishers, Inc., 10 East 53rd
Street, New York, NY 10022. Published simultaneously in Canada by Fitzhenry &
Whiteside, Limited, Toronto.

FIRST EDITION

Designer: Jim Mennick

Library of Congress Cataloging in Publication Data

Branson, Mark Lau.
  THE READER'S GUIDE TO THE BEST EVANGELICAL BOOKS.

  1. Theology—Bibliography. 2. Evangelicalism—Bibliography. 3. Bibliography—
Best books—Theology. 4. Bibliography—Best books—Evangelicalism. I. Title.
Z7751.B77   1982 [BR118]   016.2   81-48205
ISBN 0-06-061046-8

82 83 84 85 86 10 9 8 7 6 5 4 3 2 1

089246

I used to think that dedicating a book to one's spouse was merely a "nice touch." Now I understand the price paid by an author's marriage partner! So, to

NINA WAI HUNG LAU BRANSON

whose name appropriately means "Intelligent Rainbow" and to our parents

ROBERT AND JEAN BRANSON
SET CHAU AND CHIU HUNG LAU

in gratefulness for their love.

Contents

Acknowledgments

I have benefited from the views, reviews, comments, guidance, and expertise of many. As editor of *TSF Bulletin,* I not only have the advantage of publishing many book reviews, but many faithful associates and contributors also provided additions and suggestions, especially Clark Pinnock, Paul Mickey, Donald Dayton, Robert Hubbard, Grant Osborne, Steve Davis, Richard Mouw, David Gill, Donald Tinder, Keith Yandell, David Lowes Watson and Bernard Ramm. Inter-Varsity Christian Fellowship granted the working arrangements needed to take on such a project.

Writing retreats and accommodations were provided by David and Ruth Adeney, the Berkeley Presbyterian Missionary Homes, New College of Berkeley, Mike and Char Hayes, and Paul Thompson.

The concept and editorial guidance came from Roy M. Carlisle of Harper & Row, and Melissa Stoker kept me informed and encouraged. Carol Brown and John Young deserve special thanks for their invaluable contributions to Part One, The Christian Life.

Research, typing, and administrative help came from John Duff, Shelley Thron, Mihae Sunu, Terri Olson, Lois Hart, Sue Richardson, and Jean Gross.

Greg and Laura Ikehara-Martin, John Hobbins, and especially Mike Hayes and Tom McAlpine became partners during many phases of the work, providing affirmation, research, suggestions, and help with composition. I am thankful for such friends.

Abbreviations

The following abbreviations of publishers' names follow individual book titles in the bibliographies. Some publishers, infrequently cited, are noted in unabbreviated form.

It is, of course, impossible to keep track of titles that go out of print, or even publishing houses that cease to publish. We have tried to include books that are still obtainable. Some, however, are out-of-print; those are probably available at libraries or used-book stores.

AP	Abingdon Press
AG	Augsburg Publishing House
BBH	Baker Book House
DC	Doubleday & Company
FHR	Fleming H. Revell Company
FP	Fortress Press
GL/R	Gospel Light/Regal Books
HR	Harper & Row, Publishers
HP	Herald Press
IVP	Inter-Varsity Press
JKP	John Knox Press
McP	Macmillan Publishing Company
MP	Moody Press
OB	Orbis Books
OUP	Oxford University Press
PP	Paulist Press
TH	Tyndale House Publishers
WP	The Westminster Press
WBE	William B. Eerdmans Publishing Company
WCL	William Carey Library
WB	Word, Inc.
ZC	The Zondervan Corporation

Author's Note

Throughout the guide the reader will find lists of favorite books, selected by leaders in the church. The first five books are those named as most influential in that person's personal life; the second five are those most influential in that person's professional life. Even though that is an artificial distinction, it gives more variety to the selections. We specifically requested lists from a wide variety of leaders and made it clear that the lists do not have to include evangelical books. Our intent was growth and the broadening of horizons. Although many contributors listed the Bible and various reference tools for Bible study, those items have been omitted. The contributors are listed alphabetically.

How to Use This Guide

St. Paul encourages Timothy to join him in Rome, adding, "Bring . . . also the books, and above all the parchments."

There has been no time in the history of Christianity when books have not been supremely important for the growth and preservation of the church. There have been times when anti-intellectual strains and anti–freedom of thought movements have crippled the church and stunted the growth of its members. And there certainly have been, and still are, repressive societies that attempt to eradicate Christian literature. But the impulse to reflect on the wonder and nature of God's activity in human history is never long shackled. In North America today we see a renaissance of quality Christian books of every type written to encourage, reassure, challenge, inform, and guide the church universal. These books are also a vehicle for expressing biblical values in a culture where they are not the norm. This is especially true of that movement in the church known as evangelicalism.

This guide was compiled to bring some light to the path through the stacks and stacks of books written primarily by and for evangelicals. That is not to say that other theological and spiritual perspectives are not valuable, or even that they are not included. Although not all the authors listed in the bibliographies would identify themselves as evangelicals, bibliographic selections generally stay within the parameters of classical orthodox thought. Further elaboration on contemporary evangelicalism (and, therefore, on book selection) can be found in the opening section of Part II.

We are writing for the educated layperson, the university student, the beginning seminarian, and the pastor. Access to the most worthwhile books, and help in evaluating those resources, will provide the reader with guidelines for establishing priorities. Selections are limited to the 1950–1980 era, with a focus on more recent materials.

Readers should keep in mind that books are consciously written at varying levels, from introductory to advanced, and include all stages in between. People who want to grow, rather than just confirm what they already understand or believe, should choose some books beyond their reach. Stretching always promotes healthy growth. It may be helpful to read more difficult books with friends, discussing them together, to bridge the gap in any individual's lack of comprehension and knowledge.

It is self-evident that Christians have always maintained different emphases in belief. Again, in order to grow, reading should go beyond the borders of individual denominational, theological, or spiritual knowledge and experience. Because of these considerations we strongly urge readers to choose books in Part II as well as in Part I.

Part I is a preliminary attempt to assess books about the Christian life, many of which are generally more popular. There is no pretension toward comprehensiveness. Part II, "The Bible, the Church, and the World," is for the more serious reader, although help is provided for those venturing into new territory. Part II begins with the Bible, obviously the basis and reference point of all further study. Discussion then shifts to the church, which is first discussed historically, then as the producer of theology, and then as the contemporary agent of the Kingdom. Finally, in the broader context of the world, Christian ethics and the Christian professional life are considered.

We pray that these essays and bibliographies will be of some help to the many Christians who find the maze and quantity of books published today a bit intimidating. Each topic is prefaced by introductory comments, including an evaluation of the most significant books. Following the introductory paragraphs, a more detailed, annotated list is provided.

An asterisk following a title indicates that the book is discussed in the paragraphs just preceding the list. A dagger (†) identifies books suitable for one's initial exposure to a topic.

PART I

The Christian Life

DISCIPLESHIP

Bookstores are filled with innumerable volumes providing goals, steps, definitions, and methods for Christian discipleship. Books that offer theological depth, serious biblical reflection, or an understanding of spirituality that moves beyond human-centeredness are more rare. The books that follow fall into the latter category; they focus on the individual believer and the various dimensions of growth in Christian maturity.

Donald Kraybill's *The Upside-Down Kingdom* does not avoid all of the "unreasonable" and "unrealistic" teachings of Jesus. With clear accounts from the gospels and a grasp of our modern life, Kraybill answers many of the excuses and rationalizations that limit faithfulness in a Christian's life. Relationships to politics, economics, enemies, and society's "outsiders" are dealt with as Kraybill focuses on Jesus' temptation, his sermon in Nazareth, the responses of various hearers, and the messages of the parables. This volume is both refreshing and provocative, as the surprises of Jesus' Kingdom ought to be.

C. S. Lewis's *Mere Christianity* has become the standard by which other modern apologetics are measured. Transcending denominational lines, Lewis offers a powerful apologetic on the deity of Christ. Once that is taken care of, he goes on to describe Christian behavior in a manner so biblically sound as to be offensive to no one. This little book continues to have influence nearly twenty years after it was written.

With explanations and suggestions that are realistic (taking the struggles seriously) and encouraging (hope is central in the Kingdom), John White's *The Fight* is a helpful introduction to Christian discipleship. Chapters on Bible study, witnessing, prayer, guidance, temptation, and fellowship offer comments that provide practical steps alongside the often overwhelming call to a new way of life.

Few books have made as broad and as deep an impact as has Dietrich Bonhoeffer's *The Cost of Discipleship*. Challenging the "cheap grace" too often dispensed by churches and theologians, Bonhoeffer focuses on Jesus' call for the Christian to "come and die." The Christian life is costly because we are to follow; it is filled with grace because we are to follow Jesus. The Sermon on the Mount is central to Jesus' teaching, and Bonhoeffer provides clear exposition that brings it into modern life. Skip recent "Jesus and me and isn't it wonderful" books and read Bonhoeffer several times.

Elizabeth O'Connor's *Letters to Scattered Pilgrims* weaves together seemingly unrelated topics (reflection, journal writing, money, personal identity) into a congruent, insightful whole. O'Connor's writing penetrates the complexities of human identity (composed of intellect, emotions, and history) and offers insights into wholeness, growth, and faithfulness. Her guidance for journal writing and the ways personal journals can enter into group life will provide new options for many Christians. The issue of money, which often causes defensiveness, receives gentle, biblical attention. *Letters to Scattered Pilgrims* deserves a long life in both personal and group settings.

Also tying together the inner and outer dimensions of the Christian life is Henri Nouwen's *Reaching Out*. The reader is encouraged to "reach out" to one's own depth, to others, and to God. Loneliness is to be remolded into beneficial solitude, hostility toward the world is transformed into hospitality, and illusions about God become prayer. Nouwen is neither wordy nor irrelevant. Readers will sense that they are understood by Nouwen, and in earlier frustrations find new hope.

In *Common Roots: A Call to Evangelical Maturity*, Robert Webber offers a well-balanced overview of important topics in Christian growth. The church, worship, theology, missions, and spirituality receive biblical and practical direction. Webber's concern for evangelism includes sensitivity to cross-cultural issues, the place of Christian education, and issues in the church's relationship with society. Helpful bibliographies are included.

A different approach is taken by J. I. Packer in *Knowing God*.

His is a more doctrinal work, examining God's attributes and describing appropriate responses. The strictly Reformed viewpoint is most clear in the fourth chapter, in which Packer opposes any visual representation of Christ on the grounds of the commandment against idolatry. Although many consider his position mistaken, the rest of the book is more generally acceptable.

Two good introductions to the Christian faith are *Beginning with God,* by James Sire, and *Welcome to the Family,* by William Wells. *Beginning with God* is a short, simply written, doctrinal introduction to the faith. Sire writes clearly, and although the book could be read by a high school student, an adult would not at all feel talked down to. *Welcome to the Family* is actually three short books in one cover. Wells begins by relating the nature and significance of the Bible: its inspiration, format, interpretation, and basic contents. The second part, the longest and most valuable of the three, is an engagingly written, brief church history. The last two chapters are very short summaries of the Christian life and evangelism. Each chapter concludes with a concise annotated bibliography.

In *Caring Enough to Confront,* David Augsburger offers helpful insights into the skills of nonaggressive confrontation. Augsburger believes that confrontation is essential for healthy relationships and as a part of true caring. He offers dialogues for healthy and unhealthy confrontation, reasons why healthy confrontation is necessary, and ways to apply his theories.

Though Edith Schaeffer's *Affliction* tends to be wordy, it offers an explanation of why a God of compassion allows his children to suffer. Several theories are offered, one of which is that God, never allowing us to suffer more than we can bear, uses our afflictions to minister to others similarly afflicted. What makes this book a cut above others on the same subject is that Schaeffer relies much more on Scripture than on personal experience.

With suffering and disease in the world, does the gospel of Jesus Christ have any relevance today? In *The Timelessness of Jesus Christ,* Richard Halverson says yes. In an intelligent presentation, Halverson points out that Christ, as the great physician, was not content to deal with the symptoms when he had the power to heal the disease. This, Halverson says, makes Christ's message relevant today and always.

[3]

Augsburger, David. *Caring Enough to Confront.** GL/R, 1973.

Bonhoeffer, Dietrich. *The Cost of Discipleship.** McP, 1959.

Campolo, Anthony, Jr. *The Success Fantasy.* Victor Books, 1980. Americans, including American evangelicals, almost universally pursue money, power, and prestige; biblical teachings have been twisted, societal and family pressures add to the confusion; Campolo offers stories, humor, and thoughtful insights for Christian adults.

Dobson, James. *Emotions: Can You Trust Them?* GL/R, 1980. A helpful guide offering advice on distinguishing reality from emotionalism.

Engstrom, Ted W., and David J. Juroe. *The Work Trap.* FHR, 1979. An insightful look at the meaning of work and the problems with being a "workaholic"; helpful guides for evaluation and for changing patterns of behavior concerning the priorities of self, family, church, and work.

Friesen, Garry. *Decision Making and the Will of God.* Multnomah Press, 1980. Part of Multnomah's excellent Critical Concern Series, dealing with the will of God using the following questions: Does God have a perfect will for every Christian? May a Christian exercise choice and still be in God's will? Can you be 100 percent sure of God's individual will for your life? Unexpected and helpful answers.

Good, Phyllis, and Donald Kraybill. *Perils of Professionalism.* HP, 1982. In an age of structures that operate on the basis of power, Christians need to find ways for power to be shared so that the gifts of others are realized.

Halverson, Richard. *The Timelessness of Jesus Christ: His Relevance in Today's World.** GL/R, 1982.

Hitt, Russell T. *How Christians Grow.* OUP, 1979. Through personal stories and biblical reflection, focuses on the Christian's identity (rather than belief or behavior); includes sacraments, prayer, fellowship, suffering, hope.

Howard, Richard. *Newness of Life.* Beacon/Baler, 1975. Uses Pauline material to study who Christians are to be and what they are to do.

Hunter, A. M. *Christ and the Kingdom.* Servant, 1980. A brief expository look at Jesus' life, focusing on the Sermon on the Mount and on the parables; emphasizes God the Father, the new people centered in Christ, and the cross as normative.

Kraybill, Donald B. *The Upside-Down Kingdom.** HP, 1978.

LaHaye, Tim. *The Spirit Controlled Temperament.* TH, 1966. If any book by LaHaye must be read, this should be the one. All the others are merely re-arranged presentations.

Lewis, C. S. *Mere Christianity.** McP, 1964.

McGinnis, Alan L. *The Friendship Factor: How to Get Closer to the People You Care For.* AG, 1979. A skillful exposition of the aspects of friendship, not relying too heavily on Scripture, but valuable nonetheless.

Merton, Thomas. *Life and Holiness.* DC, 1964. A fine introduction to the spiritual life by this prolific and influential Catholic author; a good work of his with which to begin.

Minirith, Frank B., and Paul Meier. *Happiness Is a Choice.* BBH, 1977. An excellent manual on the causes and cures of depression; readable by the layperson and helpful for everyone.

Nouwen, Henri J. M. *Intimacy.* HR, 1981. Stages toward faith are discussed for several areas of a person's life—sexuality (the most helpful chapter), prayer, community, and ministry.

———. *Making All Things New.* HR, 1981. A basic introduction to the need for self-questioning, the invitation to life with Jesus, and the interrelationship between solitude and community.

———. *Reaching Out.** DC, 1975.

O'Connor, Elizabeth. *Letters to Scattered Pilgrims.** HR, 1979.

Ortiz, Juan Carlos. *Disciple.* Creation House, 1975. A powerful call to practical love in the church, with many examples from the author's experience as a pastor in Argentina.

Packer, J. I. *I Want to Be a Christian.* TH, 1977. An introduction to Christian beliefs and behavior using the Apostle's Creed, a discussion of baptism, the Lord's Prayer, and the Ten Commandments.

———. *Knowing God.** IVP, 1973.

Pippert, Rebecca M. *Out of the Saltshaker: Evangelism as a Way of Life.* IVP, 1979. A good manual on individual evangelism.

Plantinga, Theodore. *Learning to Live with Evil.* WBE, 1982.

Expected soon; should be a helpful theological and practical volume on the nature of evil and appropriate human responses.

Richards, Larry, and Paul Johnson, M.D. *Death and the Caring Community*. Multnomah Press, 1980. An unusual book, another in the Critical Concern Series. Talks of the needs of the terminally ill and the response of the caring community, then offers a training course in caring for the dying.

Schaeffer, Edith. *Affliction.** FHR, 1978.

Sire, James W. *Beginning with God.** IVP, 1981.

Smedes, Lewis B. *Love Within Limits*. WBE, 1978. A meditation on I Corinthians 13, with discussion questions at the end of each chapter.

Smith, M. Blaine. *Knowing God's Will*. IVP, 1979. A thorough and reasonable treatment of an important subject.

Smith, Tilman. *In Favor of Growing Older*. HP, 1982. A "living more with less" guide for those 55 and older; topics include money, faith, sexuality.

Stott, John R. W. *Basic Christianity*. IVP, 1958. An introduction to the Christian faith through a study of the person and work of Jesus.

————. *Understanding Christ*. ZC, 1979. Called "an inquiry into the theology of prepositions." Stott here examines words that meaningfully express the Christian's relationship with Jesus—words such as through, on, in, under, with. A helpful, basic guide.

Swindoll, Charles R. *Three Steps Forward, Two Steps Back*. Nelson, 1980. Swindoll offers encouragement from Scripture for those who feel discouraged by constant setbacks.

Tozer, A. W. *Pursuit of God*. Christian Publications, 1948. A classic on the thirst for God appropriate to the Christian life.

Webber, Robert E. *Common Roots: A Call to Evangelical Maturity.** ZC, 1978.

Wells, William P. *Welcome to the Family.** IVP, 1979.

Wenger, J. C. *Disciples of Jesus*. HP, 1952. A pamphlet explaining the basics of following Jesus from an Anabaptist-Mennonite viewpoint.

White, John. *The Fight.** IVP, 1976.

SPIRITUALITY

The specific areas of prayer, meditation, contemplation, and other spiritual disciplines have benefited recently from the bridging of old gaps. Meditation has often been dismissed as too "Eastern," and the biblical models were ignored. Mystical and contemplative resources have been relegated by Protestants to medieval Catholicism. Now we have valuable writings that make these biblical forms of spirituality more accessible to anyone.

Elizabeth O'Connor's *Search for Silence* is an introductory guide to meditation which recognizes that the journey deep within oneself, to that "home" where the Holy Spirit lives, is a difficult and usually ignored pilgrimage. The encounter with both the light side and dark side of ourselves requires faith and time. O'Connor will find many readers identifying with her comments about fear—fear of being alone, fear of abandonment, fear of failure. The "confession of our humanity" allows us to move beyond shallow façades, to admit our need for each other, and to acknowledge our inability to love. Confession does not end in powerless mediocrity, but allows us to move deeper into ourselves and thus makes the giving and receiving of love a possibility. The Sermon on the Mount is then no longer an ideal, but a sensible, realistic norm. O'Connor, in the second section, shows how the inward journey relates to our work, witness, and service in the world. Prayer and action must be linked together.

Solitude, celibacy, prayer, and contemplation are the four topics discussed in Henri Nouwen's *Clowning in Rome*. As our lives tangle with fears, anger, and fragmentation, solitude can offer the possibility of wholeness, love, and service. Celibacy is related to the need for a sanctuary, and Nouwen shows the relevance for this concept beyond the sexual connotations. The mind's constant churning with thoughts can be transformed into unceasing prayer. Finally, contemplation allows a person to "see things as they really are." Perceptive vision can then allow the minister to "make visible" God's work.

In *Thomas Merton: Contemplative Critic*, Nouwen's perceptive understanding of spirituality allows us to meet a twentieth-century Catholic monk. The first half of the book provides a survey of trends in Merton's life—such as "sarcasm to contemplation," "conquering solitude," and "unmasking the illusion." The same headings are used in the second half, where the text is made up solely of excerpts from Merton's writings. This is the place to start exploring Merton's works.

The many dimensions of biblical prayer are found in John White's *Daring to Draw Near.* Abraham's pleading for Sodom and Gomorrah, Jacob's wrestling with an angel, David's confessing and dancing, and Jesus' prayers on the cross are among those selected for commentary. Such prayers teach us about more than simply prayer itself; they teach us about God and the cosmos. The context of each prayer, the character of the one praying, and the response of God provide the reader with material that shows modern struggles to be very appropriate settings for biblical prayer.

Donald Bloesch, in *The Struggle of Prayer,* uses a typology that sets in opposition mystical and prophetic prayer. He only grudgingly accepts as legitimate a small mystical element in prophetic prayer, also termed "biblical prayer." This is a valuable Reformed contribution.

A more balanced work is *True Prayer* by the Anglican Kenneth Leech. Profusely illustrated with quotes from spiritual writers throughout the history and traditions of the church, Leech's work puts prayer in the context of the whole Christian life. Another excellent work, this from an Eastern Orthodox perspective, is *Beginning to Pray,* by Anthony Bloom. In spite of the title, it is not just for beginners; it is both a theological and practical treatise.

Richard Foster's *Celebration of Discipline* provides a valuable introduction to the interconnectedness of inward, outward, and corporate disciplines. Brief explanations, helpful suggestions, and hopeful encouragement keep the reader moving through an array of topics. Meditation, prayer, fasting, study, simplicity, solitude, submission, service, confession, worship, guidance, and celebration—the temptation is to pick and choose, but Foster writes that they are all part of a whole, and that spiritual growth comes as the strands become a fabric.

Bloesch, Donald. *The Struggle of Prayer.** HR, 1980.
Bloom, Anthony. *Beginning to Pray.** PP, 1970.
Chambers, Oswald. *My Utmost for His Highest.* Dodd, Mead,

1935. A devotional classic comprised of 366 Scripture verses with commentary by Chambers.

Colliander, Tito. *Daily Light on the Daily Path.* ZC, n.d. A year's worth of King James scriptural mosaics. Similar works are available in the Living, New International, and New American Standard Versions of the Bible.

Donders, Joseph G. *Jesus, the Stranger; Jesus, the Way; Jesus, Heaven on Earth; The Jesus Community.* OB, 1978; 1979; 1980; 1981. A Kenyan Roman Catholic professor offers sermons (narrative poems) in which Jesus becomes relevant, powerful, compassionate; useful for meditation.

Ellul, Jacques. *Prayer and Modern Man.* Seabury, 1973. "Modern Man" has no desire, sees no need, does not know how to pray. Challenges false definitions, faulty reasons for prayer, thus offering a penetrating rethinking about the what and why of prayer; highly recommended.

Foster, Richard J. *Celebration of Discipline.** HR, 1978.

_____. *Freedom of Simplicity.* HR, 1981. Inward and outward aspects of simplicity receive insights from Bible study, church history, and modern dilemmas; the freedom from self-deception and from bondage to the demands of an individual's surroundings can be obtained; appreciates the complexity of the problem and offers practical suggestions.

Hallesby, O. *Prayer.* AG, 1931. A very good general book on the theory and practice of prayer by a Norwegian Lutheran.

Kelsey, Morton T. *Adventure Inward.* AG, 1980. A helpful guide to journal writing, including practical ideas, useful comments on dreams and imagination, and a bibliography.

_____. *Encounter with God.* Bethany, 1972. Explains and describes the reality of human encounter with God.

_____. *The Other Side of Silence.* PP, 1976. An apologetic for and guide to meditation; draws on biblical and psychological resources, especially the role of imagination.

Leech, Kenneth. *True Prayer.** HR, 1980.

Lindskoog, Kathryn. *The Gift of Dreams.* HR, 1979. Dreams are seen from biblical, personal, historical, psychological, and physiological perspectives; as gifts from God, dreams can be received as guides toward self-understanding and wholeness.

[9]

Merton, Thomas. *Contemplative Prayer*. DC, 1969. An introduction from a Roman Catholic monastic perspective; well written, containing very little of the influence of oriental religions found in some of his other books.

Murray, Andrew. *With Christ in the School of Prayer*. FHR, 1953. A warm devotional treatise by a South African Reformed pastor of the last century.

Nouwen, Henri J. M. *Clowning in Rome*.* DC, 1979.

————. *Thomas Merton: Contemplative Critic*.* Fides/Claretian, 1972.

O'Connor, Elizabeth. *Our Many Selves*. HR, 1971. The fractured inner life of the believer can be healed through activities of prayer and ministry; confession of your own judgmental attitudes leads to an empathy for others; personal suffering can provide a creative source for wholeness.

————. *Search for Silence*.* WB, 1972.

Peterson, Eugene H. *A Long Obedience in the Same Direction*. IVP, 1979. The Songs of Ascents (Psalms 120–134) provide meditation material on God's fidelity and the believer's opportunity for joy.

Rinker, Rosalind. *Prayer: Conversing with God*. ZC, 1959. A personably written encouragement to prayer based on the fact that talking with God is, after all, talking with a real person.

Schmemann, Alexander. *For the Life of the World*. St. Vladimir's Press, 1973. From an Eastern Orthodox perspective; the church and the world are the settings for the Christian's "incarnational spirituality."

Thielicke, Helmut. *Being a Christian When the Chips Are Down*. FP, 1979. The Christian need not suppress fears and suffering; Christian values, forgiveness, love, and death are seen in light of God's faithfulness; special events and holidays are a source of hope.

White, John. *Daring to Draw Near*.* IVP, 1977.

Williams, Rowan. *Christian Spirituality*. JKP, 1980. Explores theology and spirituality from a historical viewpoint; looks at Paul, Augustine, Bernard, Aquinas, Luther, St. John of the Cross.

Wolff, Pierre. *May I Hate God?* PP, 1979. Anger and even hatred toward God also often produce guilt and more estrangement; this book is for those who suffer and yet desire renewed intimacy with God.

LOVE, MARRIAGE, FAMILY, AND SEXUALITY

A subject that has received a great deal of attention in Christian books, especially in the last few years, is marriage. With the surrounding culture discouraging such traditional Christian values as the importance of the family and the permanence of marriage, many have written books to help Christians to cope with these stresses.

One hopeful aspect that is becoming more common is the recognition that the customary hierarchical view of marriage needs re-examination. One of the best works from an egalitarian perspective on the nature of marriage is Patricia Gundry's *Heirs Together,* a study in biblical materials, contemporary society, and practical ideas. The biblical studies offer careful, beneficial comments about principles of interpretation. Readers who are unconvinced about the appropriateness of egalitarian marriage will be helped by an extensive discussion of relevant questions and the roots of commonly held prejudices. Gundry's book is an unusual combination—its gentle, personal, and pragmatic writing is mixed with scholarship.

Concerning sexuality, Lewis Smedes's *Sex for Christians* discusses who we are as sexual beings (in light of the creation, the fall, and redemption), and then goes on to deal with behavior. Smedes writes for the single person as well as those who are married. Especially insightful is the chapter broadening the meaning of "fidelity" from merely physical behavior to include a more thorough understanding of faithfulness—one that is loving, vulnerable, and creative.

Several evangelicals have seen fit to write "Christian sex manuals," to some derision from both within and without the church. Of these manuals, one of the most detailed and clearly written is *The Gift of Sex,* by Clifford and Joyce Penner. Although it is thorough on the mechanics of sex, it does not ignore the spiritual and emotional aspects. Included are eighteen "sexual enhancement exercises" (most of which are of a nonmuscular sort).

A concern for most couples is the regulation of conception,

and one technique gaining popularity due to the mounting evidence against the safety of chemical and mechanical contraceptives is Natural Family Planning. The method has advanced beyond the stage of "Vatican roulette," and a simple but complete guide is *No-Pill, No-Risk Birth Control,* by Nona Aguilar.

Many books have been written on child-rearing from a Christian perspective. One recent work that stands out is called *Parenting for Peace and Justice,* by Kathleen and James McGinnis. This is a guide for parents on how to raise children with values of simplicity, nonviolence, equality, and prayer. It concludes with a five-and-a-half page annotated bibliography of additional resources.

Achtemeier, Elizabeth. *The Committed Marriage.* WP, 1976. A theological and practical study; readable. Very helpful.

Aguilar, Nona. *No-Pill, No-Risk Birth Control.** Rawson, Wade, 1980.

Atkinson, David. *Homosexuals in the Christian Fellowship.* WBE, 1979. Following a very good survey of literature (church and secular), Atkinson explores biblical, psychological, social, medical, and anthropological issues; includes suggestions for the church.

————. *To Have and to Hold.* WB, 1979. Survey including biblical teachings about marriage, divorce, and the Christian community (church) as prophetic and pastoral; provides an overview of church history and suggestions for our modern era in which social reality and government regulations have presented an almost overwhelming challenge to the church. This work came from an evangelical study group in England.

Bromiley, Geoffrey W. *God and Marriage.* WBE, 1980. A valuable theological study that develops symbolic links concerning the union between persons and the union between God and his people.

Dobson, James. *Dare to Discipline.* TH, 1970. On the place of discipline in child-rearing; traditional, but not as strict as the title might suggest.

————. *Hide or Seek.* FHR, 1979. Advice on raising children with adequate self-esteem; so traditional that its utility for girls is questionable.

Gundry, Patricia. *Heirs Together.* * ZC, 1980.

LaHaye, Tim and Beverly. *Act of Marriage.* ZC, 1976. Notable primarily as the first of the contemporary Christian sex manuals.

Lovelace, Richard F. *Homosexuality and the Church.* FHR, 1978. Surveys church history, contemporary society, and recent happenings in denominational settings; provides helpful comments on biblical, theological, and ministerial issues.

McGinnis, Kathleen and James. *Parenting for Peace and Justice.* * OB, 1981.

Oraker, James R. *Almost Grown: A Guide for Parents of Teenagers.* HR, 1980. Psychological, physical, and spiritual stages of teenager growth are sources of stress; comments here help parents know what to expect and offer guidelines for healthy interaction.

Penner, Clifford and Joyce. *The Gift of Sex.* * WB, 1981.

Scanzoni, John. *Love and Negotiate: Creative Conflict in Marriage.* WB, 1979. Based on an egalitarian view of the marriage partnership; offers guidelines, models, tools, and encouragement for decision making; shows the appropriateness and hope of "mutual submission."

Shedd, Charlie W. *Letters to Karen.* AP, 1965. *Letters to Philip.* Jove, 1968. Traditional advice to his children on married life, such as husband: take charge; wife: swoon. Very breezy style.

Smedes, Lewis B. *Sex for Christians.* * WBE, 1976.

Trobisch, Walter. *I Married You.* HR, 1971. Well-written book on the nature of marriage, set in an African context.

Wheat, Ed. *Love Life for Every Married Couple.* ZC, 1980. On love in marriage—how to fall in, stay in, and rekindle. Good chapter on "how to save your marriage alone."

White, John. *Eros Defiled.* IVP, 1977. A helpful approach to the meaning of sexuality and the problems of sexual sins; sees the responsibility of Christians as agents of healing, forgiving, guiding.

White, Mel. *Lust: The Other Side of Love.* FHR, 1978. Contemporary problems of sexual fantasies, guilt, and temptation are seen in light of biblical accounts; God's values, love, and grace are helpful sources for wholeness.

Williams, Don. *The Bond That Breaks: Will Homosexuality*

Split the Church? GL/R, 1978. A responsible approach to biblical materials, pastoral concerns, and social pressures; better than the title implies.

BIOGRAPHY AND TESTIMONY

The genre of biography is one of the oldest forms of literature in the church. In the early centuries, accounts of martyrdom were common reading material, as were apocryphal stories of the apostles. Today's Christian testimonies may not be so dramatic, but they serve the same purpose of glorifying God and strengthening faith by showing how he has worked in our own time with people similar to us.

One of the best modern Christian autobiographies is *The Hiding Place,* by Corrie ten Boom. This is the enthralling story of a middle-aged watch-mender sent to a German concentration camp during World War II for her work hiding Jews. Another tale of God at work in adversity is *Joni,* by Joni Eareckson. An account of an athletic young woman's struggles dealing with her sudden quadriplegia, it is one of the better narrative answers to the problem of pain. *Born Again,* by Charles Colson, is the autobiographical conversion story of the famous Watergate figure. It is fascinating not only for the personal aspects, but also for the history of the scandal. Sheldon Vanauken's *A Severe Mercy* is a captivating love and conversion story by a friend of C. S. Lewis, eighteen of whose letters are included.

Buechner, Frederick. *The Sacred Journey.* HR, 1982. Spiritual autobiography of a Presbyterian minister and author. Beautifully written, with reflections on time, love, and God.

Colson, Charles W. *Born Again.** Chosen Books, 1976.

Day, Dorothy. *The Long Loneliness.* 1952. Reprint. HR, 1981. The remarkable autobiography of one of the founders of the Catholic Worker Movement.

Eareckson, Joni. *Joni.** ZC, 1976.

Elliot, Elisabeth. *Shadow of the Almighty.* HR, 1958. A biography of her husband, Jim, martyred missionary to the Auca Indians of Ecuador.

Magnusson, Sally. *The Flying Scotsman.* Quartet, 1981. A

rather disappointing biography of Eric Liddell, subject of the Academy Award–winning film *Chariots of Fire;* will be appreciated most for information concerning his life as a missionary to China after his Olympic victory.

Spink, Kathryn. *The Miracle of Love.* HR, 1981. The most detailed account of the work of Mother Teresa of Calcutta and the Missionaries of Charity.

ten Boom, Corrie. *The Hiding Place.** FHR, 1971.

Vanauken, Sheldon. *A Severe Mercy.** HR, 1977.

MISCELLANEOUS LITERATURE

THE INKLINGS

No guide to the best evangelical books of the last thirty years can neglect to find a place for the Inklings. This group of Oxford intellectuals met frequently to discuss various works in progress during the 1930s and '40s.

The most celebrated member was C. S. Lewis, probably the most influential Christian writer of the century. (A good measure of influence is the number of studies on an author in proportion to original works by that author. For Lewis, this is difficult to determine in absolute number; the standard bibliography, however, is 23 pages long; the ten-year-old annotated checklist of writings on Lewis is 253 pages.) His work ranges from children's fantasy to technical literary criticism, but in Christian circles, he is generally best known as the author of *Mere Christianity, The Screwtape Letters,* and *The Chronicles of Narnia. Mere Christianity* started as three slim volumes of radio talks given by Lewis in the early 1940s. They contain a highly suggestive apologetic for and description of the Christian faith on a variety of grounds, primarily philosophical. His ability to use images to bring to life aspects of the faith is one of the most appealing features of his works. *The Screwtape Letters* is ostensibly a volume of advisory correspondence from an older devil to a younger. This reverse approach of offering spiritual advice has an unusual appeal, and a number of poor imitations have been produced to excoriate their authors' pet moral and theological peeves. *The Chronicles of Narnia* are seven volumes of children's fantasy published between 1950 and 1956. They portray a fictional land called Narnia, wherein Christ, veiled in a lion's form, reigns supreme. The symbolism, though obvious, is not overdone.

Another of the Inklings (who, by the way, *did* find the symbolism of Narnia overdone) was J. R. R. Tolkien. Tolkien, a devout Roman Catholic, is best known for his works of fantasy, *The Hobbit, The Lord of the Rings,* and *The Silmarillion.* The first-named was written for children; the second, a sequel, was written more for adults. Both recount adventures in the invented world of Middle Earth. They are, however, only sidelights of Tolkien's real first love for most of his adult life, *The Silmarillion.* Unlike the first two works named, this is not fantasy, but a detailed mythology and history of Middle Earth, mostly preceding the events recorded in *The Hobbit* and *The Lord of the Rings.* While without the appeal of almost constant perils, *The Silmarillion* has the attraction of a more stately style and evocative imagery. His faith is more obvious in this book as well, and it becomes explicit in the essay "On Fairy-Stories" in *A Tolkien Reader.*

A less-known member of the Inklings was Charles Williams. The author of seven unusual novels, a number of plays, biographies, literary studies, poems, and theological works, he is somewhat more difficult to understand than Lewis or Tolkien. His novels, for example, have as main themes the quest of the Holy Grail (*War in Heaven*), doppelgängers (*Descent into Hell*), and what happens when platonic ideals get loosed into our world and start absorbing their reflections (*The Place of the Lion*). The excessively didactic character of some passages does not detract from the excitement of these "supernatural thrillers," as they have been described.

An author not technically part of the Inklings, but closely related to them in thought, is Dorothy L. Sayers. Besides her popular Lord Peter Wimsey mysteries and her translations of Dante, she wrote works of theology and apologetics. Her *Mind of the Maker* is a significant contribution to the literature of theological studies of creativity. A collection of essays, *The Whimsical Christian,* is a much more penetrating work of apologetics than the title suggests.

Carpenter, Humphrey. *The Inklings.* Houghton Mifflin, 1978. The most important biographical study of the group; particularly helpful for Williams, about whom little is in print.

Lewis, C. S. *The Chronicles of Narnia.** McP, 1950–1956.

_____. *The Great Divorce.* McP, 1946. An unusual story of a bus trip by the narrator and some inhabitants of hell to the outskirts of heaven, where heavenly occupants attempt to convince them to remain.

_____. *Mere Christianity.** McP, 1952.

_____. *Miracles.* McP, 1947. A philosophical case for their possibility, more tightly argued than most of his other books.

_____. *The Screwtape Letters.** McP, 1943.

_____. *The Space Trilogy.* McP, 1938–1946. Three science fiction novels with religious themes. *That Hideous Strength,* the third, was greatly influenced by Charles Williams.

_____. *Till We Have Faces.* Harcourt Brace Jovanovich, 1957. A retelling of the myth of Cupid and Psyche; considered by Lewis as his best book.

_____. *The Weight of Glory.* McP, 1949. A representative collection of essays. The title essay, actually a sermon, is a gem.

Sayers, Dorothy L. Lord Peter Wimsey mystery/detective novels. 13 vols. Avon.

_____. *The Mind of the Maker.** HR, 1941/1979.

_____. *The Whimsical Christian.** McP, 1978.

Tolkien, J. R. R. *The Hobbit.** Houghton Mifflin, 1938.

_____. *The Lord of the Rings.** Houghton Mifflin, 1954–1955.

_____. *The Silmarillion.** Houghton Mifflin, 1977.

_____. *A Tolkien Reader.** Ballantine, 1966.

Williams, Charles. *Descent into Hell.** WBE, 1965.

_____. *Descent of the Dove.* WBE, 1965. A history of the Holy Spirit in the church.

_____. *The Place of the Lion.** WBE, 1965.

_____. *Taliessin Through Logres.* WBE, 1974. Three long Arthurian poems by Williams with commentary by C. S. Lewis; difficult, but rewarding.

_____. *War in Heaven.** WBE, 1965.

FICTION

The problem of the relationship between Christianity and fiction is a difficult one, a part of the general question of Christianity and art. What makes a work of fiction Christian? Is it authorship or theme? There are Christians such as Walker Percy, Larry Woiwode, and John Updike who write "mainstream" fiction; without a careful reading of their work, or additional knowledge, one might well not guess their faith. On the other hand, in a recent anthology of "Christian fantasy," *Visions of Wonder*, editors Boyer and Zahorski include three non-Christian writers for their "intriguing and sympathetic perspectives on the Christian tradition" (p. 15).

The books discussed in this section are all by Christians. The focus is on works with spiritual themes, but the expression of the faith of the authors is not always obvious. Fantasy has been a favorite medium of writing for many Christians, as the works of the Inklings show. Tolkien, following Sayers, has suggested that creativity is part of the image of God, and to create an alternative world is a suitable exercise of this God-like creativity. *Visions of Wonder* includes a good selection of lesser-known fantasy stories, particularly valuable for the first reprinting of Charles Williams's only published short story.

A favorite among adults and children is Madeleine L'Engle. *A Wrinkle in Time* won the Newbery medal in children's literature, and the other volumes in her trilogy, *A Wind in the Door* and *A Swiftly Tilting Planet,* are equally exciting and imaginative. An additional series about the Austin family is adventurous and realistic. L'Engle is able to provide stories that not only entertain but reflect on issues of world view, life and death, ethics, love, power, evil, and good.

Another fantasy novel of unusual power is *The Book of the Dun Cow,* by Walter Wangerin. Like Tolkien in *The Lord of the Rings,* Wangerin sets a cosmic battle between good and evil in the hands of ordinary mortals, in this case principally a rooster. There is a trifle more humor in this than in Tolkien, and it is an altogether captivating book. A more realistic, futuristic novel is *The Last Western,* by Thomas Klise. Written in a near-journalistic, choppy style, it is the story of a multiracial baseball star who joins the "Silent Servants of the Used, Abused, and

Utterly Screwed Up" and then becomes Pope. It is, if anything, even more intriguing than this description. Another futuristic novel of an entirely opposite sort is *The Seven Last Years,* by Carol Balizet. The perspective is revealed in the acknowledgments, one of which is to "Hal Lindsey, whose book started it all." Although the book is not a paragon of literary quality, and the author's notions of the sins preceding "the End" are old-fashioned, much worse fiction has been written on the subject, and little better.

Two authors who have received wide recognition in the secular marketplace (probably wider than in the Christian) are Frederick Buechner and Flannery O'Connor. Buechner's latest novel, *Godric,* is a masterful work of historical autobiographical fiction based on a genuine saint's life. It is a well-wrought portrait of a very human holiness. Although written in a deliberately archaic style, readers who persist through even a few of the short chapters will find the going easy. Flannery O'Connor wrote two novels and a number of short stories; the novels and one volume of stories are available conveniently in *Three.* A Southern Catholic, her fiction is set in the South of the 1930s and '40s. Her characters and plots are grotesque (in one story a traveling Bible salesman steals a crippled woman's artificial leg while pretending to seduce her, or be seduced by her); her style is faultless. To complaints that the oddity of her work contradicted her faith, she replied that to the deaf one has to shout, and to the blind one must write large. She is undoubtedly one of the greatest American writers of the century.

Balizet, Carol. *The Seven Last Years.** Chosen Books, 1978.

Boyer, Robert H., and Kenneth J. Zahorski, eds. *Visions of Wonder.** Avon, 1981.

Bremkamp, Gloria Howe. *Horn of the Ram.* Christian Herald, 1982. A novel of Rahab and the battle of Jericho, exciting despite the poor literary quality.

Buechner, Frederick. *Godric.** Atheneum, 1980.

Hurnard, Hannah. *Hind's Feet on High Places.* TH, 1977. An overwritten and superspiritual allegory of sanctification, found helpful by many.

Klise, Thomas S. *The Last Western.** Argus, 1974.

Landorf, Joyce. *I Came to Love You Late.* FHR, 1977. A fairly well-written novel of Mary, brother of Lazarus.

L'Engle, Madeleine. *The Arm of the Swordfish*. Dell, 1965.

―――. *Meet the Austins*. Dell, 1981.

―――. *The Moon by Night*. Dell, 1963.

―――. *A Ring of Endless Light*. Dell, 1980.

―――. *A Swiftly Tilting Planet*.* Dell, 1978.

―――. *A Wind in the Door*.* Dell, 1973.

―――. *A Wrinkle in Time*.* Dell, 1962.

―――. *The Young Unicorns*. Dell, 1968.

Nelson, Shirley. *The Last Year of the War*. HR, 1978. An excellent, engrossing novel set at "Calvary Bible Institute" in Chicago during World War II.

O'Connor, Flannery. *Three*.* New American Library, 1980.

Wangerin, Walter. *The Book of the Dun Cow*.* HR, 1978.

CHILDREN'S BOOKS

In this age of television, when children are conditioned to turn their minds off in order to be entertained, parents would do well to provide their offspring with good books. The child who has learned to love reading has the key to a most satisfying form of recreation, as well as to true learning. Few experiences stay with us until adulthood like the memory of a good book.

Parents need not feel that they must avoid Christian books to give their children good literature, but where does one start? There are two books designed to give parents advice on building a good library—both secular and Christian—for their children. They are *How to Grow a Young Reader,* by John and Kathryn Lindskoog, and *Honey for a Child's Heart,* by Gladys Hunt. The more up-to-date *How to Grow a Young Reader* leans more toward teaching the parent how to instill a love of reading in the child, and showing how to discern the values being taught in the book. Books are used as examples throughout. On the other hand, Hunt mentions few books in the body of the text of *Honey for a Child's Heart,* leaving that to an excellent bibliography at the end. For convenience it is divided into categories, each further divided into three age divisions, a most useful tool for parents. In the body of the book Hunt explains how to select a good book, how to read to a child, how a book influences a child, and much more. Both books are a must.

Picture books are important for young children, and there are some marvelous ones to choose from. Peter Spier's *Noah's Ark,* a

Caldecott Medal winner, is especially charming. His pictures teem with energy, and parent as well as child could spend hours without seeing all there is to see.

The complete text of the book of Jonah from the New International Version of the Bible is reproduced in *Jonah*. That's not so unusual, but a clever twist is provided in the illustrations. Jonah is beautifully portrayed as a timid mouse and the citizens of Ninevah as fearsome cats. Lovely pastel colors enhance the illustrations.

For the more traditional Bible story picture-book reader, there's Ken Taylor's *Bible in Pictures for Little Eyes*. Each page has a picture with a short paragraph of text just the right length for short attention spans, followed by elementary questions for discussion.

Also available for the younger child is a series of over eighty books called *Arch Books*. Each is colorfully illustrated and tells a short Bible story in a personal way.

*Arch Books.** Concordia, 1979.

Bartholomew. *Jimmy and the White Lie*. Concordia, 1976. What happens when Jimmy tells a "little" lie—how the lie develops into a monster, and how Jimmy rids himself of the burdensome thing.

Doan, Eleanor. *A Child's Treasury of Verse*. ZC, 1977. A big collection of favorite poems, both classic and modern, arranged by subject from adventure to Christian graces, and whimsically illustrated by Nancy Munger.

Hunt, Gladys. *Honey for a Child's Heart.** ZC, 1969.

Jahsmann, Allan H., and Martin P. Simon. *Little Visits with God*. Concordia, 1957. For families who lean toward more traditional devotional material, this book has proven to be very popular.

*Jonah.** Crossway Books, 1981.

Lindskoog, John and Kathryn. *How to Grow a Young Reader.** David C. Cook, 1978.

Marxhausen, Joanne. *Three in One: Picture of God*. Concordia, 1973. Using an apple as a teaching aid, Marxhausen explains the doctrine of the Trinity to children. Parents can learn from this one too!

Peterson, Lorraine. *If God Loves Me Why Can't I Get My Locker Open?* Bethany, 1980. For older children, answers to the more difficult questions they ask about God, always related to their everyday situations.

Spier, Peter. *Noah's Ark.** DC, 1977.

Taylor, Ken. *Bible in Pictures for Little Eyes.** MP, 1956.

INSPIRATIONAL AND GIFT

This category is difficult to define. It includes books that are rarely bought for oneself, that are frequently illustrated, and that appeal more to the heart than to the intellect. This is not to say that the others in this chapter are intellectually arid, or that these are particularly mindless, but that the main purpose of these books is to uplift and encourage readers in their Christian life.

A moving and unusual book of this sort is Martin Bell's *Way of the Wolf.* Stories, poems, songs, and meditations present the gospel in new images. A more traditional work is *A Shepherd Looks at Psalm 23,* by Phillip Keller. This is a collection of devotional reflections on the twenty-third psalm by a former shepherd. *Hope for the Flowers,* by Trina Paulus, is a clever, cartoon-illustrated parable of the Christian life. The two main lessons are that it's nice to be nice, and you must be born again.

Bell, Martin. *The Way of the Wolf.** Seabury, 1970.

Brand, Paul, and Philip Yancey. *Fearfully and Wonderfully Made.* ZC, 1980. Brand, a leprosy expert and surgeon, draws comparisons between the human body and the body of Christ.

Keller, Phillip. *A Shepherd Looks at Psalm 23.** ZC, 1970.

Kiemel, Ann. *It's Incredible.* TH, 1977. A representative title of this author; written in pseudo–free verse, telling how God has worked in her life and ministry.

Paulus, Trina. *Hope for the Flowers.** PP, 1972.

Reeve, Pamela. *Parables by the Sea.* Multnomah Press, 1976. Illustrated with attractive photographs, tells how Reeve was taught theological lessons by means of a shell, a tide-pool, and the waves.

Swindoll, Charles R. *Killing Giants, Pulling Thorns.* Multnomah Press, 1978. Powerful but readable book on various problems in the Christian life, such as loneliness, depression, and pessimism; magnificent photographs.

Wilkerson, David, ed. *The Jesus Person Pocket Promise Book.* GL/R, 1972. Eight hundred promises from the Bible; a handy collection, even though the texts are not always in context.

FAVORITE BOOKS

DONALD BLOESCH

Personal

Evangelical Catechism, by the Evangelical Synod of North America
The Pilgrim's Progress, by John Bunyan
The Cost of Discipleship, by Dietrich Bonhoeffer
Our Faith, by Emil Brunner
Prayer, by Friedrich Heiler
Pensées, by Blaise Pascal

Professional

Lectures on Romans, by Martin Luther
Institutes of the Christian Religion, by John Calvin
Church Dogmatics, by Karl Barth
Agape and Eros, by Anders Nygren
Philosophical Fragments, by Søren Kierkegaard
The Confessions of Saint Augustine
Christ and Culture, by H. Richard Niebuhr

PAT BOONE

Personal

The Cross and the Switchblade, by David Wilkerson
Prayer Is Invading the Impossible, by Jack Hayford
Rees Howells: Intercessor, by Norman P. Grubb
They Speak with Other Tongues, by John Sherrill
God's Smuggler, by Brother Andrew

Professional

Profiles in Courage, by John F. Kennedy
Through Gates of Splendor, by Elisabeth Elliot
The Greatest Salesman in the World, by Og Mandino

JILL BRISCOE

Personal

Life on the Highest Plane, by Ruth Paxson
C. T. Studd, by Norman P. Grubb
The Screwtape Letters, by C. S. Lewis
Becoming a Christian, by John Stott
Studies of the Four Gospels, by Campell Morgan

JOHN COBB

Personal

The Perennial Philosophy, by Aldous Huxley
Testament of Devotion, by Thomas Kelly
The Healing Light, by Agnes Sanford
A Private and Public Faith, by William Stringfellow
The Wounded Healer, by Henri Nouwen

Professional

Process and Reality, by Alfred North Whitehead
The Nature and Destiny of Man, by Reinhold Niebuhr
Theology and the Philosophy of Science, by Wolfhart Pannen-
    berg
The Crucified God, by Jürgen Moltmann
A Theology of Liberation, by Gustavo Gutiérrez

DONALD W. DAYTON

Personal

Purity of Heart, by Søren Kierkegaard
Forty-Four Sermons, by John Wesley, and other writings
Shantung Compound, by Langdon Gilkey
The Blumhardt Reader, by Vernard Eller
Christoph Blumhardt and His Message, by R. Lejeune
Five Sermons and a Tract by Luther Lee, edited by Donald W.
    Dayton

Professional

Church Dogmatics, by Karl Barth
Institutes of the Christian Religion, by John Calvin

The Politics of Jesus, by John Howard Yoder
Nature and Purposes of the Gospels, by R. V. G. Tasker
Biblical Theology in Crisis, by Brevard Childs

DONALD DEFFNER

Personal

Mere Christianity, by C. S. Lewis
A Reason to Live, A Reason to Die, by John Powell
Life Together, by Dietrich Bonhoeffer
Plain Christianity, by J. B. Phillips
Something More, by Catherine Marshall

Professional

The Estranged God: Modern Man's Search for Belief, by Anthony Padavano
The Church's Mission to the Educated American, by Joel H. Nederhood
Mission Trends #2: Evangelization, edited by Gerald Anderson and Thomas Stransky
The Picaresque Saint, by R. W. B. Lewis
God Our Contemporary, by J. B. Phillips

JAMES DOBSON

Personal

History of the English-Speaking People, by Winston Churchill
Death of a President, by William Manchester
Mortal Lessons: Notes in the Art of Surgery, by Richard Selzer
What Really Happened to the Class of '65? by Michael Medved and David Wallechinsky

Professional

Better Late Than Early, by Raymond Moore
The Rebuilding of Psychology, by Gary Collins
Parents in Pain, by John White
The Dynamics of Development: Euthenic Pediatrics, by Dorothy Whipple
Men in Midlife Crisis, by Jim Conway
Toddlers and Parents, by T. Berry Brazelton
The Brain: The Last Frontier, by Richard Restak

PART II

The Bible, the Church, and the World

AN OVERVIEW OF EVANGELICALISM

Because the social and church environments help determine what questions evangelicals must face, the evangelical spectrum of recent decades can be better grasped through surveying those forces that helped mold it. The 1970s, for example, were marked with conferences that helped shape the identity of evangelicalism—the most notable being Evangelicals for Social Action and the Lausanne Congress on World Evangelization.

Evangelicalism's roots, though reaching into different soils, can be traced with substantial benefits. A studied look at the multifaceted evangelicalism of the 1980s brings into focus segments of the church which, on the surface, have little in common. Few would have predicted that the descendants of the fundamentalists of the early 1900s would hold company with the descendants of their theological rivals, the Pentecostals. Some who left their fundamentalist tradition for less authoritarian strains of the faith are joined by the "post-liberals," who likewise discovered the poverty of their heritage. Revivalist streams are contributors not only of their concern for an individual's "decision for God," but also for the link between spiritual and societal renewal as modeled during the various widespread awakenings. As Christianity was preached, an array of social issues came to the fore—slavery, women's suffrage, rights of factory workers, child labor, and so forth.

Those in the more "orthodox" traditions (Roman Catholic, Eastern Orthodox, Episcopalian, Lutheran) are more often finding active, internal renewal forces in their midst. The aftermath of Vatican II provided, among other results, an increased emphasis on lay Bible study. Episcopalians have benefited from the (originally Roman Catholic) Cursillo renewal movement as well as various charismatic influences. Finally, the Believer's Church traditions, including Anabaptists, Mennonites and Brethren, have brought a renewed focus on "radical discipleship" to contemporary evangelicals. No formal definition of "evangelical" would encompass all these trajectories, yet a sufficient commonality exists to allow for dialogue, cooperative ventures, respect, and, in this book, an appreciation for each other's writings.

After an era during which many conservative Christians withdrew from the mainstream of American culture, setting up their own schools, denominations, publishing houses, and magazines, the tide has changed. The groups that, perceiving themselves as outsiders, sought arenas for power and influence, now must decide how to handle that power. Pentecostals wanted to be recognized by the National Association of Evangelicals during the 1940s. Fundamentalists, still smarting from the Scopes Monkey Trial, have come back in force as the Moral Majority. Evangelical scholars are surfacing not only in the Evangelical Theological Society and at conservative institutions, but also at "mainline" schools and in the midst of professional societies like the American Academy of Religion, the Society of Biblical Literature, and the American Theological Society.

In addition to increased variety, visibility, and influence, evangelicals are well served by internal self-criticism. Through publications and conferences, opportunities for redirection are provided. "The Chicago Declaration" in 1973 brought a forceful reawakening to the sociopolitical and economic concerns of biblical faith. The Lausanne Congress on World Evangelization (1974) provided energy, direction, and international cooperation to evangelism concerns. "The Chicago Call" of 1977 fostered a much-needed appreciation for the church's deeper roots, including early creeds, sacraments, and other more "orthodox" concerns. In 1980 "An Evangelical Commitment to Simple Lifestyle" again voiced the biblical call to economic stewardship that exhibits responsible financial actions in light of the world's hungry. These conferences, and their resulting statements and commentaries, received not only the attention of news coverage at the time but have had an ongoing influence on the church and the world.

Significant prophetic writings also come through several major evangelical periodicals, most notably *Sojourners, The Other Side,* and *Radix.* Trends, critiques, challenges, and defense swirling around the evangelical church find expression in *Christian Scholars Review, Christianity Today, Eternity, The Reformed Journal, Wittenberg Door, Leadership, Pastoral Renewal, TSF Bulletin, HIS, Moody Monthly, Christian Herald,* and many other independent, denominational, or renewal magazines. Also, several recent books have chronicled and commented on the evangelical world.

George Marsden, in *Fundamentalism and American Culture,* traces the forces that interacted during the late 1800s and early 1900s to form fundamentalism. While several major ingredients—revivalism, millennialism, dispensationalism, and holiness teachings, among others—brought both divergence and commonness into the conservative church coalition, the basic characteristic of all the parties was an opposition to modernism. The rise of Darwinism along with theological liberalism provided the required targets. The strengths of differing forces varied. Sometimes Calvinism, from the Princeton setting, dominated opinions. At other times or in other locations, Pietism was the major influence. Fundamentalists' self-identity ranged from "establishment" to "outsider." Their views on the human intellect varied from trust to denigration. Yet with all of the variables, fundamentalists stood firm in opposing the culture's modernist trends in theology and in evolutionary theories, whether biological or sociological.

Allyn Russell's *Voices of American Fundamentalism* provides a needed corrective to the stereotyping of early fundamentalists as anti-intellectual, intransigent, and feisty. Russell's insightful, lively biographical sketches on influential leaders include William Jennings Bryan, J. Gresham Machen, and five others.

Donald Dayton looks at a different history in *Discovering an Evangelical Heritage.* Wesleyan and Holiness influences of the nineteenth century moved with forceful, biblically informed leadership to bring about social change. Their understanding of sin and salvation required that Christians not only respond personally to God's offer of forgiveness and call to spiritual maturity, but that God's concern for a just society become our concern. Though any achievement was by God's grace, and any "final victory" required the arrival of the millennium, significant changes were not only possible but obligatory. Biblical mandates offered no escape from this responsibility. This holistic view of the Christian message was also present in other conservative traditions, but soon became sidetracked through what David Moberg called *The Great Reversal*. This theological/sociological commentary on the early twentieth century properly laments the loss of this holism and proposes needed correctives. Those changes are being experienced today under the influence of previously mentioned conferences and periodicals, along with the preaching and teaching now heard in many churches. However, the conservative reawakening to the sociopolitical messages of the Bible has taken more than one direction. Quebedeaux and Webber offer further help on those variations (see below).

Donald Bloesch's *The Evangelical Renaissance* traces the resurgence of evangelical life as seen in renewal movements, publishing houses, and seminaries. Bloesch finds strength in the pietistic roots while also valuing the influence of Karl Barth. Finally, Bloesch voices a warning against foes, such as those who preach an "easy salvation" (which ignores the meaning of the cross), civil religion, biblical rationalism, evangelical infighting, and an emphasis on showmanship and public relations techniques. A genuine renewal will bring a rediscovery of both catholic and evangelical roots, and salvation will have both individual and social dimensions.

The chronicling of evangelical trends has also been done by Richard Quebedeaux. In *The New Charismatics* he looks at that movement's history, beliefs, variations, personalities, and priorities. *The Young Evangelicals* provides a comparison of the "establishment" evangelicals, with their fundamentalist roots, and the new generation educated in the shadow of the 1960s Civil Rights Movement and Vietnam War protests. The positive contributions of biblical criticism gain more acceptance and nonevangelical theologians are read not only for target practice but also for worthwhile ideas and formulations. Quebedeaux's chronicling continues with *The Worldly Evangelicals,* in which he notes that the emerging coalitions provided sufficient strength to foster all the temptations of upward mobility and power.

Through sociological analysis, he looks at theology, church and parachurch structures, people, and events. Quebedeaux's desire to spot new trends sometimes undercuts his ability to discern steadier, broader currents, but no one else provides such a thorough sociological survey of modern evangelicalism.

Thirteen essays are included in *The Evangelicals,* edited by David Wells and John Woodbridge. The orthodoxy of the nineteenth century, with its sociopolitical involvement, collided with German skepticism. A defensive, at times anti-intellectual civil religion was the result. However, since the 1940s there has emerged an enlightened orthodoxy that once again exhibits a social conscience. These essays also examine current beliefs, personalities, comparisons with other channels of christendom, and relationships with society (science, politics, and so forth). Writers include Gerstner, Kantzer, Holmer, Pannell, Bentley, Marsden, Moberg, and Marty. The Marty essay views evangelicals as the heirs of healthy nineteenth-century orthodoxy, and sees contemporary liberals and fundamentalists as "modern deviants."

Richard Coleman's *Issues of Theological Conflict* compares evangelical beliefs to other strands of theology. Crucial doctrines are seen not only as they are currently explained by evangelicals and liberals, but also in light of developments that helped create current differences. Coleman also looks at approaches to social involvement as indicative of beliefs. His explanations will promote understanding and opportunities for mutual influence.

Of a more polemical nature is J. I. Packer's *Fundamentalism and the Word of God.* This is a serious, scholarly defense, with a bit of a British slant. Issues of authority, Scripture, and faith and reason are seen in light of liberalism. Packer's explanations are accurate and the selected issues are central to the continuing dialogue.

In-house discussions also prove helpful for understanding evangelical beliefs. Robert Johnston's *Evangelicals at an Impasse* examines four current issues: biblical inspiration, the role of women, social ethics, and homosexuality. By looking at such specific issues, theological and cultural biases can be observed. The influences of both traditions and contemporary sociological studies become apparent in one's biblical interpretations. Johnston helps evangelicals understand themselves by providing a mirror for such reflections.

[31]

The strengths and weaknesses of evangelical theology can be highlighted through comparisons with other contemporary schools of thought, as in *Evangelicals and Liberation,* edited by Carl Armerding. An overview of liberation theology is given, with special focus on Gutiérrez. Biblical, theological, sociological, and ecclesiological issues are examined. Authors Hamilton, Knapp, Conn, and Pinnock not only offer expositions on liberation theology but also indicate lessons for North Americans.

Two other recent volumes can help orient a reader to current discussions. Stanley Gundry and Alan Johnson edited *Tensions in Contemporary Theology,* which includes papers by Ramm, Grounds, and others on the theology of hope, recent Roman Catholic theology, and the radical theologies of the 1960s. Following the thirtieth annual meeting of the Evangelical Theological Society, Kenneth Kantzer and Stanley Gundry produced *Perspectives on Evangelical Theology.* Except for Montgomery's ill-informed comments on biblical criticism, the contributions are generally insightful and often provocative. Christology, election, dispensationalism, liberation theology, and process theology are among the subjects receiving the attention of such scholars as Pinnock, Sider, Howe, and Henry.

Though poorly titled, Robert Webber's *The Moral Majority: Right or Wrong?* may provide the best positioning for contemporary evangelicals. Webber looks at the World Council of Churches (WCC) on the left and at the Moral Majority (MM) on the right, and calls for a "prophetic centrist" position. In critiquing the two extremes, Webber notes, for example, that the WCC supports revolutionary causes as a means to establishing justice, and the MM supports the Pentagon for similar reasons—both are militaristic in their pursuits of values considered appropriate to the Kingdom of God. Webber demonstrates other similarities in economic arenas. Evangelicals should be prophetic as they seek to correct institutions and individuals, and they should be "centrists" when compared with various ideologies. If Webber is heard, evangelicals, and the church as a whole, will be healthier.

All of these concerns (roots, issues, biblical interpretation, theology, ethics) receive more thorough attention in the following chapters. The principles that guided the selection of topics and books will not always be obvious; because American evangelicalism cannot be defined, books cannot be easily sorted. Although many authors cited here would not identify themselves as "evangelical," they represent positions that offer faithful, informed direction for the Christian church. None of these is so "liberal" or "modernist" as to deserve such labels of rejection. "Evangelical" can be either a self-designation or a term for that coalescing group described above. That vision or hope requires new definitions, bridges, and communication.

The insights of one author or tradition can be complemented by reading outside that viewpoint. The wealth of orthodoxy can meet the liveliness of the charismatics. The Anabaptists, despised by both Reformers and Roman Catholics, have much to teach both. Post–Vatican II Roman Catholicism brings fresh insights into spiritual and theological studies. A common concern for biblical authority, the Lordship of Jesus Christ, and the ongoing ministry of the Holy Spirit pervade all the different traditions. A concern for self-correction and an increasing commitment to a unitive evangelicalism will be necessary as the temptations of power and reductionism continue to threaten.

Several bibliographies by others provide different evaluations or more detailed listings in particular areas. In that this volume offers neither a thorough guide to commentaries nor comments on the more technical biblical studies, readers may want to consult these other guides.

John Bollier's *The Literature of Theology* is a useful research guide by a nonevangelical for advanced students and pastors. Especially noteworthy are his listings of other bibliographies and guides to periodicals. On a more popular level is Cyril Barber's *The Minister's Library*. This is written specifically to help the pastor organize and build a library. Barber's list is somewhat more extensive than mine and his evaluations, generally shorter, are from a more conservative viewpoint.

On the Old Testament, *Old Testament Books for Pastor and Teacher,* by Brevard Childs, and *Old Testament Commentary Survey,* by John Goldingay and Robert Hubbard, provide insightful guidelines on research tools and commentaries. For New Testament study, *Bibliographical Guide to New Testament Research,* by R. T. France, and *New Testament Commentary Survey,* by Anthony Thiselton and Don Carson offer worthwhile guidance. A new series of bibliographies is being edited by David Aune and Mark Lau Branson. The first in the series, David Aune's *Jesus and the Synoptic Gospels,* offers comments on over 900 books. Other volumes will cover Old Testament, intertestamental, New Testament, and second-century writings.

Armerding, Carl E., ed. *Evangelicals and Liberation.** Presbyterian and Reformed/BBH, 1977.

Barr, James. *Fundamentalism.* WP, 1978. Believes that evangelicals are more influenced by their doctrine of biblical inerrancy than by a literal approach to Scripture; Barr, as an outside critic, offers helpful insights.

Bloesch, Donald G. *The Evangelical Renaissance.** WBE, 1973.

Brown, Hubert L. *Black and Mennonite.* HP, 1976. A man with two heritages explores the roots of Anabaptism and contributions of Black theology; finds common ground on issues of suffering, oppression, community; helpful bibliography.

Coleman, Richard J. *Issues of Theological Conflict.** 2nd ed. WBE, 1980.

Dayton, Donald. *Discovering an Evangelical Heritage.**† HR, 1976.

Fackre, Gabriel. *The Religious Right and Christian Faith.* WBE, 1982. Expected soon; a theological evaluation of this religious, political, and sociological phenomenon.

Gundry, Stanley N., and Alan R. Johnson. *Tensions in Contemporary Theology.** MP, 1976.

Hearne, Virginia, ed. *Our Struggle to Serve: The Stories of Fifteen Evangelical Women.* WB, 1979. Bibliographical sketches; includes Gallagher, Finger, Mollenkott.

Inch, Morris A. *The Evangelical Challenge.* WP, 1978. An often oversimplified look at evangelicals and their "success"; explores roots, theology, strategy, self-perception.

Johnston, Robert K. *Evangelicals at an Impasse.** JKP, 1979.

Kantzer, Kenneth, and Stanley Gundry. *Perspectives on Evangelical Theology.** BBH, 1979.

Kraus, C. Norman. *Evangelicalism and Anabaptism.* HP, 1979. Evangelicalism, interpreted as postfundamentalism, is explained with its many and varied recent causes, tangents, theologies; urges mutual respect and hopes for cross-fertilization—this particular relationship will be key in coming years.

Marsden, George M. *Fundamentalism and American Culture: The Shaping of Twentieth Century Evangelicalism 1870–1925.** OUP, 1980.

Marty, Martin E. *The Public Church: Mainline—Evangelical—Catholic.* Crossroad, 1981. Just released—very helpful in discerning the shape of the American church in light of a new coalescence of peoples, relationships, similarities, and causes.

Moberg, David O. *The Great Reversal: Evangelism versus Social Concern.**† Lippincott, 1972.

Packer, J. I. *Fundamentalism and the Word of God.** WBE, 1958.

Padilla, Rene C. *The New Face of Evangelicalism.* IVP, 1976. The most insightful, provocative commentary on the Lausanne statement; Savage examines the church, Chao looks at leadership; also Henry, Stott, Escobar, Snyder, Costas and Griffiths. Deserves a continuing readership.

Quebedeaux, Richard. *By What Authority: The Rise of Personality Cults in American Christianity.* HR, 1982. A historical, sociological analysis of contemporary popular religion, the effects of media, the American search for heroes and glamour, and the resulting confusion concerning authority, accountability, and truth.

———. *The New Charismatics.** HR, 1983.

———. *The Worldly Evangelicals.** HR, 1978.

———. *The Young Evangelicals.** HR, 1974.

Rogers, Jack. *Confessions of a Conservative Evangelical.* WP, 1974. A personal, reflective narrative that follows Rogers from an "uptight" conservatism into a more holistic, evangelical position; discusses accompanying changes in values, theology, approaches to church authority, social views.

Russell, Allyn E. *Voices of American Fundamentalism.** WP, 1976.

Sider, Ronald J. *The Chicago Declaration.* Creation House, 1974. A commentary on "The Chicago Declaration" which focused attention on the economic, social, political implications of the gospel; this gathering was an impetus, being the formation of Evangelicals for Social Action.

Webber, Robert E. *The Moral Majority: Right or Wrong?**† Crossways, 1981.

Webber, Robert, and Donald Bloesch, eds. *The Orthodox Evangelicals*. Thomas Nelson, 1978. A commentary on the proceedings and outcome of the conference that issued "The Chicago Call"; seeks greater appreciation of roots and of orthodox plurality. Essays by Lovelace, Nicole, Howard, and others.

Weber, Timothy P. *Living in the Shadow of the Second Coming*. OUP, 1979. An insightful analysis of how conservative Christians have been influenced by their understanding of the Second Coming; the loss of millenarian dreams about America gave way to disillusionment and escapist theories gained dominance.

Wells, David R., and John D. Woodbridge, eds. *The Evangelicals*.* AP, 1975.

Woodbridge, John D., Mark A. Noll, and Nathan O. Hatch. *The Gospel in America*. ZC, 1979. A look at evangelicalism through topical studies; intellectual issues, the church, and relationship with the world—uneven but helpful.

Bibliographies

Aune, David. *Jesus and the Synoptic Gospels*.* Theological Students Fellowship, 1980.

Barber, Cyril J. *The Minister's Library*.* BBH, 1974. With periodic additional supplements.

Bollier, John A. *The Literature of Theology: A Guide for Students and Pastors*.* WP, 1979.

Childs, Brevard S. *Old Testament Books for Pastor and Teacher*.* WP, 1976.

Essential Books for Christian Ministry. Southwestern Baptist Theological Seminary, 1972.

France, R. T. *Bibliographical Guide to New Testament Research*.* 2d ed. JSOT Press (Eisenbrauns), 1979.

Goldingay, John, and Robert Hubbard. *Old Testament Commentary Survey*.* Rev. Theological Students Fellowship, 1981.

Grier, W. J. *The Best Books: A Guide to Christian Literature*. Banner of Truth, 1968.

Hurd, J. C., Jr. *A Bibliography of New Testament Bibliographies*. Seabury, 1966.

Metzger, B. M. *Index to Periodical Literature on Christ and the Gospels*. WBE, 1962.

Scholer, D. M. *A Basic Bibliographic Guide for New Testament Exegesis*. WBE, 1973.

Thiselton, Anthony, and Don Carson. *New Testament Commentary Survey*.* Rev. Theological Students Fellowship, 1977.

Trotti, John, ed. *Aids to a Theological Library*. Scholars Press, 1977.

THE BIBLE

INTRODUCTION

Evangelicals claim a unique relationship with the Bible: they value it as authoritative, giving it reverence beyond human reason or historical traditions. The Bible is to be understood clearly in its own context, then applied to all areas of life. At both levels of study—understanding and application—evangelicals have produced a massive amount of literature. Some books are technical treatments of scholarly "minutia," while others are oversimplified in their approaches, often forfeiting understanding in their rush toward "relevance." There are, however, many excellent evangelical resources for understanding and pursuing all dimensions of Bible study.

Whether the goal is personal study—either devotional or intellectual—or the preparation of a sermon, the basic process of study should include the following: (1) an overview of the historical setting of the writer and the intended readers; (2) accurate definitions of words and concepts, based upon an understanding of those original readers; (3) a grasp of the purpose and meaning of the passage in its own context; (4) pursuit of theological and ethical issues as they are illuminated by the text; and (5) prayerful, expectant attempts at understanding what the passage means for today's society and for the believer.

Few tasks are as exciting or worthwhile as intensive Bible study. The following sections in this chapter will provide guidance for choosing the right tools to aid in that task. Most sections will be divided into separate listings for (1) the whole Bible, (2) the Old Testament, and (3) the New Testament.

SEE ALSO What Christians Believe: Revelation and Inspiration.

GENERAL REFERENCE AND STUDY TOOLS

The most indispensable tool for Bible study is a Bible dictionary, with its detailed alphabetical listing of the people, places, objects, doctrines, events, and writings of the Bible. If, for instance, you need the location of Bethsaida, a history of the prophet Isaiah, a brief summary of the biblical references to baptism, an outline of the Acts of the Apostles, or information about the types and uses of bread, the Bible dictionary is the first place to turn.

The *New Bible Dictionary, Second Edition* has just been released. A team of scholars from England, North America, and Australia has updated articles, maps, pictures, and bibliographies and added new articles. This is a first-class production, abreast of scholarship in archeology and biblical studies. The material is also available in a beautiful, colorful, three-volume set, *The Illustrated Bible Dictionary*.

For more extensive, scholarly information on New Testament words and concepts, the *New International Dictionary of New Testament Theology* is a worthwhile resource, examining the historical and theological development of a broad range of New Testament concepts. Edited by Colin Brown, this is a translation and expansion of a German work, most usable by the more serious student. Because some concepts are placed in unexpected locations, use of the indices is necessary.

A second indispensable tool is an exhaustive Bible concordance, to assist the reader in discerning meaning and in locating related passages. The concordance should "match" one's Bible, since concordances are keyed to specific Bible translations.

A Bible encyclopedia is also useful for further research. Usually more exhaustive than a Bible dictionary, offering further elaboration on biblical issues and often continuing on into church history and contemporary concerns, an encyclopedia offers benefits for families as well as students and pastors. The *International Standard Bible Encyclopedia,* which represents the mainstream of the best in American evangelical biblical scholarship, is currently being revised under the editorship of Geoffrey Bromiley. The first two volumes (Volume 1, 1979; Volume 2, 1982) indicate that this is a successful mustering of evangelical scholarship. Four volumes are projected, to appear at intervals of one to two years. Bibliographies conclude the major articles.

Another helpful study tool is the "introduction" or "survey." Geared for the serious student, an introduction provides historical and literary information on each biblical book, then proceeds to offer comments on the message of that book. Scholarly debates about authorship, dating, geography, and audience are usually included. Although a good dictionary usually contains sufficient information for a layperson, a good introduction may provide impetus and guidance for more extensive study.

Such a volume is available from Frederic Bush, David Hubbard, and William LaSor. Titled *Old Testament Survey: The Message, Form, and Background of the Old Testament,* it is arranged according to the order of the Massoretic text (law, then prophets, then writings). Each book is set in its historical surroundings; then its major messages are explored. The writers display expertise in using contemporary critical methods to help the reader more fully understand and appreciate the role a book had in its own day and how it can be received by the modern church. If the biblical book is not written in a form that is readily outlined, these authors do not force an outline onto it. While analysis of a text may reveal its various layers of history and composition, that analysis is not allowed to interfere with a clear grasp of the book as it has finally come to be included in the Jewish and Christian scriptures. Such information about a book's formation can be important for understanding the message, but the authority of the Bible lies in its current form. Another welcome feature of this volume is its awareness of socioethical issues in the Old Testament. It is almost inconceivable that themes concerning property, human relationships, national and international justice, and inappropriate uses of violence have so often gone unnoticed by evangelicals. Old Testament books provide a wealth of writings about spiritual, emotional, societal, ethical, and international issues. Bush, Hubbard, and LaSor help uncover those riches.

Two other Old Testament introductions deserve mention. The central value of Brevard Childs's *Introduction to the Old Testament as Scripture* is his elucidation of the theological core of each biblical writer. Fully abreast of modern scholarship, Childs is a needed guide, calling Bible scholars to tend more closely to the final form in which the church has received this collection of ancient writings. Several introductory essays discuss the history of Old Testament introductions, the "Problem of the Canon," "Canon and Criticism," and "Text and Canon." Although this volume will probably be useful only to more advanced students, the church will benefit if its message is heeded.

R. K. Harrison's *Introduction to the Old Testament* has been considered the classical conservative work in this area. His outlines and expositions are helpful, and there is a wealth of archeological, historical, and literary information present. However, the value of these contributions is limited by a preoccupation with older issues, periodic polemics, and omission of concern for the form, message, and socio-ethical issues of each book.

New Testament introductions similarly vary in quality and emphases. Ralph P. Martin, in his *New Testament Foundations,* shows the capacity to work effectively with critical tools while not losing sight of the central concern of understanding the message. He is weak on ethical issues but strong on theological and more narrowly defined spiritual concerns. Volume I, on the gospels, explains background information and discusses "How the gospels came to be." Then each work is examined on its own terms and, finally, messages are related to both the early church and today's needs. Volume II, covering the rest of the New Testament, again describes the setting and purpose of each document. Martin is at his best when dealing with Paul, especially in that theological concerns are not lost. Some conservatives will object to his denial of Pauline authorship for Ephesians or of Petrine authorship for II Peter, yet Martin is cautious, and explains such conclusions carefully without denigrating the authority of Scripture.

W. G. Kümmel has also provided a commendable volume. His *Introduction to the New Testament,* though classified as conservative among German writings, is to the left of Martin. Kümmel is especially helpful in explaining the historical background of biblical books and in discerning the central messages of Scripture.

Donald Guthrie's *New Testament Introduction* is a thoroughly evangelical volume that contributes to the classical discussions about dates, authorship, historical reliability, and purpose, and then proceeds to offer comments on the content of each book.

Bibliographical notes offer guidance for further study. At times, Guthrie tends to be stodgy, and he fails to pay adequate attention to socio-ethical concerns.

Everett F. Harrison, on the other hand, handles the purpose and content of New Testament books with more sensitivity to the theological and ethical issues. This *Introduction to the New Testament* is briefer than the others, informed on scholarly issues, yet not too complex for lay readers.

Whole Bible

Bromiley, Geoffrey. *International Standard Bible Encyclopedia.** 2 vols. to date. WBE, 1979–.

Brown, Colin. *New International Dictionary of New Testament Theology.* 3 vols. ZC, 1975–78.*

Danker, F. W. *Multipurpose Tools for Bible Study.* Concordia, 1970. A very good guide to various types of reference books on the Bible.

Douglas, J. D., ed. *The New Bible Dictionary, Second Edition**† and *The Illustrated Bible Dictionary* (3 vols.). TH, 1981. Same content, the latter having color and a much higher price. The earlier *NBD* (WBE, 1962) is still very serviceable.

Eerdmans Concise Bible Encyclopedia. WBE, 1980. Very brief, introductory reference tool; good for family use or easy traveling.

Eerdmans Concise Bible Handbook. WBE, 1980. An introductory book-by-book guide; very basic.

Harris, L., G. Archer, and B. Waltke. *Theological Workbook of the Old Testament.* MP, 1981. A useful word-study book keyed to Strong's concordance for easy use; helpful for a summary of word usage, limited for theological depth.

Hughes, Gerald, and Stephen Travis. *Harper's Introduction to the Bible.* HR, 1981. A good basic study guide to the books and events of the Bible; includes history, culture, and geography.

Packer, James I., Merrill C. Tenney, and William White. *The Bible Almanac.* Thomas Nelson, 1980. An elementary guide to the people and cultures of Bible times.

Tenney, Merrill C. *The Zondervan Pictorial Bible Dictionary.*

ZC, 1963. A conservative dictionary that provides basic information on people, places, events, and topics in the Bible; little scholarly interaction.

Tenney, Merrill C., et al., eds. *Zondervan Pictorial Encyclopedia of the Bible.* 5 vols. ZC, 1975–76. A conservative, and sometimes rudimentary work; special attention to themes and doctrines, with bibliographies.

Old Testament

Archer, Gleason L. *A Survey of Old Testament Introduction.* MP, 1973. A conservative work which tends to be polemical.

Bush, Frederic William, David Allan Hubbard, and William Sanford LaSor. *Old Testament Survey: The Message, Form, and Background of the Old Testament.* * WBE, 1981.

Childs, Brevard. *Introduction to the Old Testament as Scripture.* * FP, 1979.

Harrison, R. K. *Introduction to the Old Testament.* * WBE, 1969.

Schultz, Samuel J. *The Old Testament Speaks.* 3rd ed. HR,. 1980. A college-level survey which provides a basic, non-critical survey of OT content; includes OT history and literature.

van Ruler, Arnold A. *The Christian Church and the Old Testament.* WBE, 1971. A Dutch theologian calls on the church to accept the OT as authoritative, and to study and follow its teachings; especially good in surveying OT piety and cultic practices.

New Testament

Barker, Glenn W., William L. Lane, and J. Ramsey Michaels. *The New Testament Speaks.* HR, 1969. A good evangelical college-level exposition of the purpose and message of the NT; includes helpful historical information.

Gundry, Robert H. *A Survey of the New Testament.* ZC, 1982. A very good introductory textbook; follows a book-by-book format and discusses historical and literary issues; includes excellent discussion questions.

Guthrie, Donald, *New Testament Introduction.* * Rev. IVP, 1981.

Harrison, Everett F. *Introduction to the New Testament.** 2d ed. WBE, 1971.

Hiebert, David E. *An Introduction to the New Testament.* 3 vols., Rev. MP, 1975–1977. A conservative work which provides background information and an outline for each book; in challenging modern critical studies, confuses methods with results.

Kümmel, W. G. *Introduction to the New Testament.** Rev. AP, 1975.

Martin, Ralph P. *New Testament Foundations: A Guide for Christian Students.** 2 vols. WBE, 1975, 1978.

Bible History and Archeology

The books of the Bible were influenced by the historical events at the time of their writing. In fact, many of them provide records and interpretations of political, religious, or personal occurrences. In turn, these writings often affected history. Knowing the historical background of each era simplifies grasping the meaning and significance of biblical writings. Such a historical understanding can come from thoughtful, inductive study of the passage, from other books, and from archeology.

Several volumes that spell out the history of Bible times are available. John Bright's *A History of Israel,* recently revised, gives an appreciable survey of Old Testament times up through the Maccabean revolt in the second century B.C. He discusses relevant information about cultures in the vicinity of Palestine and offers insights into the theological ramifications of ancient practices. Bright's valuable work indicates an awareness of the latest archeological discoveries and respect for biblical authority. A more popular, though equally learned, presentation is F. F. Bruce's *Israel and the Nations.* There is a rich suggestiveness, inviting careful study, in his discussion of those events, peoples, and divine activities that intertwine throughout the Old Testament.

Too often overlooked is the period between the testaments. Bruce Metzger's *An Introduction to the Apocrypha* provides historical information, a condensation of each of the apocryphal books, and a helpful commentary. He also discusses New Testament allusions to these writings and the church's varied history in dealing with them. Not only does this material provide a relevant backdrop for understanding the New Testament itself, but one can also learn about those who were actively seeking God in the turbulent times before Christ.

C. F. D. Moule's *The Birth of the New Testament,* recently updated, deals not only with history, but also with theological issues. It is not properly a New Testament introduction, because it does not provide a systematic look at each writer or segment. Rather, it is a very competent survey of the historical context surrounding the birthing of the New Testament. Form and redaction criticism are used with careful expertise as Moule helps the reader closely examine New Testament texts to discover origins and purposes. A useful bibliography is included.

F. F. Bruce's *New Testament History* provides essential information about cultures, governments, religions, and events as they correlate with the life of Jesus and the early years of the Christian church. His grasp of Roman and Jewish history, combined with an insightful knowledge of biblical writings, result in an erudite textbook.

Because archeological investigation continues, discoveries and interpretive reports are never-ending. Although most projects will not result in finds that directly relate to the Bible, any information about surrounding cultures can provide helpful information about the cities, laws, business transactions, language, and history of the entire area. Keith Schoville's *Biblical Archeology in Focus* is a textbook on the whole enterprise of archeology, both of biblical history and of history outside biblical times. He defines the tasks, describes the history, and surveys sites both within and beyond the Holy Lands. Maps, photographs, and bibliographies add to the value of his presentation. Edwin Yamauchi's *The Stones and the Scriptures,* a more popular introduction, maintains an appropriate, scholarly caution. The author interacts with contemporary biblical scholars who may have too easily dismissed the historical reliability of biblical writings. He works with both testaments to provide an informed and expectant account of current research.

The architect of modern studies in archeological history is William F. Albright, whose volumes (and those of his students) abound. William Dever recently updated Albright's *Archeology of Palestine,* a well-organized, thoroughly informed presentation of methods, excavation sites, and appropriate correlations with biblical materials.

Two magazines will be helpful to readers wishing to keep abreast of the more popular results of archeological research. *Biblical Archeology Review* and the *Biblical Archeologist* explain work underway, comment on relevant biblical passages, and provide excitement for biblical study.

One specific area of New Testament history that draws special attention is the life of Jesus. The most helpful overall survey is that by Everett F. Harrison. *A Short Life of Christ* takes the major events and teachings of Jesus and weaves them together to discern the themes that occur most often. This overview interacts with questions of historicity and offers theological and apologetic comments. Harrison's biblical and theological strengths, however, do not suffice for the needed interaction with the social, political, and economic issues that were so significant in Jesus' ministry.

I. Howard Marshall, in *I Believe in the Historical Jesus,* provides a preliminary outline on the methodology of historical study. It includes issues such as the interrelationship of history and the supernatural, the nature of the gospels, and how we can determine those facts about which we can have assured knowledge. *The Method and Message of Jesus' Teaching,* by Robert H. Stein, focuses on the content and manner of Jesus' teaching and actually provides a valuable contribution to studies on the history of Jesus. Stein explores Jesus' use of speaking forms and techniques (overstatement, metaphors, riddles, and so on), as well as the intertwining by Jesus of teaching and action—the essence of the gospel. Topical studies (such as Kingdom of God, Fatherhood of God, Ethics, Christology) provide further expansion on key issues. Readers are given both an insightful analysis of Jesus' life and a guide toward beneficial educational methodology.

Andre Trocmé's *Jesus and the Nonviolent Revolution* illuminates areas often omitted by others. The Old Testament concept of the Jubilee Year is shown to be present in Jesus' activities and teachings. After giving us a perceptive view of the history of violence and nonviolence in Jewish culture, Trocmé carries those themes into Jesus' life. He concludes that believers, because of their freedom as forgiven people, are able to care about other people and work toward justice. John H. Yoder's *Politics of Jesus* (discussed under biblical theology), parallels Trocmé's thought.

Whole Bible

Albright, William F. *The Archeology of Palestine.** Penguin, 1949.

———. *History, Archeology and Christian Humanism.* McGraw-Hill, 1964. Brilliant essays on the development of classical and modern atheism and theistic humanism; shows relevance of recent archeological discoveries bearing on the study of Christianity.

———. *New Horizons in Biblical Legend.* OUP, 1966. Brief lectures on OT and NT archeology.

Blaiklock, E. M. *The Zondervan Pictorial Bible Atlas.* ZC, 1972. Probably the best inexpensive atlas.

Finegan, Jack. *Discovering Israel.* WBE, 1981. Historical and archeological studies, photographs, timetables, and maps provide a helpful guide to Israel, whether for reasons of travel, Bible study, or for understanding current events.

LaSor, William Sanford. *Great Personalities of the Bible.* FHR, 1965. Examines over thirty Bible characters, discussing the faith, values, strengths, and weaknesses of each, as well as implications for modern readers.

Lewis, Jack P. *Archaeological Backgrounds to Bible People.* BBH, 1971. Archeological and biblical materials are used to formulate these sixty-three sketches of persons related to biblical history; an informative, nontechnical reference book.

National Geographic Society. *Everyday Life in Bible Times.* National Geographic Society, 1967. A beautiful guide to Bible lands; maps and pictures.

Pictorial Archive. *Student Map Manual: Historical Geography of the Bible Lands.* ZC, 1979. An excellent (though expensive) volume; maps, indices, references to secondary literature, and excavation reports.

Schoville, Keith. *Biblical Archeology in Focus.** BBH, 1978.

Thompson, John A. *Archeology and the Bible.* WBE, 1962. A helpful, recently updated survey of archeological materials relating to each biblical period.

Wilson, Clifford A. *Rocks, Relics, and Biblical Reliability.* ZC, 1977. A conservative, sometimes sensationalist, introductory account that appreciates the Albright school.

Wiseman, Donald J., and Edwin Yamauchi. *Archaeology and the Bible: An Introductory Study.* ZC, 1979. Introduces the method and relevance of biblical archeology; includes comments on dating methods and limitations of such research.

Yamauchi, Edwin. *The Stones and the Scriptures.**† IVP, 1972.

Old Testament and Apocrypha

Albright, W. F. *Yahweh and the Gods of Canaan: A Historical Analysis of Two Contrasting Faiths.* DC, 1968. A biblical and archeological study; very insightful.

Bright, John. *A History of Israel.** 3rd ed. WP, 1981.

Bruce, F. F. *Israel and the Nations.**† WBE, 1963.

Davis, John J., and John C. Whitcomb. *A History of Israel from Conquest to Exile.* BBH, 1980. Three earlier volumes have been combined into a conservative, somewhat noncritical survey covering portions of OT history.

Harrison, R. K. *Old Testament Times.* WBE, 1970. A conservative scholar examines the nations and cultures surrounding Israel and discusses how that backdrop aids understanding of the OT.

Kitchen, K. A. *Ancient Orient and Old Testament.* IVP, 1966. This leading evangelical archeologist compares OT accounts with what is known about other cultures in the eastern Mediterranean.

_____. *The Bible in Its World: The Bible and Archaeology Today.* IVP, 1978. Focuses on the OT, especially concerning recent discoveries at Ebla; too much interpretation too soon on this dig.

Metzger, Bruce M. *An Introduction to the Apocrypha.** OUP, 1977.

New Testament

Anderson, J. N. D. *Christianity: The Witness of History.* IVP, 1969. A lawyer provides a basic introduction to historical questions about Jesus.

Barrett, C. K., ed. *The New Testament Background: Selected Documents.* HR, 1961. A collection of writings by or about those who lived just prior to the time of the New Testament.

Bruce, F. F. *New Testament History.**† DC, 1974.

_____. *Jesus and Christian Origins Outside the New Testament.* WBE, 1974. A brilliant presentation and analysis of materials undergirding NT studies.

————. *The New Testament Documents: Are They Reliable?* Rev. WBE, 1960. Originally published in 1943; by focusing on Luke's historical writings and showing the collaboration of nonbiblical sources, offers an excellent case for the dependability of the NT.

Finegan, Jack. *The Archeology of the NT: The Life of Jesus and the Beginning of the Early Church.* Princeton University Press, 1969. An excellent, cautious account by an evangelical scholar.

Gasque, Ward, and Ralph P. Martin. *Apostolic History of the Gospel.* WBE, 1970. A collection of essays in honor of F. F. Bruce; Ellis, Ladd, and Marshall contribute to those on the Acts; Morris, Moule, and Reicke are included in the Pauline section.

Guthrie, Donald. *The Apostles.* ZC, 1975. Traces early church happenings with a focus on Acts; a nontechnical narrative of biblical history; most worthwhile as an introductory overview.

Metzger, Bruce M. *The New Testament: Its Background, Growth, and Content.* AP, 1965. Political, social, philosophical, and religious factors of Palestinian Judaism and Greco-Roman culture are covered; literary and canonicity questions are also discussed; erudite.

Moule, C. F. D. *The Birth of the New Testament.** HR, 1981.

Perkins, Pheme. *The Gnostic Dialogue: The Early Church and the Crisis of Gnosticism.* PP, 1980. An excellent, technical work on the effects of first-century Gnosticism on early Christianity.

Reicke, Bo. *The New Testament Era: The World of the Bible from 500 B.C. to A.D. 100.* FP, 1968. A brief, informative volume by a Basel professor.

Robinson, J. A. T. *Can We Trust the Bible?* WBE, 1977. A popular version of *Redating the New Testament.*

————. *Redating the New Testament.* WP, 1976. A liberal scholar provides a thorough, detailed study concluding that all NT books were written before A.D. 70; believes critics have formulated later dates to substantiate biased theologies.

Tenney, Merrill C. *New Testament Times.* WBE, 1965. A conservative scholar surveys the cultures surrounding Palestine before and during the NT era.

Yamauchi, Edwin. *The Archaeology of New Testament Cities in Asia Minor*. BBH, 1980. A survey of the archeological history of towns mentioned in the NT.

———. *Harper's World of the New Testament*. HR, 1981. A good brief, basic guide to the geography, politics, religions, and societies of the first century; beautiful photography.

History—Life of Jesus

Anderson, C. C. *Critical Quests of Jesus*. WBE, 1969. *The Historical Jesus: A Continuing Quest*. WBE, 1972. Surveys of contemporary scholarly debates, concluding that properly used historical research tools are appropriate for studying the life of Jesus; disappointingly thin at times.

Cullmann, Oscar. *Jesus and the Revolutionaries*. HR, 1970. An insightful study into Jesus' relationship with the Zealots.

France, R. T. *I Came to Set the Earth on Fire: A Portrait of Jesus*.† IVP, 1975. A helpful, brief introduction to Jesus' life.

Fuller, R. H. *The Formation of the Resurrection Narratives*. McP, 1971. A careful discussion of the NT evidence on the resurrection of Jesus from every possible angle.

Green, Michael. *Man Alive!* IVP, 1968. A historical and theological study on the resurrection; introductory, stimulating.

Guthrie, Donald. *Jesus the Messiah*. ZC, 1972. A nontechnical, somewhat reflective, and practical look at the major events and teachings of Jesus; useful for study group material.

———. *A Shorter Life of Christ*. ZC, 1970. A brief look at the first-century milieu and a summary of the gospel narratives.

Harrison, Everett F. *A Short Life of Christ*.*† WBE, 1968.

Henry, Carl F. H., ed. *Jesus of Nazareth: Savior and Lord*. WBE, 1966. Includes a number of very helpful essays on historical and theological issues.

Hoehner, Harold W. *Chronological Aspects of the Life of Christ*. ZC, 1977. Concerned with sequencing gospel events when possible.

Marshall, I. Howard. *I Believe in the Historical Jesus*.* WBE, 1977.

———. *The Work of Christ*. ZC, 1970. Summarizes the theological interpretations of each NT writer, then looks at the whole to discover unifying themes.

Stanton, G. N. *Jesus of Nazareth in New Testament Preaching.*
IVP, 1974. An informed analysis of preaching (especially
in Acts) to discern the importance early Christians placed
on the historical life of Jesus.

Stein, Robert H. *The Method and Message of Jesus' Teachings.** WP, 1978.

Trocmé, Andre. *Jesus and the Nonviolent Revolution.** HP,
1974.

Trueblood, Elton. *The Humor of Christ.* HR, 1964. An insightful look at passages which reveal Jesus' wit.

van den Loos, H. *The Miracles of Jesus.* Brill, 1965. A comprehensive listing and examination of the miracle narratives,
analyzing philosophical and historical questions; maintains
the historicity of these events.

SEE ALSO Biblical Theology: Christology and What Christians
Believe: Jesus Christ.

BIBLICAL INTERPRETATION AND STUDY

When trying to understand a friend's comments, a person
must pay close attention to what the friend is trying to say.
People generally have reasons for what they say, and misunderstanding often occurs when those reasons are missed. As the
careful listener perceives the crucial issues, appropriate questions can reveal even more relevant information.

In a similar manner, in order to understand and apply scriptural teachings, the student must ask the right questions. If a
student were to open the book of Romans and ask for an account of Jesus' life on earth, the report would be all too sketchy.
However, questions about human rebellion and God's righteousness would bring out very worthwhile material. Similarly,
if contemporary scientific questions were posed to the early
chapters of Genesis or to the creation account in Job 38, somewhat confused reports would come forth. On the other hand,
questions about the powerfulness of God's word or about God's
role for humans in his creation will reveal abundant teachings.

Inductive Bible study attempts to listen closely to the text in
order to discern what questions are needed for further understanding. In beginning studies the key questions are as simple
as: What does the text say? How does it say it? Who wrote it?
To whom was it written? Why was it written? What does it
teach concerning a faithful hearer about personal spirituality?

about one's relationship with others? about economic, political or social issues? What implications does it have for me today? More advanced students can be helped by more sophisticated methods, such as historical criticism, literary criticism, and redaction criticism.

Grant Osborne and Stephen Woodward have authored *Handbook for Bible Study*, a competent, well-organized guide to various methods of Bible study. They discuss the value and limitations of assorted inductive approaches and offer helpful "how-to's" as well as a guide to other study tools.

The classical textbook by evangelical scholar Bernard Ramm is *Protestant Biblical Interpretation*. A survey of various types of biblical literature (historical narratives, poetry, letters) is followed by guidelines on appropriate study tools for each. Although Ramm interacts with theories, principles, and methods of more advanced interpretive work, the needs of the collegian and beginning seminarian will be ably served.

Biblical criticism continues to be an arena of much debate. The word "criticism" does not mean that the Bible is being criticized, though that can happen; it is a term from literary disciplines meaning "analysis." For example, textual critics study ancient manuscripts in order to discover the earliest text of Bible books. Source criticism uncovers the oral and written sources that lie behind a book; Luke mentions his use of these resources in his opening verses. Redaction critics realize that any writer, such as Luke, was selective in collecting and explaining history. They attempt to discern what ideas, principles, or historical circumstances governed such editing (redacting). It should be noted that some conservative scholars, appropriately aware of problems stemming from modern studies, have often overreacted. Because they disagree with the results achieved, they then criticize scholarly methods. However, those results are often the product of faulty presuppositions or careless research. The scholarly methods should not be criticized for such improper application.

An introductory volume to current biblical studies has been edited by Colin Brown: *History, Criticism, and Faith*. Along with F. F. Bruce, R. T. France, and Gordon Wenham, Brown surveys various academic issues like mythology, the sources of the Pentateuch, the authenticity of Jesus' words as recorded in the gospels, and how individual faith relates to historical events.

Two recent critics of contemporary biblical analysis are Harry

R. Boer (*The Bible and Higher Criticism*) and Gerhard Maier (*The End of the Historical-Critical Method*). These provocative studies spell out the errors and difficulties they believe to be caused by prejudiced researchers. The presuppositions of the scholar sometimes have more impact on the results of study than does the Bible. These two books can help students maintain a healthy caution and balance in interpretive work.

John Bright in *The Authority of the Old Testament* provides helpful comments on the appropriate uses of the Old Testament by today's church. He surveys various methods of study and issues a clear call for Christians to regain the valuable materials of these sacred writings. George E. Ladd's *The New Testament and Criticism* is an informed, valuable guide to various methods of biblical studies. Ladd examines critical approaches (linguistic, literary, historical, form, and comparative religion studies), offers definitions and evaluations, and proposes a "critical-theological" method. This volume serves well as an introduction to critical approaches or as a means of gaining perspective for more advanced students.

For those desiring to partake of the scholarly "cutting edge" of this topic, two recent volumes are most helpful. I. Howard Marshall edited *New Testament Interpretation: Essays on Principles and Methods,* which includes noteworthy essays by F. F. Bruce (on the history of biblical criticism), Marshall (on historical criticism), Smalley (on redaction criticism), and Goldingay (on semantics). R. T. France and David Wenham edited *Gospel Perspectives: Studies of History and Tradition in the Four Gospels,* an informed collection of essays on many topics concerning the relationship of these gospels to matters of historicity. These volumes were produced by biblical scholars who participate in the activities of the Tyndale House, a British research organization composed of evangelical scholars.

Whole Bible

Boer, Harry R. *The Bible and Higher Criticism.** WBE, 1981.
    Published in 1975 under the title *Above the Battle.*
Brown, Colin, ed. *History, Criticism and Faith.**† IVP, 1976.
Brown, Raymond E. *The Critical Meaning of the Bible.* PP,
    1981. Responsible use of critical study methods helps the
    church in its constant need to be self-critical, learning, and

more biblically faithful; Brown provides a clear overview of Roman Catholic issues and hopes for renewed vigor in biblical study and appropriation.

Gasque, W. W., and W. S. LaSor. *Scripture, Tradition, and Interpretation.* WBE, 1978. A very good collection of essays in honor of Everett Harrison.

Harrison, R. K., Bruce Waltke, Donald Guthrie, and Gordon Fee. *Biblical Criticism: Historical, Literary, and Textual.* ZC, 1978. A good, basic guide by conservative scholars; more up-to-date on textual criticism than on literary criticism.

Maier, Gerhard. *The End of the Historical-Critical Method.** Concordia, 1977.

Osborne, Grant R., and Stephen E. Woodward. *Handbook for Bible Study.*†* BBH, 1979.

Ramm, Bernard. *Protestant Biblical Interpretation.** BBH, 1970.

Smart, J. D. *The Interpretation of Scripture.* WP, 1969. A very good guide, aware of contemporary issues; especially cognizant of the church's need for clear biblical understanding. Sympathetic with evangelical concerns, although Smart would not use that label for himself.

Tollers, Vincent L., and John R. Maier. *The Bible in Its Literary Milieu: Contemporary Essays.* WBE, 1979. Twenty-five essays on various types of biblical criticism and the current state of biblical scholarship; uneven in quality, with a few excellent contributions.

Tuttle, Gary. *Biblical and Near Eastern Studies: Essays in Honor of William Sanford LaSor.* WBE, 1978. Twenty-two essays in honor of William LaSor, focusing on the OT and on OT issues in the NT; some very valuable, others less so.

Virkler, Henry. *Hermeneutics: Principles and Processes of Biblical Interpretation.* BBH, 1981. A good conservative textbook written to walk a student through the interpretive process.

Wink, Walter. *The Bible in Human Transformation.* FP, 1973. Faced with liberal methods which fail to allow the Scriptures to speak to modern needs, Wink works toward a new paradigm; should receive a wide readership.

Yoder, Perry. *From Word to Life.†* HP, 1982. Modern study

methods are explained and demonstrated, providing a helpful guide to inductive methodology; students and laypersons can benefit from the "how-to's" of study and the guidelines toward application of that which is learned.

Old Testament

Bimson, John. *Redating the Exodus and Conquest.* The Almond Press, 1981. An excellent, exciting case for a fifteenth-century exodus; abreast of modern scholarship.

Bright, John. *The Authority of the Old Testament.** Reprint. BBH, 1975.

Hawthorne, Gerald F. *Current Issues in Biblical and Patristic Interpretation.* WBE, 1975. Insightful essays on contemporary scholarly issues.

Payne, J. Barton, ed. *New Perspectives on the Old Testament.* WB, 1970. An Evangelical Theological Society collection of essays which indicates cautious openness to some contemporary study methods; still confuses results with methods at times.

New Testament

Finegan, Jack. *Encountering New Testament Manuscripts.* WBE, 1974. Instills excitement about the task of textual criticism.

France, R. T., and David Wenham. *Gospel Perspectives: Studies of History and Tradition in the Four Gospels.** 2 vols. JSOT Press (Eisenbrauns), 1980.

Greenlee, J. H. *An Introduction to New Testament Textual Criticism.* WBE, 1964. A good introduction to the work of textual criticism.

Kistemaker, Simon J. *The Gospels in Current Study.* Rev. BBH, 1980. A conservative introduction to critical study of the gospels; sometimes too polemical; confuses methods with results.

Ladd, George E. *The New Testament and Criticism.** WBE, 1967.

Marshall, I. Howard, ed. *New Testament Interpretation: Essays on Principles and Methods.** WBE, 1977.

Metzger, B. M. *The Text of the New Testament: Its Transmission, Corruption, and Restoration.* OUP, 1968. The best basic guide to textual criticism by the leading scholar in this field; concerns both tasks and methods.

Morris, Leon. *Apocalyptic*. WBE, 1972. A noteworthy introduction to this literary style, its characteristics, and uses in the NT.

Palmer, H. *The Logic of Gospel Criticism*. St. Martin's, 1968. A penetrating analysis of critical methods, indicating inconsistencies and limitations; very good.

Ridderbos, Herman. *The Authority of the New Testament Scriptures*. BBH, 1963. A conservative critique of modern biblical analysis, though also appreciates such study tools when used with an eye toward the uniqueness of the Bible as more than a historical book.

Thiselton, Anthony. *The Two Horizons: New Testament Hermeneutics and Philosophical Description*. WBE, 1980. An excellent, very technical work on the relationship of philosophy to hermeneutics; examines the contributions of Heidegger, Bultmann, Gadamer, and Wittgenstein.

COMMENTARIES

The purpose of a commentary is to provide adequate historical information and an analysis of the text, so the reader can better understand the meaning and significance of a book or passage. Commentaries can be found at varying levels of thoroughness, from a brief overview to technical scrutiny based on the Hebrew and Greek texts. Although most commentators seek to be objective, most will nevertheless project their own traditions onto the results. When understood, this can actually be a strength for those using commentaries. By noting the background of the writers and consulting varying works, different nuances and insights can be found.

Single-volume commentaries provide quick, easy reference for those times when minimal background or exposition is needed. Concerning sets, the advice is "be selective." The quality will vary with each volume, though general comments on some such projects can offer limited guidance. Readers can be encouraged by the wealth of available works currently being produced.

Commentaries that cover only a particular passage, such as the Sermon on the Mount or Jesus' parables, follow the comments concerning single-volume works and sets. Finally, a cou-

ple of commentaries for each book of the Bible are listed alphabetically. At times this was a frustrating project, because those
works by evangelicals are not necessarily (although increasingly
so) the most worthwhile contributions.

In biblical studies, few doubt that older commentaries very
often have an edge on more contemporary works. Calvin and
Luther, to name two of the best examples, generally show an
ability to discern the central core of biblical writers. Spurgeon's
works certainly demonstrate the strengths of Puritan sensitivities. Such riches should not be lost to modern students.

More complete guides to commentaries are also available. On
the Old Testament, John Goldingay and Robert Hubbard have
written *Old Testament Commentary Survey* and Brevard Childs
has offered *Old Testament Books for Pastor and Teacher*. Anthony Thiselton and Don Carson authored *New Testament
Commentary Survey*. All are fairly comprehensive and include a
broad spectrum of theological positions.

Guides to Commentaries

Childs, Brevard S. *Old Testament Books for Pastor and Teacher.**
     WP, 1977.
Goldingay, John, and Robert Hubbard. *Old Testament Com-
     mentary Survey.** Rev. Theological Students Fellowship/
     IVP, 1981.
Thiselton, Anthony, and Don Carson. *New Testament Com-
     mentary Survey.** Rev. Theological Students Fellowship/
     IVP, 1977.

One-Volume Commentaries

Guthrie, Donald, ed. *The New Bible Commentary: Revised.*†
     WBE, 1970. In addition to helpful commentaries on each
     book, offers a number of valuable articles on issues relating
     to Bible research; edited in England, includes American
     writers.
Howley, G. *The New Layman's Bible Commentary in One
     Volume.*† ZC, 1979. The most recent production by British
     editors, usually on par with *The New Bible Commentary;*
     aimed more toward lay readership.
McTavis, John, and Harold Wells, eds. *Karl Barth: Preaching
     Through the Christian Year.* WBE, 1978. An invaluable

collection of the exegetical footnotes from Barth's *Dogmatics;* cross-referencing with the index volume of the *Dogmatics* is needed for finding specific passages.

Commentary Sets

The Bible Speaks Today.† John R. W. Stott, ed. IVP. A helpful, fairly popular series developed for laypeople. Offers comments on each passage and suggests the relevance of the message for contemporary hearers.

The Broadman Bible Commentary. C. J. Allen, ed. 7 vols. Broadman. A moderately conservative series from Southern Baptist scholars.

The Expositor's Bible Commentary on NIV. Frank Gaebelein, ed. ZC. Though commendable for attempting to directly serve the preacher, this series is disappointingly shallow so far. Harris and Longenecker are exceptions, and we anticipate others.

Good News Bible Commentary.† Carl Armerding and W. Ward Gasque, eds. HR. A new series, scheduled to begin in 1983, written for laypeople and based on the Good News Version; early writers include Bruce, Hagner, and Palmer.

Harper New Testament Commentaries. Henry Chadwick, ed. HR. Being selectively reprinted by Baker as *Thornapple Commentaries.* Vary theologically, the few by evangelicals being noteworthy; verse-by-verse thoroughness, aimed toward more advanced readers.

The New Century Bible. Ronald Clements and Matthew Black, eds. Oliphants. A conservatively critical series currently being reprinted by WBE (with minor updating) in paperback; mainly exegetical with little theological help, often stodgy.

New International Commentaries. R. K. Harrison and F. F. Bruce, eds. WBE. Often the most helpful of evangelical contributions. Quality varies depending on how thoroughly an author deals with background, exegesis and theology; language abilities would be helpful for the reader at times.

Tyndale Commentaries. D. J. Wiseman and R. V. G. Tasker, eds. OT by IVP, NT by WBE. Though appearing to be shorter than comparable volumes in the New International series, size of type and fewer lines given to biblical text make them almost equal in quantity. These are often strong on exegesis, a benefit of much British work, but theological and ethical reflections are more sketchy; accessible to laypersons.

The Wesleyan Bible Commentary. Charles W. Carter, Ralph Earle, and W. Ralph Thompson, eds. 6 vols. WBE. Rooted in the Wesleyan-Holiness tradition, these volumes offer conservative approaches to biblical study; often noncritical in outlook. Perhaps the re-awakening and fresh perspectives in the younger generation of Wesleyan scholars will bring forth new offerings.

The Word Bible Commentaries. David Hubbard, Glenn Barker, John Watts, and Ralph Martin, eds. 52 vols. WB. Aimed toward the more advanced student or pastor, this series works directly with the Hebrew and Greek text. In addition to offering a fresh translation with text-critical and philological notes, each pericope receives careful interpretation through the use of appropriate critical methodology. Contributors are all among leading evangelical scholars in the U.S. and elsewhere.

Commentaries on Selected Passages

Parables

Bailey, Kenneth E. *Poet and Peasant*. WBE, 1976. *Through Peasant Eyes: More Lucan Parables*. WBE, 1980. The literary and historical analysis of Jesus' parables are provided with valuable insights from Bailey's unique research and lengthy residence in the Middle East. By discussing these stories with Lebanese peasants, Bailey gains new understanding. Exciting and provocative interpretations result.

Jeremias, Joachim. *Rediscovering the Parables*. Scribners, 1966. A helpful model of redactional work, including sufficient historical and literary comments.

Kistemaker, Simon. *The Parables of Jesus*. BBH, 1980. A conservative Reformed scholar discusses the literary and historical milieu of Jesus' teaching and offers expositions of several parables.

Perkins, Pheme. *Hearing the Parables of Jesus*. PP, 1981. Perkins explains the what and why of parables, giving direction on reading these passages. Here helpful expositions also include ethical implications, too often overlooked by others.

Stein, Robert H. *An Introduction to the Parables of Jesus.* WP, 1981. Following explanations on the purpose, setting, and interpretation, Stein offers commentary on over fifteen parables; very helpful for laypersons, students, pastors.

Thielicke, Helmut. *The Waiting Father.*† Reprint. HR, 1959. An eminent German scholar-pastor preaches on several of Jesus' parables. Sound interpretive work and relevant links with today's world highlight these expositions. Several parables omitted here are exposited in *Christ and the Meaning of Life* (BBH, 1975).

Sermon on the Mount

Driver, John. *Kingdom Citizens.*† HP, 1980. A much-needed exposition on the Sermon on the Mount, offering competent exegesis and a call to discipleship; these passages are not seen as a utopian dream but as the description of a way of peace and justice lived out by Jesus and sought by the New Testament church.

Guelich, Robert A. *The Sermon on the Mount: A Foundation for Understanding.* WB, 1982. A comprehensive, scholarly volume that ably sets the sermon within the context of Matthew's Gospel, pursues questions regarding Jesus and Old Testament Law, and provides careful exegesis, analysis, and commentary; valuable for advanced students and pastors.

Thielicke, Helmut. *Life Can Begin Again.*† FP, 1963. The penetrating German pastor-theologian preaches on the Sermon on the Mount.

Others

Jeremias, Joachim. *The Prayers of Jesus.* FP, 1978. A brief yet valuable redactional work on selected passages from the gospels.

Thielicke, Helmut. *Between Heaven and Earth.*† HR, 1965. The temptation of Jesus receives attention in this series of sermons; a helpful grasp of the gospel passages is followed by illuminating comments on present-day parallels.

Abbreviations

In the book-by-book listing of the Bible that follows, these abbreviations are used, to avoid repetition of sometimes rather lengthy commentary titles. More detailed information on some of the commentaries themselves can be found in the bibliographic lists earlier in this chapter.

AB	*Anchor Bible,* DC
BST	*The Bible Speaks Today,* IVP†
CBC	*Cambridge Bible Commentary,* Cambridge University Press
CGTC	*Cambridge Greek Testament Commentary,* Cambridge University Press
EBC	*Expositor's Bible Commentary,* ZC
HNTC	*Harper's New Testament Commentaries,* HR
IB	*The Interpreter's Bible,* AP
ICC	*The International Critical Commentary,* T&T Clark
NBC	*The New Bible Commentary: Revised,* WBE
NC	*New Century Bible,* Attic Press, Rep., WBE, in process
NICNT	*New International Commentary on the New Testament,* WBE
NICOT	*New International Commentary on the Old Testament,* WBE
NIGTC	*New International Greek Testament Commentary,* WBE
NLBC	*The New Layman's Bible Commentary,* ZC
OTL	*Old Testament Library,* WP
TB	*Torch Bible Commentary,* SCM/McP
TNTC	*Tyndale New Testament Commentaries,* WBE
TOTC	*Tyndale Old Testament Commentaries,* IVP
WBC	*The Wesleyan Bible Commentary,* BBH

Old Testament Commentaries
Genesis

Kidner, Derek. *TOTC*. 1967. More thorough than it appears; emphasis on exegesis.

Thielicke, Helmut. *How the World Began*. FP, 1964. A helpful theological exposition on chapters 1–11.

von Rad, Gerhard. *OTL*. 1966. Though certain critical conclusions lead to a loss of the literary whole, the exegetical and theological dimensions provide a valuable resource.

Exodus

Childs, Brevard S. *OTL*. 1974. An exceptional theological commentary with textual, compositional, and historical considerations; also shows the relevance of Exodus to the rest of the OT and to the NT.

Cole, R. Alan. *TOTC*. 1973. A brief, conservative work; emphasis on exegesis.

Leviticus

Harrison, R. K. *TOTC*. 1980. Historical and exegetical value.

Wenham, Gordon. *NICOT*. 1979. Very helpful, with both exegesis and theological dimensions.

Numbers

Wenham, Gordon. *TOTC*. 1981. Competent historical and exegetical work, followed by appropriate comments on the relevance of this book for today.

Deuteronomy

Craigie, Peter C. *NICOT*. 1976. Emphasis on cultural background and theological meaning.

Thompson, J. A. *TOTC*. 1974. Historical and exegetical value and a discussion of major themes as they relate to modern times.

Wright, G. E. *IB*. 1956. Cautiously critical, rich with theological insights.

Joshua

Bright, John. *IB*. 1956. Reviews liberal critical positions and offers a helpful, brief commentary.

Woudstra, Marten H. *NICOT.* 1981. Offers historical, exegetical, and theological insights.

Judges

Bruce, F. F. *NBC.* 1970. A brief section with exegetical and theological value.

Cundall, Arthur E. *TOTC.* 1968. Historical and exegetical analysis.

Hercus, John. *God Is God.* Hodder, 1971. Thematic development, especially valuable as an introduction to the messages from the lives of the judges.

Ruth

Baldwin, Joyce G. *NBC.* 1970. Though brief, offers valuable insights.

Campbell, Edward F. *AB.* Thorough exegesis, rich background material, theological emphasis.

Knight, George A. F. *TB.* Rev. 1956. Shorter and somewhat more popular; thought-provoking on meaning/theology.

Morris, Leon. *TOTC.* 1968. Historical and exegetical emphasis.

Samuel

Hercus, John. *Pages from God's Casebook.* IVP, 1967. *David.* IVP, 1967. Popular expositions on Saul's and David's lives.

Herzberg, Hans W. *OTL.* 1965. Historical insights developed with attention toward themes for preaching, by a moderately conservative German scholar.

Payne, D. F. *NBC.* 1970. Exegetical comments and several relevant articles included as appendices.

Kings

Ellul, Jacques. *The Politics of God and the Politics of Man.* WBE, 1972. Stimulating theological analysis of selected chapters.

LaSor, William. *NBC.* 1970. Cultural and historical information with occasional theological insights.

Chronicles, Ezra, Nehemiah

Ackroyd, Peter R. *TB.* 2 vols., 1973. Helpful exegetically and theologically on the Chronicles; not as valuable on Ezra and Nehemiah.

Coggins, R. J. *CBC.* 1976. All four books receive theological interpretations.

Kidner, Derek. *TOTC*. 1979. Covers Ezra and Nehemiah only. Though not as insightful as his work on Genesis, still helpful with historical and exegetical comments.

Esther

Baldwin, Joyce G. *NBC*. 1970. Though brief, helpful with history and exegesis.

Knight, George A. F. *TB*. 1955. Includes Song of Songs and Lamentations. Moderately conservative, theologically insightful.

Job

Andersen, Francis I. *TOTC*. 1976. Exegetically helpful, alert to theological and spiritual issues.

Gordis, Robert. *Koheleth*. Ktav, 1978. An informative, insightful work by a conservative Jewish scholar.

Psalms

Kidner, Derek. *TOTC*. 2 vols., 1973. Exegetically helpful with illuminating spiritual insights.

Weiser, Artur. *OTL*. 1962. Uses form critical methods appropriately to discern theological messages.

Proverbs

Kidner, Derek. *TOTC*. 1964. Valuable for exegesis and for insightful topical studies arising from the text. Excellent introduction.

von Rad, Gerhard. *Wisdom in Israel*. AP, 1972. Though not necessarily evangelical, offers an insightful theological guide to wisdom literature.

Ecclesiastes

Gordis, Robert. *Koheleth: A Man and His World*. Reprint. Schocken, 1968. A conservative Jewish work with spiritual sensitivity.

Kidner, Derek. *BST*. 1976. A fresh, relevant exposition.

Song of Songs

Glickman, S. Craig. *Song for Lovers*. IVP, 1977. Helpful interpretive work, recognizing this writing as a sensual, human love story, but strains to maintain a male hierarchy bias.

Knight, George A. F. *TB*. 1955. With Esther and Lamentations. Though brief, beneficial for theological reflection.

Isaiah

Jones, D. R. *TB,* chapters 56–66. 1964. With Joel. Capable for exegesis and for comments on Christian appropriations.

Mauchline, John. *TB,* chapters 1–39. 1962. Exegetically helpful, moderately conservative.

Smart, James D. *History and Theology in Second Isaiah.* Chapters 35 and 40–66. WP, 1965. Rich theologically.

Westermann, Claus. *OTL,* chapters 40–66. Sensitive, close reading of the text with appropriate form-critical comments.

Young, E. J. *Isaiah.* 3 vols. WBE, 1965–72. Exegetically valuable, often noncritical and polemical.

Jeremiah

Bright, John. *AB*. 1965. Exegetically, historically, and theologically insightful; includes a lively new translation.

Thompson, John A. *NICOT.* 1980. Historical dimensions open the text for meaningful exposition.

Lamentations

Harrison, R. K. *TOTC*. 1973. With Jeremiah. Historically helpful.

Hillers, Delbert R. *AB*. 1973. Exegetically and theologically valuable, moderately conservative.

Ezekiel

Eichrodt, Walther. *OTL*. 1970. Theologically and exegetically helpful; textual rearrangement not always convincing.

Taylor, John B. *TOTC*. 1969. Valuable for historical background.

Daniel

Baldwin, Joyce G. *TOTC*. 1978. Helpful for history and exegesis.

Wallace, Ronald S. *BST*. 1979. Valuable exposition.

Walvoord, John. *Daniel: The Key to Prophetic Revelation.* MP, 1969. Thorough and informed dispensational interpretation.

Young, Edward J. *NICOT*. 1949. Erudite, though at times stodgy.

Hosea

Andersen, Francis I., and David N. Freedman. *AB*. 1980. Extensive work on historical and linguistic issues, theologically helpful.

Mayes, James L. *OTL*. 1969. Theologically insightful, form-critical work that is moderately conservative.

Joel, Obadiah, Jonah, Micah

Allen, Leslie C. *NICOT*. 1976. Helpful with background on all four; some theological value.

Ellul, Jacques. *The Judgment of Jonah*. WBE, 1971. Exposition on the theological core for modern society.

Fretheim, Terence. *The Message of Jonah: A Theological Commentary*. AG, 1977. Valuable exposition; theology with applications to life.

Mayes, James L. *OTL*. 1976. Valuable exegetically and theologically, moderately conservative.

Watts, John D. W. *Obadiah: A Critical, Exegetical Commentary*. WBE, 1969. Valuable for exegesis and theology.

Amos

Mayes, James L. *OTL*. 1969. Exegetically helpful, moderately conservative.

Motyer, J. A. *BST*. 1975. Exposition with exegetical insights.

Nahum, Habakkuk, Zephaniah

Watts, John D. W. *CBC*. 1975. Also includes Joel, Obadiah, Jonah. Historical setting developed with valuable comments on exegesis.

Haggai, Zechariah, Malachi

Baldwin, Joyce G. *TOTC*. 1972. Valuable for historical analysis and for exegesis.

New Testament Commentaries
Matthew

Gundry, Robert H. *The Gospel According to Matthew*. WBE, 1981. Provocative comments on literary and theological aspects; highlights Jesus' relationship with the law and Christian discipleship; not thoroughly up-to-date on other literature, yet a most helpful pathfinding volume of evangelical scholarship.

Hill, David. *NC*. 1972. Offers good summaries of other important studies but does not push much further; readable and helpful as a primer.

Schweizer, Eduard. *JKP*. 1975. Although overstating the Hellenistic influence, ably provides a scholarly theological work that interacts thoroughly (perhaps *too* thoroughly) with the companion volume on Mark.

Mark

Cranfield, C. E. B. *CGTC*. 1959. Based on the Greek text; sometimes defensive of conservative positions as over against form criticism, yet not overly polemic; academic yet practical.

Lane, William. *NICNT*. 1973. Valuable for historical information, with occasional theological insights.

Luke

Cassidy, Richard. *Jesus, Politics and Society.* OB, 1979. Insightful, faithful guide to Jesus' life and era; fills in areas usually omitted by others.

Ellis, E. Earle. *NC*. 2d ed., 1980. Mainly exegetical; discerns elements of theological message.

Fitzmyer, Joseph A., S.J. *AB*. 1982. Volume I on chapters 1–8 is a valuable, moderately evangelical work that provides deep exegetical analysis and helpful structural comments and discerns the theological continuity of Luke; Volume II expected soon.

Marshall, I. Howard. *NIGTC*. 1978. Exhaustive exegesis on the Greek text, yet does not discover theological threads which lead to an overall understanding of the message.

John

Barrett, C. K. *The Gospel According to St. John.* 2nd ed. Allenson, 1978. Helpful exegetically on the Greek text; moderately conservative.

Brown, Raymond E. *AB*. 2 vols., 1971. Historical and theological dimensions developed; valuable work by a Roman Catholic biblical scholar.

Morris, Leon. *NICNT.* 1970. In addition to a fairly thorough discussion of authorship and date, offers adequate exegesis and comments on the book's relevance.

Acts

Bruce, F. F. *NICNT.* 1954. An exciting historical text on the church's development.

Longenecker, Richard. *EBC.* 1980. Updates Bruce; some historical and theological value.

Romans

Barth, Karl. *The Epistle to the Romans.* OUP, 1968. This volume was the focus of Barth's break from liberalism; rich theologically.

Cranfield, C. E. B. *ICC.* 1975–79. A model of lucidity and depth; first in the new series of the *ICC.*

Käsemann, Ernst. WBE, 1980. Theologically helpful, occasionally sidetracked by German Lutheran issues; profitable interaction with contemporary scholarship.

I Corinthians

Barrett, C. K. *HNTC.* Rev., 1971. Exegetically helpful with occasional theological insights and sensitivity to church concerns.

Bruce, F. F. *NC.* 1980. Includes II Cor. Fairly sparse, helpful historically.

II Corinthians

Barrett, C. K. *HNTC.* 1974. Mainly exegetical, occasional theological value and comments on church issues.

Harris, M. J. *EBC.* 1974. Brief, with a few nuggets; his contribution to the *NIGTC* series can be anticipated.

Hughes, Philip. *NC.* 1962. Valuable in discussing the history of the times and the function of the book throughout church history.

Galatians

Bruce, F. F. *NIGTC.* 1982. Drawing on his vast knowledge of Pauline thought and New Testament history, Bruce provides a long-needed, thorough study on Galatians.

Burton, E. de W. *ICC*. 1921. Though older, this remains a most thorough, detailed work, of exegetical and theological value; contains some strange comments on christology.

Guthrie, Donald. *NC*. 1969. Some exegetical and historical value; weak on theology.

Ephesians

Barth, Marcus. *AB*. 2 vols., 1974. Unsurpassed in historical and theological value, though some believe his theology biases his textual interpretation.

Robinson, J. Armitage. *St. Paul's Epistle to the Ephesians*. 1922. Reprint. Kregel, 1979. Helpful, with history, exegesis, and theology.

Philippians

Barth, Karl. SCM, 1962. Valuable as a theological exposition.

Beare, F. W. *HNTC*. 1962. A concise, theologically aware work.

Martin, Ralph. *NC*. 1980. Historical and exegetical emphasis with helpful interaction with contemporary scholarship.

Colossians, Philemon

Martin, Ralph. *NC*. 1974. Valuable for background, exegesis, and theology.

Moule, C. F. D. *CGTC*. 1957. Thoughtful theological comments based on helpful exegesis.

Thessalonians

Best, Ernest. *HNTC*. 1972. A moderately conservative volume with beneficial exegesis and notes.

Morris, Leon. *NICNT*. 1959. Less thorough, although still valuable in all areas.

Pastoral Epistles

Guthrie, Donald. *TNTC*. 1957. Helpful with exegesis.

Kelly, J. N. D. *HNTC*. 1963. Reprint. BBH, 1981. A model work for overall interpretative presentation; also interacts with radical critics.

Hebrews

Barclay, William. *Daily Study Bible*. WP, 1976. Some exegetical value with beneficial comments on the practical message.

Bruce, F. F. *NICNT.* 1964. One of the best in this series; offers clear exegesis and exposition.

Hughes, P. E. *The Epistle to the Hebrews.* WBE, 1977. Insightful on the role of this letter throughout church history; helpful historical comments on the text.

Montefiore, Hugh. *HNTC.* 1964. Though brief, helpful with exegesis, history, and theology.

James

Adamson, James. *NICNT.* 1976. Insightful comments on the message based on alertness to context and theological issues.

Davids, Peter. *NIGTC.* 1982. A valuable study that explores the influence of wisdom literature and apocalyptic literature and favors the later as more significant; technical yet readable.

Laws, Sophie. *HNTC.* 1980. A very readable, moderately evangelical work that helpfully indicates Jewish and Hellenistic influences; provides good exegetical and theological notes.

Peter, Jude

Beare, F. W. *The First Epistle of Peter.* Blackwell, 1970. On the Greek text, scholarly yet sensitive to spiritual issues.

Green, E. M. B. *TNTC.* 1971. On II Peter and Jude. Helpful background and exegesis.

Kelly, J. N. D. *HNTC.* 1969. Helpful comparisons between I and II Peter and good historical comments. Sees liturgical elements in I Peter.

Johannine Epistles

Marshall, I. Howard. *NICNT.* 1978. Resourceful for exegesis and comments on the text.

Stott, John R. W. *TNTC.* 1964. Informed exegesis and structure; insights on practical implications.

Revelation

Beasley-Murray, G. R. *NC.* 1974. Introductory essays offer advantages; literary structure also informed.

Ellul, Jacques. *Apocalypse.* Seabury, 1977. Penetrates to the central theological-ethical message for the first century and for modern-day readers.

Ladd, George E. *Revelation.* WBE, 1972. Informed exegesis with theological insights.

Mounce, Robert. *NICNT.* 1977. Exegetical value with occasional theological comments.

Sweet, J. P. *Revelation.* WP, 1979. Historical and exegetical value.

BIBLICAL THEOLOGY

The pursuit of understanding the theology of biblical writers is called "biblical theology." Some authors work with the whole Bible or with either testament, discerning the threads of meaning running through certain books. Others select a particular topic (such as "Holy Spirit") and study what one or several biblical writers believe about that topic. Those who develop "systematic theology" build on this work, expounding it in terms of more modern forms of thought, knitting the views of the biblical sources into a more consistent, unified statement.

For a clear survey of the complex field of biblical theology, two volumes of Gerhard Hasel are needed. *Old Testament Theology* and *New Testament Theology,* both subtitled "Basic Issues in the Current Debate," provide brief, understandable accounts of contemporary writers and methods. These summaries, along with bibliographies and an exposition of Hasel's own agenda, are valuable for students, laypersons, and pastors. *Biblical Theology in Crisis,* by Brevard Childs, also offers a survey of the history of the discipline, with a focus on the uniquely American scene as it has developed over the last half-century. Childs has not only offered critiques of mainstream liberal, neo-orthodox, and conservative methods; he also continues to provide hopeful directions for biblical studies that serve the church.

A helpful, inclusive biblical theology from the Wesleyan-Holiness tradition, entitled *God, Man, and Salvation,* has been written by W. T. Purkiser, Richard S. Taylor, and Willard S. Taylor. Though not too opaque for the layperson, issues in contemporary scholarly discussions are not omitted. Theological themes are traced through both testaments, and clarifying summaries are included. The central focus of this work is salvation. Another approach is that by F. F. Bruce. Though not specifically designed as a biblical theology, his *New Testament Development of Old Testament Themes* can easily serve as such, especially as an introduction. Topics such as "rule of God," "salvation," and "servant of God" are shown to have noteworthy development in both testaments. The integrity of both testaments is maintained, because Bruce lets each passage be understood in its own context.

Elmer Martens works with a question in Exodus 5 as a thematic focus: "God, what are you up to?" *God's Design* provides an insightful, well-organized tour through the eras of Old Testament history and literature. God has an agenda, which his dealings with the Hebrew people begin to reveal. Throughout Martens's book, special paragraphs concentrate on such "theological reflections" as liberation theology, power, and warfare. Walter Kaiser's *Toward an Old Testament Theology,* focusing on "promise," is less successful. A justified faith in God's intentions for the future too easily causes one to miss God's current activity and desires. Thus "promise" as a focusing theme fails to encompass either the broad richness or the heart of the Old Testament. However, Kaiser does provide helpful insights into the difficult task of discovering congruent threads through these varied writings. Likewise, R. E. Clements, in *Old Testament Theology: A Fresh Approach,* uncovers crucial issues throughout Old Testament books. His discussion of methodology is especially noteworthy, and the themes he selects for exposition are doubtlessly central: the God of Israel, the People of God, the Old Testament as Law, and the Old Testament as Promise. This multiple-strand approach actually parallels suggestions in Hasel.

Leonard Goppelt's *Theology of the New Testament, Volume 1* provides enough of a basis to predict that this new two-volume set will be a pacesetter. The careful biblical exegesis is woven into rich themes in systematic theology. Volume 1, subtitled "The ministry of Jesus in its theological significance," focuses on the Kingdom of God, repentance, Jesus' self-understanding, Jesus and the church, and the resurrection. Goppelt helpfully discerns how Jesus, considering his hearers in each setting, varies his teachings accordingly—thus "demanding" repentance from the religious hierarchy and "offering" forgiveness to those who are usually socially marginalized.

George Ladd's *A Theology of the New Testament* works with four divisions (Synoptics, John, Paul, others) in developing theological strands. A difficulty arises in not letting each synoptic writer (Matthew, Mark, Luke) speak clearly for himself. Similarly, clustering Pauline work as monolithic in nature misses valuable distinctions in each book. Overall, though, Ladd does penetrate the theological core of the New Testament and interacts with expertise in contemporary scholarly debates. Especially helpful is Ladd's exposition concerning the overlapping ages (present evil age and the Kingdom of God), though an essay should have helped introduce this concept.

Donald Guthrie's *New Testament Theology* takes a topical approach, following the development of a theme through each New Testament contribution. His topics include God, man, christology, the Holy Spirit, ethics, and five others. While Guthrie shows some appreciation for literary analysis, critical tools are not given much respect. His approach to ethics shows an appreciated concern for human character and individual sanctification, but lacks an understanding of biblical social ethics. This is a large book, and the immense amount of material does provide valuable insights into some doctrinal concerns.

James D. G. Dunn's *Unity and Diversity of the New Testament* seeks to let each writer speak for himself. The unique, and often differing, viewpoints are part of the richness of the Bible. Dunn finds the central unity in the congruence between the presentation of the historical Jesus and the beliefs about an exalted Christ. Too often Dunn concentrates on the various writers' differing elements in great detail, giving little attention to their unifying themes. He tends to confuse surface issues of form with deeper issues of content, which are often more congruent. However, the value of Dunn, helping one discover unique messages, should not be lost due to his overindulgence.

For an alert, lucid introduction to New Testament theology, one should read F. F. Bruce's *The Message of the New Testament*. Bruce uses a thematic approach to guide readers through overviews and highlights of the entire New Testament, in surprisingly brief form.

Christology, the study of beliefs about Jesus Christ, is of central concern for evangelicals. Some writers use the titles given to Jesus (Son of God, Son of Man, Lord, Savior) as indicators. Oscar Cullmann's *The Christology of the New Testament* clusters these terms into four areas: earthly work, future work, present work, and pre-existence. Cullmann notes that these classifications can only offer general sorting help and are not rigidly sustainable. While this approach is worth exploring, and Cullmann's work is better than others, it tends to lose the pre-passion life of Jesus. This is not inherent in the method, but probably more a result of the tendencies in Reformed thinking in European-American theology.

John H. Yoder overcomes this difficulty in *The Politics of Jesus*. By focusing on the activities and teachings of Jesus, Yoder demonstrates that the personal and social ethics of the gospels were not "interim ethics," or merely idealistic, but provide a normative guide for believers. In many ways, Yoder penetrates the core of christology in this presentation, though it should be complemented by Marshall or Moule. A christology should not omit significant ingredients of Jesus' life: his birth, his works of compassion and justice, his preparation of disciples, his teachings, his passion and death, his resurrection and ascension. Yoder has restored much of the content of Jesus' life to theological discussion. His emphasis on the years between Jesus' baptism and his crucifixion grants required attention to the centrality of his interaction with rulers and authorities, issues of violence, economic concerns, and other "political" issues.

I. Howard Marshall's *The Origins of New Testament Christology* is a noteworthy guide to pre-Pauline thinking. In pursuing Jesus' own christology, Marshall's informed use of critical study methods and lucid explanation of Jesus' relationship with messianic concepts from Judaism offers a useful starting point for understanding this theological discussion. Similarly, C. F. D. Moule, in *The Origin of Christology,* emphasizes the impact Jesus himself had on various New Testament developments as followers sought to understand their Lord. This volume is probably the most worthwhile product coming out of the recent British debates about the incarnation.

James D. G. Dunn offers a more extensive study in *Christology in the Making: A New Testament Inquiry into the Origins of the Doctrine of the Incarnation*. He calls for an emphasis on both the incarnation and the resurrection as the most profitable path toward an informed christology. Unfortunately, Dunn's asset, his emphasis on the differing theological beliefs of New Testament writers, easily becomes a liability; he seems to assume that the more full or complete theories are of the latest possible dates. For example, Jesus' self-conscious divinity is seen as a later development in the thinking of the church, one that was then read back into the gospel stories.

For an almost author-by-author survey on the atonement, Leon Morris's *The Cross in the New Testament* is helpful. The exegetical and theological dimensions are valuable in delineating various aspects of Jesus' work on the cross.

Paul's theology is often given special attention. F. F. Bruce's *Paul: Apostle of the Heart Set Free* works with biography, history, and theology to paint a lucid, colorful picture of this pacesetting thinker and activist. Bruce sets up the backdrop of politics, economics, religions, and customs as a stage for Paul. Topics receiving development include eschatology, law, flesh and spirit, baptism and the Lord's Supper, and Paul's "gospel." Bruce is disappointing in his exposition of Paul's interfacing with Old Testament law, although as a whole this proves to be a most worthwhile guide to the man and his theology. In dealing with the specific issue of Paul's interpretation of Jesus, Bruce's *Paul and Jesus* offers an insightful introduction.

Herman N. Ridderbos's *Paul: An Outline of His Theology* is a valuable exegetical work on Paul's writings and an informed survey of modern scholarly discussions. Ridderbos develops a "redemptive-historical" interpretive key for understanding Paul's message. These twin foci tie together a concern for seeing God's involvement in the salvation process and a recognition that history offers the location in which that activity occurs.

SEE ALSO What Christians Believe.

General

Bruce, F. F. *New Testament Development of Old Testament Themes.**† WBE, 1969.

Childs, Brevard S. *Biblical Theology in Crisis.** WP, 1970.

Lehman, Chester K. *Biblical Theology.* 2 vols. HP, 1971, 1974. Develops the theological insights of each biblical book, then discerns the flow of common streams; though a Mennonite scholar, he often appears to be strongly influenced by Reformed perspectives.

Purkiser, W. T., Richard S. Taylor, and Willard S. Taylor. *God, Man and Salvation.** Beacon Hill, 1977.

Themes in Both Testaments

Baker, D. L. *Two Testaments: One Bible.* IVP, 1976. Mainly a survey of modern approaches to the question of continuity;

defends the essential theological unity of the Bible.

Ellis, Edward Earle. *Prophecy and Hermeneutics in Early Christianity*. WBE, 1978. A fairly technical examination of leadership and biblical interpretation in the NT church; misses the socio-ethical significance of prophecy.

France, R. T. *Jesus and the Old Testament*. IVP, 1971. A careful, insightful study of Jesus' appropriation of OT Scripture.

Guinan, Michael E. *Gospel Poverty, Witness to the Risen Christ*. PP, 1981. Examines the varied biblical teachings on money, concluding that poverty is an evil and riches are a danger, yet avoids the trap of any ideological camp; much more than a book on money because it sees all the ties between poverty and the essence of the gospel.

Kline, Meredith G. *By Oath Consigned*. WBE, 1968. Near Eastern studies are used to form the background for comparing OT circumcision with NT baptism.

Ladd, George E. *The Gospel of the Kingdom: Scriptural Studies in the Kingdom of God*. WBE, 1964. An insightful survey of teachings on the subject of the Kingdom.

LaSor, William Sanford. *Israel: A Biblical View*. WBE, 1976. A helpful introduction which examines the relationship of Israel and the church; the two are not seen as totally merged into one NT concept.

Longenecker, Richard. *Biblical Exegesis in the Apostolic Period*. WBE, 1975. A careful analysis of how NT writers used OT Scripture; attempts to discern first-century cultural issues that influenced interpretation and thereby learn how, in our modern culture, we are to work at interpretation.

Morris, Leon. *Testaments of Love*. WBE, 1981. Partially spurred on by modern misuse of the word "love," a leading evangelical biblical scholar offers an extensive study of what the Bible teaches, how love is expressed by God and by humans, and how we are to respond to love; includes comments on how God works for justice and even his wrath is an extension of his love.

Robertson, O. Palmer. *The Christ of the Covenants*. Presbyterian and Reformed, 1980. In formulating a basis for covenant theology, OT covenants are examined as trajectories toward Jesus.

Sloan, Robert B. *The Favorable Year of the Lord: A Study of*

Jubilary Theology in the Gospel of Luke. Schola, 1977. A technical development of the Levitical "Jubilee Year" as it relates to Jesus' actions and teachings; this dissertation will no doubt be followed by additional studies.

Old Testament Theology

Clements, R. E. *Old Testament Theology: A Fresh Approach.** JKP, 1979.

Dyrness, William. *Themes in Old Testament Theology.*† IVP, 1979. A topical arrangement with brief, clear theological development of OT issues.

Goldingay, John. *Approaches to Old Testament Theology.* IVP, 1982. A helpful guide to various approaches currently employed in OT biblical theology.

Hasel, Gerhard. *Old Testament Theology: Basic Issues in the Current Debate.** Rev. WBE, 1975.

Kaiser, Walter. *Toward an Old Testament Theology.** BBH, 1978.

Martens, Elmer A. *God's Design: A Focus on Old Testament Theology.** BBH, 1981.

Terrien, Samuel. *The Elusive Presence: Toward a New Biblical Theology.* HR, 1978. Though not consistently evangelical, provides a helpful development of biblical materials around the theme of God's existence as both hidden and revealed.

Old Testament Themes

Bright, John. *Covenant and Promise: The Prophetic Understanding of the Future of Pre-Exilic Israel.* WP, 1976. Examines varying messages of seventh- and eighth-century prophets, weaving together history, biblical exegesis, and theological insights applicable for the church today; very profitable.

Brueggemann, Walter. *The Land.* FP, 1977. Stimulating, at times heavy, series of theological reflections on the theme of "land" in the Old Testament.

DeVries, S. J. *Yesterday, Today and Tomorrow: Time and History in the Old Testament.* WBE, 1975. Examines the Hebrew concept of time; careful exegesis.

Kline, Meredith G. *The Structure of Authority.* WBE, 1972. Parallels the covenant models of the ancient Near East with those of the Bible; uses this information to argue for earlier dates than are often assumed by more liberal scholars.

Limburg, James. *The Prophets and the Powerless.* JKP, 1977. A needed reply to evangelical "foretelling," with insightful exposition of prophetic "forthtelling" concerning several ethical issues.

Payne, David F. *Kingdoms of the Lord.* WBE, 1981. A four-part study of the history of the Hebrew Kingdom, its enemies, its prophets, and the faith of the nation; lively, informative overview of political and spiritual issues in light of archeology and biblical records.

Westermann, Claus. *The Genesis Accounts of Creation.* FP, 1964. A theological exposition of the creation accounts; accepts the documentary hypothesis, which many scholars reject, but the insights here deserve appreciation.

Wolff, Hans Walter. *Anthropology of the Old Testament.* FP, 1974. Valuable treatment of such subjects as human nature, life and death, and work; critical approach should not limit more conservative readers from these treasures.

New Testament Theology

Bruce, F. F. *Peter, Stephen, James, and John: Studies in Non-Pauline Christianity.* WBE, 1979. Though often too sketchy and disappointingly thin on theological implications, these lectures offer a beginning survey of this material.

_____. *The Message of the New Testament.**† WBE, 1973.

Dunn, James D. G. *The Unity and Diversity of the New Testament.** WP, 1977.

Goppelt, Leonard. *Theology of the New Testament, Volume 1.** WBE, 1981.

Guelich, Robert A., ed. *Unity and Diversity in New Testament Theology.* WBE, 1978. Many theological issues receive attention in this collection honoring George E. Ladd.

Guthrie, Donald. *New Testament Theology.** IVP, 1981.

Hasel, Gerhard. *New Testament Theology: Basic Issues in the Current Debate.** WBE, 1978.

Jeremias, Joachim. *New Testament Theology, Volume I.* Scribners, 1971. Builds on exegetical resources, offers moderately conservative theological insights.

Kümmel, W. G. *The Theology of the New Testament According*

to Its Major Witnesses: Jesus, Paul, John. AP, 1973. A well-organized, generally conservative work by a German NT scholar.

Ladd, George E. *A Theology of the New Testament.** WBE, 1974.

Richardson, Alan. *An Introduction to the Theology of the New Testament.* HR, 1958. Topically arranged; helpful, brief explanations.

Smart, James D. *The Past, Present, and Future of Biblical Theology.* WP, 1979. Urges the church to know the theology of biblical writers; probes for unifying elements; challenges critics of the discipline.

New Testament Themes

Banks, Robert. *Paul's Idea of Community.* WBE, 1980. Counters those who read Paul as overly individualistic; shows the church as that which called believers away from the law and from selfishness; weak on the institutional guidelines of the pastoral letters.

Banks, Robert, ed. *Reconciliation and Hope: New Testament Essays on Atonement and Eschatology Presented to L. L. Morris.* WBE, 1974. These biblical themes receive careful exegetical and theological attention.

Brown, R. E. *The Birth of the Messiah: A Commentary on the Infancy Narratives in Matthew and Luke.* DC, 1977. The most comprehensive commentary on the birth narratives of Matthew and Luke; complex issues receive careful exegetical and theological attention from a Roman Catholic scholar.

————. *The Virginal Conception and Bodily Resurrection of Jesus.* PP, 1973. A Roman Catholic NT scholar offers careful exegetical comments and theological insights on two important events.

Bruce, F. F. *The Time Is Fulfilled.* WBE, 1978. Five passages are selected from NT books (Mark, John, Romans, Hebrews, Revelation) and developed for their theological relevance as uniting OT and NT themes for the church.

Cullmann, Oscar. *Early Christian Worship.* SCM, 1953. Discusses the first century milieu, the life of Jesus, early church preaching, and liturgy, with special reference to worship materials from the Revelation and the Johannine letters.

Dunn, James D. G. *Jesus and the Spirit: A Study of the Religious and Charismatic Experience of Jesus and the First-Century Christians as Reflected in the New Testament.* WP, 1975. An informative, well-organized study on the relationship of the Spirit to Jesus and early Christians.

Hill, David. *New Testament Prophecy.* JKP, 1979. Following introductory background material on the OT and on John the Baptist, the concept of a "prophet" is given helpful treatment throughout the NT writings; carefully studies the prophet's relationship with God and role in the church.

Hurley, James B. *Man and Woman in Biblical Perspective.* ZC, 1981. One of the more thorough biblical studies that focuses on exegetical methods; somewhat restricted by his own cultural biases (aren't we all?), and thus provides conservative conclusions.

Knight, George William, III. *The New Testament Teaching on the Role Relationship of Men and Women.* BBH, 1977. An exegetical study that concludes men and women are equal while intrinsically defined for differing roles; oversimplifies the issues and overlooks the "exceptions" throughout the NT.

Longenecker, Richard N. *The Christology of Early Jewish Christianity.* BBH, 1970. An insightful study on NT materials, based on OT concepts, about Jesus; "Messiah" and "Lord" receive special attention as the diversity of early theology unfolds.

Longenecker, R. N., and M. C. Tenney, eds. *New Directions in New Testament Study.* ZC, 1974. A collection of essays by evangelical scholars, some very helpful.

Martin, Ralph P. *Reconciliation.* JKP, 1981. The Hebrew focus on justification and the Greco-Roman concern for countering evil forces provide the backdrop for studying reconciliation as it concerns the relationships of God to humans and humans to humans.

————. *Worship in the Early Church.* FHR, 1964. With an appreciation for Jewish traditions, Martin looks at NT prayers, hymns, confessions, teachings about stewardship, the role of the Bible, and the institution of sacraments.

Metzger, B. M. "The Ascension of Jesus." *Historical and Literary Studies*. Brill, 1968. A brief (ten page) study which offers careful exegesis and comments.

Tetlon, Elizabeth M. *Women and Ministry in the New Testament*. PP, 1980. The historical setting of Judaic culture, the Roman Empire, and the growing NT church provide clarifying dimensions for this helpful exegetical and practical study by a Roman Catholic scholar.

Williams, Don. *The Apostle Paul and Women in the Church*. GL/R, 1977. Analyzes every Pauline passage that refers to Christian women, whether in theological teachings or in passing historical comments; offers helpful interpretation for the contemporary church.

Christology

Cullmann, Oscar. *The Christology of the New Testament.** WP, 1959.

Dunn, J. D. G. *Christology in the Making: A New Testament Inquiry into the Origins of the Doctrine of the Incarnation.** WP, 1980.

Jeremias, Joachim. *New Testament Theology, Volume I*. Scribners, 1971. Focuses on the teaching of the gospels and the role of Jesus in theology; scholarly, erudite work.

Marshall, I. Howard. *The Origins of New Testament Christology.** IVP, 1976.

Morris, Leon. *The Apostolic Preaching of the Cross*. WBE, 1955. With his usual biblical expertise, Morris examines the OT, first-century language use, and Jewish literature on issues like redemption, covenant, blood, propitiation, reconciliation, and justification; this is a preliminary study to *The Cross in the New Testament*.

_____. *The Cross in the New Testament.** WBE, 1965.

Moule, C. F. D. *The Origin of Christology.** Cambridge University Press, 1977.

Yoder, John Howard. *The Politics of Jesus.**† WBE, 1972.

Paul

Bruce, F. F. *Paul: Apostle of the Heart Set Free.**† WBE, 1977.

_____. *Paul and Jesus.** WBE, 1974.

Käsemann, Ernst. *Perspectives on Paul*. FP, 1971. Various themes receive helpful comments, including anthropology, reconciliation, justification, faith, the body of Christ, and worship.

Longenecker, Richard N. *Paul, Apostle of Liberty.* BBH, 1964. An introductory text on Paul's life and teachings; historical and theological matters are given insightful treatment.

Ridderbos, Herman N. *Paul: An Outline of His Theology.** WBE, 1975.

SEE ALSO Bible History and Archeology and What Christians Believe: Jesus Christ.

FAVORITE BOOKS

E. EARLE ELLIS

Personal

Lee's Lieutenants, by D. S. Freeman
The Road to Serfdom, by F. A. Hayek
Mere Christianity, by C. S. Lewis
The Bondage of the Will, by Martin Luther
Memoirs of McCheyne, edited by A. A. Bonar

Professional

Christ and Time, by Oscar Cullmann
The Vitality of the Individual in the Thought of Ancient Israel, by A. R. Johnson
Commentaries by J. B. Lightfoot
The Origin of Paul's Religion, by J. G. Machen
The Inspiration and Authority of the Bible, by B. B. Warfield

LOWELL ERDAHL

Personal

Agenda for Biblical People, by Jim Wallis
Call to Conversion, by Jim Wallis
All Men Are Brothers, by Mahatma Gandhi
The Politics of Jesus, by John Howard Yoder
My Utmost for His Highest, by Oswald Chambers

Professional

The Prophetic Imagination, by Walter Brueggemann
The Cultural Subversion of the Biblical Faith, by James Smart
The Game of Disarmament, by Alva Myrdal

Social Power and Political Freedom, by Gene Sharp
Religion and Violence, by Robert McAfee Brown

JERRY FALWELL
Personal

The Normal Christian Life, by Watchman Nee
Rees Howells: Intercessor, by Norman P. Grubb
The Pursuit of God, by A. W. Tozer
The Power of Prayer, by R. A. Torrey
A Christian Manifesto, by Francis Schaeffer

Professional

Preaching and Preachers, by D. Martyn Lloyd-Jones
Criswell's Guidebook for Pastors, by W. A. Criswell
Lectures to My Students, by Charles Spurgeon
Walking with the Giants, by Warren Wiersbe
Battle for the Mind, by Tim LaHaye

RICHARD J. FOSTER
Personal

The Journal and Major Essays, by John Wohlman
The Healing Light, by Agnes Sanford
The Little Flowers of Saint Francis, by Brother Ugolino
Life Together, by Dietrich Bonhoeffer
Testament of Devotion, by Thomas Kelly
Shadow of the Almighty, by Elisabeth Elliot

Professional

Mere Christianity, by C. S. Lewis
Christian Perfection, by Francois Fenelon
Christian Commitment: An Apologetic, by Edward John Carnell
Call to Commitment, by Elizabeth O'Connor
The Other Side of Silence, by Morton T. Kelsey

STAN GUNDRY
Personal

Our Lord Prays for His Own, by Marcus Rainford
Holy Masquerade, by Olaf Hartman

The Problem of Wineskins, by Howard Snyder
Glad Tidings, by Dwight L. Moody
The Freedom of God, by James Daane

Professional

The Progress of Dogma, by James Orr
Evangelical Theology, by Karl Barth
Christianity and Liberalism, by J. G. Machen
The Bondage of the Will, by Martin Luther
The Freedom of the Will, by Jonathan Edwards

RICHARD C. HALVERSON

Personal

Mere Christianity, by C. S. Lewis
My Utmost for His Highest, by Oswald Chambers
Christian Perfection, by Francois Fenelon
Splendor of God, by Honore Willsie Morrow
The Problem of Wineskins, by Howard A. Snyder

Professional

The Secularist Heresy, by Harry Blamires
The Christian View of God and the World, by James Orr
The Life of Christ, by F. W. Farrar
Jesus and the Kingdom, by George E. Ladd
Missionary Methods: St. Paul's or Ours? by Roland Allen

NANCY HARDESTY

Personal

The Last Battle, by C. S. Lewis
Mysticism, by Evelyn Underhill
Complete Poems, by Carl Sandburg
The Meaning of Persons, by Paul Tournier
Compassion and Self-Hate, by Theodore Rubin and Eleanor
  Rubin

Professional

Revivalism and Social Reform, by Timothy Smith
Glimpses of Fifty Years, by Frances Willard
The Promise of the Father, by Phoebe Palmer
Beyond God the Father, by Mary Daly

Jack Hayford

Personal

Power Through Prayer, by E. M. Bounds
My Utmost for His Highest, by Oswald Chambers
The Knowledge of the Holy, by A. W. Tozer
The Burden of the Lord, by Ian MacPherson
Shadow of the Almighty, by Elisabeth Elliot

Professional

Interpretation of the New Testament, by Richard Lenski
Daily Study Bible, by William Barclay

CHRISTIAN HISTORY

The Church in History

During recent decades Christians have often overlooked the two thousand years of church history. The reasons vary: many evangelicals want to tie themselves directly into the first century, ignoring the victories and tragedies of the intervening years; many liberals write off such history because recent scholarship places us beyond the limited abilities of earlier believers, who did not possess the critical study tools that paved the way for our enlightened age. Protestants of various stripes are unable to appreciate the ways in which God has worked in the Catholic Church before and after the sixteenth-century events in Europe.

Although writers of church history, like those in other academic fields, are known for their boring collections of information, it is not difficult to find volumes that are not only accurate but that carry the reader on exciting, colorful journeys. In *Eerdmans Handbook to the History of Christianity,* edited by Tim Dowley, movements, turning points, leaders, and beliefs receive concise comments from writers such as Padilla, Gasque, and Thiselton. Through the artistic use of charts, maps, pictures, and colored pages, readers are provided with a visually attractive volume. Short quotations from primary sources, accounts about the societies surrounding the church, and the well-organized chronological arrangement help make this a volume well worth owning. *The New International Dictionary of the Christian Church,* edited by J. D. Douglas, provides almost 5,000 items arranged alphabetically—including people, places, intellectual terms, cities, societies, movements, events, beliefs, denominations, and writings. Many articles include bibliographies, and cross-referencing is made easy.

Kenneth Scott Latourette is often considered the dean of church historians. *A History of the Expansion of Christianity* provides seven volumes of historical accounts that focus on the growth in numbers and the geography of the church. Each segment analyzes phases of growth and asks questions about the content of the gospel message: how the expansion occurred, the effects of the growth on the societies involved, and the effects of those cultures on the church. The interrelationship of methods and effects receives careful attention. *Christianity in a Revolutionary Age,* also by Latourette, picks up the account in the nineteenth century, providing an even more exhaustive account of two centuries (1800–present) of worldwide church activities—Roman Catholic, Eastern Orthodox, and Protestant.

For a lucid, brief overview of the major events in church history, A. M. Renwick has written *The Story of the Church.* In viewing missions, organizations, doctrines, and impact on human life, Renwick chronicles disappointments and achievements of the church. Several other very readable volumes would furnish accounts of particular segments of that history. F. F. Bruce's *The Spreading Flame* is a conversational survey of the church from the earliest events until missionaries reached England in the early seventh century. His account of the church-state relationships before and after Constantine evidences sensitivity to this important issue. Roland Bainton's *The Church of Our Fathers* also shows that history is seldom boring, and certainly need not be written that way. The readable, often dramatic survey covers 1,500 years. Similarly, Bainton's *The Reformation of the Sixteenth Century* is a lively account of peoples, events, and beliefs of the church. There are insights into simultaneous secular history that help readers fully understand the complexity and significance of these years.

Martin Marty continues to provide an almost continuous flow of historical studies. (A friend once quipped that you can always recognize Marty: he is the gentleman writing with both hands!) *Protestantism* is a textbook on worldwide Protestant religion and culture. Marty discusses unique contributions of Protestant movements and organizations and varying elements in both the religious and cultural aspects. An exhaustive bibliography includes books, articles, little-known pamphlets, and other resources overlooked in most lists. In *Righteous Empire: The Protestant Experience in America,* Marty skillfully shows the political and social dimensions of Protestantism in North America. By working with such topics as racism, governmental politics, education, and denominational divisions, he provides a lively view of the history and impact of these churches.

Atkinson, James. *The Great Light: Luther and the Reformation.* WBE, 1968. A helpful introduction, especially on Luther.

Bainton, Roland H. *Christendom: A Short History of Christianity and Its Impact on Western Civilization.* 2 vols. HR, 1964. Originally published in a coffee-table format, these volumes argue, often convincingly, that our contemporary culture has been affected more by Christianity than by any other agents; includes bibliography.

————. *The Church of Our Fathers.** Scribners, 1969.

————. *The Reformation of the Sixteenth Century.** Beacon, 1952.

————. *Women of the Reformation.* 3 vols. AG, 1971–77. A needed, erudite augmenting of historical studies is provided as women of the church receive insightful and often inspiring analysis; bibliographies, illustrations.

Beaver, Pierce R. *American Protestant Women in World Mission (A History of the First Feminist Movement in North America).* WBE, 1980. An early, vibrant feminist movement in America was that formed by Christian women to support and even send missionaries; opposition was strong, results were far-reaching.

Brown, Dale. *Understanding Pietism.* WBE, 1978. Sees Pietists as providing helpful roots for both spiritual formation and for social change; insightful comments on Puritan impact on seventeenth-century European churches.

Bruce, F. F. *The Spreading Flame.** The Paternoster Press, 1958. Reprint. WBE, 1979.

Cairns, Earle E. *Christianity Through the Centuries.* ZC, 1981. A textbook concerning the church and the cultures around it; appreciates intellectual, economic, political, and aesthetic dimensions of societies into which the church came.

Chadwick, Owen. *The Reformation.* WBE, 1965. Historical events, peoples, beliefs, structures and worship of the Reformation; includes comments on Roman Catholic and Eastern Orthodox responses.

Douglas, J. D., ed. *The New International Dictionary of the Christian Church.** ZC, 1974.

Dowley, Tim, ed. *Eerdmans Handbook to the History of Christianity.**+ WBE, 1977.

Green, Michael. *Evangelism in the Early Church.* WBE, 1970. An exciting account of activities, theology, and growth during the first centuries.

Hardesty, Nancy. *Great Women of Faith.* BBH, 1980. Church saints, Bible scholars, preachers, educators; a needed complement for church history studies.

Hollenweger, Walter J. *The Pentecostals.* AG, 1972. An impressive survey of international scope, including people, churches, theology, interrelationships.

Latourette, Kenneth Scott. *A History of the Expansion of Christianity.** 7 vols. Reprint. ZC, 1971.

————. *Christianity in a Revolutionary Age.** 5 vols. ZC, 1973.

Marty, Martin E. *A Nation of Behavers.* University of Chicago Press, 1976. Since practice precedes the institutionalizing of structures and creeds, Marty believes American religion is better understood through viewing the activities of America's religious people; insightful chapters on six segments of the church—mainline, evangelical-fundamentalist, Pentecostal-charismatic, new religions, ethnic groups, and civil religion.

————. *The Pro and Con Book of Religious America.* Word, 1975. What is right and what is wrong with American religion? Penetrating comments and discussion-starters on descriptions like spiritual or materialistic, tolerant or prejudiced, liberating or patriarchal, humanitarian or self-seeking, prophetic or entrenched.

————. *Protestantism.** Holt, Rinehart and Winston, 1972.

————. *Righteous Empire: The Protestant Experience in America.** Dial, 1970.

McLoughlin, William G. *Revivals, Awakenings, and Reform.* University of Chicago Press, 1978. Insightful study in history on issues of personal salvation, world view shifts, and social changes in light of the presuppositions of many Americans that our destiny is to lead the world toward the millennium; discusses five reawakenings, including one that began in the 1960s.

Melton, Gordon. *The Encyclopedia of American Religions*. 2 vols. Consortium, 1979. Arranged along traditional theological lines, provides comments on groups and people with an emphasis on sociological and historical nuances.

Moyer, Elgin S. *Who Was Who in Church History*. Rev. MP, 1968. A compilation of comments on those who have influenced the church.

Nash, Ronald H., ed. *Ideas of History*. 2 vols. Dutton, 1969. On speculative studies, we read Augustine, Kant, Hegel, Marx, Toynbee, and others; on critical studies (raising questions on the role of historians), we have Mill, Dilthey, Collingwood, and others; with introductions and bibliographies.

Orr, J. Edwin. *Evangelical Awakenings*. 5 vols. Bethany, 1975. A geographical approach to revivals during the eighteenth and nineteenth centuries (South Seas, Eastern Asia, South Asia, Africa, Latin America); with bibliographies.

_____. *The Eager Feet*. MP, 1975. *The Fervent Prayer*. MP, 1974. *The Flaming Tongue*. Rev. MP, 1975. Continues the chronicling of revivals into the early twentieth century.

Piepkorn, Arthur C. *Profiles in Belief*. To date, 4 vols. bound as 3. HR, 1977–79. Brief comments on history, organization, beliefs, and interrelationships of American religious groups; better than Melton on theology and liturgy.

Ramm, Bernard L. *The Evangelical Heritage*. WB, 1973. A readable, brief survey of roots, from the early church to the present; not usually able to appreciate non-Reformed traditions.

Renwick, A. M. *The Story of the Church*.* WBE, 1960.

Shelley, Bruce L. *Church History in Plain Language*.† WB, 1982. A just-released introductory textbook, suitable for laypersons; indicates lessons of history that can provide guidance for today.

Smith, M. A. *From Christ to Constantine*. IVP, 1971. *The Church Under Seige*. IVP, 1976. Popular and informed accounts of church history on first through third centuries and fourth through ninth centuries, respectively; include illustrations and glossaries.

Spitz, Lewis W. *The Renaissance and Reformation Movements.* Rand-McNally, 1971. A textbook covering the years 1300 to 1600 on various aspects of church and culture.

Walker, G. S. M. *The Growing Storm.* WBE, 1961. Introduction to the church from 600 to 1350.

Wenger, J. C. *How Mennonites Came to Be*; *What Mennonites Believe.* HP, 1977. Brief, clear pamphlets on early Mennonite peoples and events; the latter one offers an outline of theological distinctives.

Wood, A. Skevington. *The Inextinguishable Blaze.* WBE, 1960. An introduction to the eighteenth-century Wesleyan revival.

THE HISTORY OF CHRISTIAN THOUGHT

Just as our contemporary church organizations are built on historical developments, so is our theology. Beliefs, creeds, doctrines, and dogma are the combined result of scholarly pursuits, secular thought (whether congruent with Christianity or opposed to it), the heresies of a particular age, political events in the church, and (one hopes) prayer. Peter Toon, in *The Development of Doctrine in the Church* explains the relationship between doctrinal formulas and historical settings. He indicates the methodology by which theology surfaces and discusses the contributions of various thinkers to this field of study. This brief introduction also attempts to provide biblical critiques of each phase of theological developments.

A more thorough textbook, *Historical Theology: An Introduction,* has been authored by Geoffrey Bromiley. Although uneven in its chronological account of the church's continuing theological work, the insights and explanations provided by Bromiley can often place contemporary debates into a helpful perspective that avoids unwarranted urgency and too hastily reached decisions. Today's controversies are seldom new, and enlightened understandings of history can prove to be healthy additions to the discussions.

A five-volume set by Jaroslav Pelikan (three completed) provides a comprehensive history of doctrine. *The Christian Tradition* surveys orthodoxy and heresies, systems and politics, beliefs and icons, liturgies and mystical traditions with helpful, erudite treatment. Though claiming to be written for the average reader, background in theology and church history would be helpful.

Avis, Paul L. *The Church in the Theology of the Reformers.* JKP, 1981. An analysis of various sixteenth-century thinkers, focusing on the concerns for biblical teachings and various efforts for putting them into practice; insightful.

Berkouwer, G. C. *A Half Century of Theology.* WBE, 1977. Theological themes are traced through the works of European theologians (apologetics, salvation, Scripture, faith and reason, eschatology, the church); though influenced by the author's Reformed Dutch thinking, very valuable.

Bromiley, Geoffrey W. *Historical Theology: An Introduction.** WBE, 1978.

Carnell, Edward. *The Case for Orthodox Theology.* WP, 1959. In limiting the "ground of religious authority to the Bible," Carnell defends orthodoxy against fundamentalism and liberalism.

Henry, Carl F. H. *Frontiers in Modern Theology.* MP, 1965. A conservative evaluation of European trends.

Hindson, Edward. *Introduction to Puritan Theology: A Reader.* BBH, 1976. A valuable collection of writings. Each Puritan author (including Owen, Baxter, Edwards) is heard on one topic (atonement, church, eschatology, respectively); provides a good introduction to people and theology of the era.

Hughes, P. E. *Creative Minds in Contemporary Theology.* WBE, 1969. A collection of fourteen essays concerning trends in modern theology; evaluated from a Reformed position.

Kelly, J. N. D. *Early Christian Creeds.* 3rd ed. McKay, 1972. The development and purpose of early creedal formulas, and the relationship of creeds to liturgy.

————. *Early Christian Doctrines.* 2d ed. HR, 1960. Five centuries of theological work on the basics of the Trinity, Scripture, Christology, the Holy Spirit, anthropology, ecclesiology, and eschatology—including comments on the people, councils and writings of these years; very thorough textbook.

Kirk, J. Andrew. *Liberation Theology*. JKP, 1979. Discusses briefly the history of liberation theology, offers comments on some exponents and biblical themes, and suggests some positive and negative evaluations, including the need for a better doctrine of sin; not always clear in explaining others, but generally very helpful and informed.

Klaassen, Walter. *Anabaptism in Outline*. HP, 1981. A topically arranged collection of materials which offers insightful expositions of Mennonite-Anabaptist thinking on various issues; includes christology, the Bible, and church-state issues.

Osterhaven, M. Eugene. *The Faith of the Church*. WBE, 1982. Expected soon; a look at the development of Reformed thought.

Pelikan, Jaroslav. *The Christian Tradition: A History of the Development of Doctrine.** *Volume 1: The Emergence of the Catholic Tradition (100–600); Volume 2: The Spirit of Eastern Christendom (600–1700); Volume 3: The Growth of Medieval Theology (600–1300)*. The University of Chicago Press, 1971, 1974, 1978. (Two more volumes are projected: *Volume 4: Reformation of Church and Dogma, 1300–1700; Volume 5: Christian Doctrine and Modern Culture, Since 1700*.)

Smart, James D. *Revolutionary Theology in the Making*. JKP, 1964. The Barth-Thurneysen correspondence illuminates a theological era; the years from 1914 to 1925 take on life.

Toon, Peter. *The Development of Doctrine in the Church.** WBE, 1979. Theological history is explained with clarity; each stage is compared with biblical teachings.

Toon, Peter, and James D. Spioland. *One God in Trinity*. Cornerstone, 1980. Various historical developments are surveyed in these ten very helpful essays concerning the church's early formulation of trinitarian doctrines; nontechnical.

Turner, George A. *The Vision Which Transforms*. Beacon Hill, 1964. Looks at the Wesleyan tradition from biblical, theological, and historical viewpoints.

Wynkoop, Mildred B. *Foundations of Wesleyan-Armenian Theology*. Beacon Hill, 1967. Surveys historical theology to contrast Calvinism with author's own tradition.

THEOLOGIANS

A study of the development of theology can be approached through specific theologians. Readers gain a helpful overview though secondary resources that furnish information on the life and thought of a particular contributor, as well as the resulting impact on the church's ongoing theological task.

Secondary material should not be expected to provide definitive statements, however. Instead, as one writer reflects on another's contributions, both provide revealing insights and encouragement toward further study. Bibliographical guidance can then show the way into the reading of primary sources.

Barth, Karl. *The Theology of Schleiermacher*. WBE, 1982. Expected soon; a translation of perceptive lectures.

Bethge, Eberhard. *Dietrich Bonhoeffer: Man of Vision, Man of Courage*. HR, 1970. *Costly Grace: An Illustrated Introduction to Dietrich Bonhoeffer*. HR, 1980. The first is a massive, definitive work on the man and his theology; the latter is briefer and provides a helpful parallel between his writings and his life's events.

Bolich, Gregory. *Karl Barth and Evangelicalism*. IVP, 1979. By providing expositions on evangelicals and on Barth, Bolich seeks to gain more of a hearing for Barth's theology.

Bromiley, Geoffrey W. *Introduction to the Theology of Karl Barth*. WBE, 1979. Allows Barth to speak for himself, offering a clear outline and exposition; author was a cotranslator of the *Dogmatics*.

Brown, Colin. *Karl Barth and the Christian Message*. IVP, 1967. A fair, introductory overview of Barth's theology from a British scholar.

Carnell, Edward. *The Theology of Reinhold Niebuhr*. WBE, 1960. An appreciative yet critical appraisal.

Eller, Vernard. *Thy Kingdom Come: A Blumhardt Reader*. WBE, 1980. Eller finds foreshadows of neo-orthodoxy and needed thoughts on Christianity and politics in the work of the Blumhardts.

Hamilton, Kenneth. *The System and the Gospel*. WBE, 1963. An exposition and critique of Paul Tillich's theology.

Jewett, Paul K. *Emil Brunner: An Introduction to the Man and His Thought*. IVP, 1961. Helpful in explaining and evaluating Brunner's contributions.

Jones, D. Garth. *Teilhard de Chardin*. IVP, 1969. A brief introductory survey of an influential French Roman Catholic theologian.

Klassen, William, and Walter Klassen. *The Writings of Pilgrim Marpeck*. HP, 1978. In the "Classics of the Radical Reformation" series, this story of a mining magistrate turned theologian provides an insightful guide to events, theology, and persons of early years.

Ladd, G. E. *Rudolph Bultmann*. IVP, 1964. An informed exposition on Bultmann's academic methods and results; incisive critique.

Lovelace, Richard. *The American Pietism of Cotton Mather: Origins of American Evangelicalism*. WBE, 1979. Argues that Mather provided roots for modern North Atlantic evangelicalism, and can provide needed corrective along the line of social ethics; Mather's influence is somewhat overstated.

Muggeridge, Malcolm. *A Third Testament*.† Little, Brown, 1976. Popular expositions on men who have shaped Christian thinking; includes Pascal, Kierkegaard, and others.

Outler, Albert C. *John Wesley*. OUP, 1964/1980. An appropriate anthology of Wesley's writings in which he is able to speak for himself with few comments from the editor; theology and tensions are evident in this selection.

Roberts, Robert C. *Rudolph Bultmann's Theology: A Critical Interpretation*. WBE, 1976. More complete than Ladd's (above); helpful especially for advanced students.

Schmidt, Martin. *John Wesley: A Theological Biography*. 3 vols. AP, 1963. An extensive work on Wesley's thought; Albert Outler edited the primary sources.

Tupper, E. Frank. *The Theology of Wolfhart Pannenberg*. WP, 1973. An erudite, informed exposition of Pannenberg's thought; issued before his major philosophical treatise.

Tuttle, Robert G., Jr. *John Wesley: His Life and Theology*. ZC, 1978. A conversational, informed look at the person and his spiritual life; mystics highlighted, ethics underplayed.

Wood, Skevington. *John Wesley: The Burning Heart*. Bethany, 1978. An account of his life, evangelistic ministry, and themes from his messages; weak on Wesley's social ethics.

Yoder, John H. *Legacy of Michael Sattler*. HP, 1973. A valuable contribution to the "Classics of the Radical Reformation" series; letters, papers, and history; Anabaptist thinking began to become clearer as early events passed and opportunities for further development were provided.

FAVORITE BOOKS

CARL F. H. HENRY

Personal

The Christian View of God and the World, by James Orr
Church Dogmatics, by Karl Barth
The Confessions of Saint Augustine
Miracles, by C. S. Lewis
The Life and Work of Saint Paul, by F. W. Farrar

Professional

The Republic, by Plato
Institutes of the Christian Religion, by John Calvin
Systematic Theology, by Charles Hodge
A Christian View of Men and Things, by Gordon H. Clark

CHARLES KEYSOR

Personal

Commentaries on Scripture, by John Calvin
The Knowledge of the Holy, by A. W. Tozer
Commentary on Romans, by Anders Nygren
Foundations of the Christian Faith, by James M. Boice

Professional

Christianity and Liberalism, by J. G. Machen
The Pursuit of God, by A. W. Tozer
What Ever Happened to the Human Race? by Francis
    Schaeffer and C. Everett Koop
True Spirituality, by Francis Schaeffer

BRUCE LARSON

Personal

Pilgrim's Progress, by John Bunyan
John Wesley's Journal

The Everlasting Man, by G. K. Chesterton
Various works by Henry Drummond
The Great Divorce, by C. S. Lewis

Professional

Institutes of the Christian Religion, by John Calvin
Epistle to the Romans, by Karl Barth
The Misunderstanding of the Church, by Emil Brunner
Mere Christianity, by C. S. Lewis
The Meaning of Persons, by Paul Tournier

MADELEINE L'ENGLE

Personal/Professional

The Complete Works of Shakespeare
Incognito, by Petru Dumitriu
Anglican-English writers of murder mysteries

BILL LESLIE

Personal

The Other Side of Silence, by Morton Kelsey
Celebration of Discipline, by Richard J. Foster
The Way of the Heart, by Henri Nouwen
Journey Inward, Journey Outward, by Elizabeth O'Connor
Christ and Culture, by H. Richard Niebuhr

Professional

Built as a City, by David Sheppard
Call to Commitment, by Elizabeth O'Connor
The Waiting Father, by Helmut Thielicke
Mere Christianity, by C. S. Lewis
Ask Me to Dance, by Bruce Larson

PETER MACKEY

Personal

A Man Called Peter, by Catherine Marshall
The Plague, by Albert Camus
Through Gates of Splendor, by Elisabeth Elliot

East of Eden, by John Steinbeck
Till We Have Faces, by C. S. Lewis

Professional

Mr. Jones, Meet the Master, by Peter Marshall
The Lion, the Witch, and the Wardrobe, by C. S. Lewis
Language and Reality, by Wilbur M. Urban
The Literature of the Bible, by Leland Ryken
Tree and Leaf, by J. R. R. Tolkien

JOHN MACARTHUR

Personal

A Body of Divinity, by Thomas Watson
Studies in the Sermon on the Mount, by D. Martyn Lloyd-Jones
The Imitation of Christ, by Thomas à Kempis
Treasury of Scripture Knowledge, edited by R. A. Torrey
Daily Bible Study, by William Barclay

Professional

Preacher's Portrait in the New Testament, by John R. W. Stott
Spiritual Growth, by Arthur Pink
Preaching and Preachers, by D. Martyn Lloyd-Jones

REBECCA MANLEY PIPPERT

Personal

The Fall, by Albert Camus
Wise Blood, by Flannery O'Connor
Orthodoxy, by G. K. Chesterton
Mere Christianity, by C. S. Lewis
The Brothers Karamazov, by Fyodor Dostoyevsky

Professional

Plague of Plagues, by Ralph Venning
Celebration of Discipline, by Richard J. Foster
The Wounded Healer, by Henri Nouwen
Dynamics of Spiritual Life, by Richard Lovelace
The Road Less Traveled, by Scott Peck

WHAT CHRISTIANS BELIEVE

INTRODUCTION

The work of theology is a human activity: we study the variety of ways in which God has revealed himself to us (history, Scripture, Jesus, Holy Spirit). The church's theologies, whether expressed in creeds, treatises, preaching, or activities, are never more than human efforts. God illuminates his Word and provides wisdom for the theologian, but the resulting theology is always secondary to God's direct revelation in Jesus Christ and in Scripture.

The foundation of theology consists of Bible study and biblical theology. The task of systematic theology is that of sorting biblical material into thematic categories or topics ("God, the Creator," "Jesus," or "the church," for example). The final result of systematic theology, at its best, is a clearer understanding of issues that need to be taught, preached, integrated with current concerns, and practiced.

Because systematic theology is written by theologians who are themselves products of a specific culture, it is always culture-specific. It will acquire the language, thought forms, philosophy, and literary structures of one specific culture.

Rather than allowing this culture-specific quality to be a limitation, theologians acknowledge it to be an asset. However, the cultural-specificity of systematic theology has generally been misunderstood by Christians in the European–North American culture. As theologians on other continents develop their own theologies, we too often challenge the appropriateness of their work. While believing that our corrections will be a biblical influence, we are actually more likely to be attempting to export our own philosophical systems or cultural values. Indigenous churches, while able to benefit from the scholarship of other Christian communities, will necessarily develop their own systematic theologies.

While some systematic theologians are able to provide a viable service beyond their own culture and age, such are the exceptions. Even when that quality of timelessness is attributed to certain works, those who continue to use such materials are academicians specializing in historical theology or working in the same cultural tradition as the earlier theologian. So, for instance, modern Reformed scholars will still benefit from Calvin, and Lutherans will read Luther (although "systematic" is not an adjective commonly applied to the latter). Although understanding the historical roots of contemporary theology can aid in understanding the role of the church in the modern era, systematic theologians gear their work for current problems, concerns, issues, and deficiencies.

Probably the most exciting and usable series of systematic theology is *The Evangelical Faith,* by Helmut Thielicke of West Germany. Volume I expounds the relationship of theology to modern thought forms, and its first section (particularly pages 21–137) should be required reading for anyone interested in theology. It provides an outstanding introduction to theological methodology and contemporary philosophical problems. Since Kant developed the limitations of human reason, theologians (via Schleiermacher) have emphasized more subjective theories of epistemology. This issue is crucial for anyone attempting to study and expound issues related to God and his revelation. Following these "prolegomena" Thielicke gives us, in Volume II, his Doctrine of God and Doctrine of Christ. Centering on the topic "what God has done for us," Thielicke interacts with various strands of contemporary thought, including Lutheran (his own tradition) and Reformed (Calvin), and with the work of Kierkegaard and Barth. His development of christology along the schematic of prophet-priest-king is excellent. Volume III, on the Holy Spirit, the church and eschatology, provides a view that God's activity is currently powerful and constant. The Lutheran "two kingdoms" model, in which different ethics apply in the different spheres of church and world, is, however, not as helpful. Thielicke's numerous writings are especially valuable because he knows that theology must be livable (ethics) and preachable.

Among North American theologians, no evangelical rivals the stature of Carl F. H. Henry, and, apart from the massive work of Karl Barth, no one has dealt more thoroughly with the theme of God's revelation. In *God, Revelation, and Authority,* Henry shows that he is well acquainted with the various intellectual currents of the day. In the first four volumes, subtitled *God Who Speaks and Shows,* we see his dependence on the thought of Gordon Clark. (This framework continues in the later volume, subtitled *God Who Stands, Stoops and Stays.*) Although this philosophical rationalism is the one major weakness of Henry's work, there is still much of value here. Because of the cognitive integrity of revelation, Henry demonstrates the Christian's ability to interact with various philosophical and theological systems that he believes undercut God's truth. Henry dialogues with the fideism of Barth, the views of authority expounded by Kelsey and Barr, and the many practitioners of radical biblical criticism. Rather than letting the central topic of "revelation" limit the boundaries of his work, Henry uses it as a pathway into every major theme of Christian theology. Although he does not always understand the contextual roots of theologies arising beyond the North Atlantic, and therefore misses on some of his critiques, Henry is more perceptive than most. Above all, he understands his own audience well. Few can offer the encyclopedic coverage and careful, logical development of themes as thoroughly as Henry (though he is often obtuse).

Donald G. Bloesch, a professor at the University of Dubuque Theological Seminary, has completed a two-volume set entitled *Essentials of Evangelical Theology.* In the first volume, *God, Authority, and Salvation,* Bloesch approaches his topics by interacting with a wide range of other theologians, indicating those directions he believes are faithful to orthodoxy and thus able to contribute to broader ecumenical discussions. He avoids nonessentials—hence the title—opting for larger, more inclusive topics. This first volume hints at some new ideas on foreknowledge and predestination. The second volume, *Life, Ministry, and Hope,* focuses on the Christian believer, the church, and the future. His discussion on the sacraments is especially helpful, most notably as he writes about Scripture. While cautioning the church against the danger of being reduced to solely political activities, he acknowledges the crucial social role the church must play. Overall, Bloesch is working toward a "catholic" theology that interacts with and receives help from diverse church traditions. In the end, however, he does not stray from Reformed positions.

During the last few years, there has been a significant shift in the North American theological scene. Following several years without new one-volume systematic works, several evangelical authors have now provided us with attractive, scholarly, readable, single-volume systematics.

Geoffrey Wainwright's *Doxology* uses the centerpiece of praise and worship around which to develop the usual themes of systematic theology. By focusing on worship, Wainwright leads us to a high christology, a reverent view of Scripture, and a healthy, powerful concept of the Christian church. Because Jesus Christ was worshipped by the early church, implications concerning his deity and resurrection are highlighted. The Bible is valued both as revelation and as sacrament. Because the church's life centers on worshipping the God of the Bible, it would be impossible for such a community of believers to avoid involvement in God's works of love, justice, mercy, and beckoning in the world. Wainwright also provides extensive, detailed chapters on modern ecumenical concerns. This volume is valued as creative while being faithful to evangelical concerns.

The Word of Truth, by Dale Moody, must also receive excellent recommendations. Moody shows his respect for theologians ranging from modernist to fundamentalist. He can interact just as fairly with process theology as he can with dispensationalism. The valuable contributions of contemporary historical-critical biblical studies are welcomed as Moody works through the topics of God, creation, man, sin, salvation, Christ, church, and consummation. Moody's thoughtful comments on sin (not inherited) and sacrifice (not propitiation) are most helpful. As is true of most theologies except Anabaptist, Paul's thought forms get more attention than do those of Jesus. In spite of that weakness, though, Moody has given us a first-rate systematic that deserves a wide readership and a long life.

Paul Mickey's highly recommended *Essentials of Wesleyan Theology* is irenic and scholarly. Building on the strengths of the Wesleyan tradition, he presents a creative and lucid exposition of evangelical theology. This brief volume is not only a source of good thinking for advanced students, it is also an excellent resource for laypersons who are in the beginning stages of developing a theological framework for their Christian beliefs and actions. Mickey includes a chapter on ethical implications that can help lead believers toward faithfulness in daily activities.

As more scholars have realized the wealth of revelation that comes to us as narrative, the possibility of writing theology in such narrative styles has become a contemporary option. Gabriel

Fackre, professor of theology at Andover-Newton Theological School, has given us *The Christian Story*. This is another "mini-systematic," focusing on God's acts rather than on propositional truths. Fackre encourages the reader to think through the implications of various events, finding the themes of liberation and reconciliation to be most recurring. By understanding God's activities, we are better able to discover the appropriateness of our own responses to God's revelation. A volume on salvation is expected soon.

Evangelicals have increasingly drawn on the strengths of the Anabaptist-Mennonite tradition. Paul Lederach has made this even more feasible in publishing *A Third Way*. Lederach first sets out the key affirmations of Anabaptist thought, focusing on the centrality of Jesus Christ, the primacy of God's Kingdom, and the significance of a visible and well-defined church which is the community of the Spirit. While Western Christendom has often centered its identity on the affirmation of the Apostles Creed, Lederach points out that the whole of Jesus' teachings and activities (except for his birth, death, and resurrection) are omitted. This is the uniqueness of Anabaptist theology—a continual and thorough focusing on Jesus Christ. Because Jesus provided a salvation that met the "whole person" (spiritual, physical, emotional, social), we had best not ignore any aspects of his grace. Following this section, Lederach compares and contrasts this "system" with other strands of Christian theology. An increasingly faithful response to Scripture and to Jesus is available to evangelicals as the resources of Anabaptism are comprehended.

Sets

Bloesch, Donald G. *Essentials of Evangelical Theology. Volume 1: God, Authority, and Salvation.** HR, 1978. *Volume 2: Life, Ministry, and Hope.** HR, 1979.

Boice, James M. *Foundations of the Christian Faith. Volume 1: The Sovereign God; Volume 2: God the Redeemer; Volume 3: Awakening to God; Volume 4: God and History.*† IVP, 1976–1980. A contemporary, somewhat popularized version of Calvinism.

Henry, Carl F. H. *God, Revelation, and Authority.** 5 vols. to date. WB, 1976–.

Thielicke, Helmut. *The Evangelical Faith.** 3 vols. WBE, 1974–1982.

Wiley, H. Orter. *Christian Theology.* 3 vols. Nazarene Publishing House, 1940. It has been a while since we have had a thorough systematic set from the Wesleyan-Holiness tradition; this is still a standard work.

Single-Volume Systematics

Berkhof, Hendrikus. *Christian Faith: An Introduction to the Study of the Faith.* WBE, 1979. A Dutch Reformed theologian, critical of Schleiermacher, provides a lucid, valuable systematic; different type sizes differentiate between material for scholars and that for laity.

Buswell, James Oliver. *A Systematic Theology of the Christian Religion.* ZC, 1969. A conservative, readable development of covenant theology in two volumes; Volume I deals with theism and biblical anthropology; Volume II with soteriology and eschatology.

Cone, James H. *A Black Theology of Liberation.* Lippincott, 1970. *God of the Oppressed.* Seabury, 1975. A Christian's personal and cultural history impact the way one perceives theological issues, and Cone has helped lead the way for an important stream of American liberation thinkers. Sociology and anthropology help define modern issues, and sensitivities gained highlight different biblical content than may be heard by those of different backgrounds. Hopefully non-Blacks will gain an appreciation for such theology.

Fackre, Gabriel. *The Christian Story.** WBE, 1978.

Friedman, Robert. *The Theology of Anabaptism.* HP, 1973. Anabaptism has an "existential" center but needs further conceptual work: we are justified not "in sin" but "out of sin," the way of discipleship precedes concern for salvation, grace is not primarily soteriological but creative; insightful presentation with bibliography.

Lederach, Paul M. *A Third Way.**† HP, 1980.

Marshall, I. Howard. *Pocket Guide to Christian Beliefs.* IVP, 1978. Valuable starting place for laypersons; offers definitions, biblical background, comments on key issues.

Mickey, Paul A. *Essentials of Wesleyan Theology.**† ZC, 1980.

Moody, Dale. *The Word of Truth.** WBE, 1981.

Morris, Leon. *Great Doctrines of the Bible*. IVP, 1960. A brief, introductory survey of basic orthodox themes.

Oden, Thomas C. *Agenda for Theology: Recovering Christian Roots*. HR, 1979. As a "postliberal" theologian moving toward an informed evangelical position, Oden cautions against the accommodating methods of much modern theology; contains an especially insightful discussion of the Pastoral Epistles.

Topel, L. John. *The Way to Peace, Liberation Through the Bible*. OB, 1979. Traces liberation themes through the Bible, thus providing a very readable, gentle study guide to a very important theme.

Wainwright, Geoffrey. *Doxology: The Praise of God in Worship, Doctrine, and Life.** OUP, 1980.

Weber, Otto. *Foundations of Dogmatics*. WBE, 1981. Explores the role of dogmatics as a scholarly pursuit and in relationship to the church.

Wynkoop, Mildred B. *A Theology of Love: Dynamics of Wesleyanism*. Beacon Hill, 1972. The intersection of love and holiness provides a viable center for doing theology; hermeneutics, salvation, sanctification, morality, and Wesleyan theology are discussed.

Theological Expositions of the Apostles' Creed

Barth, Karl. *Credo*. Scribners, 1962.

Pannenberg, Wolfhart. *The Apostles' Creed in the Light of Today's Questions*. WP, 1972.

Thielicke, Helmut. *I Believe: The Christian's Creed*. FP, 1968.

GOD

Theological studies that focus on God the Creator, God the Father, the Trinity, and various related topics are less abundant than one would anticipate. Each of the preceding systematic sets would include valuable material on most of these issues.

A popular and still theologically sound contribution is J. I. Packer's *Knowing God*. It serves as an excellent introduction to the Reformed tradition, yet is still very accessible to laypersons desiring materials that relate to devotional needs.

Going beyond his own involvement in the charismatic renewal, and in reflection on the Jesus movement, Thomas Smail, in

The Forgotten Father, provides a helpful theology on God the Father. Renewal is too often "need centered," and that characteristic can only be overcome when Christians place themselves at the disposal of a loving, powerful Father. This is the Father of our Lord Jesus Christ, and the one to whom the Spirit says, "Abba." Smail's volume has come at a most appropriate time.

James Houston's insightful and unique *I Believe in the Creator* works more from an aesthetic basis, developing the theological implications in ways that invite meditation rather than analysis. As a layman himself, Houston sought to write so that anyone's vocational, relational, or artistic pursuits could be rooted in God's creative work. His book is a valuable and thoughtful contribution. *The Living God,* by R. T. France, is probably the best basic introduction to theological issues in this area. Hans Küng's *Does God Exist?* is an incredible, massive development of themes, apologetics, and a call to faith by a contemporary Roman Catholic writer.

The question of theodicy, or the problem of evil, is handled with insight and clarity by C. S. Lewis in *The Problem of Pain,* and by John W. Wenham in *The Goodness of God.*

In a time when some see Satan as a myth and others join occult groups at an alarming rate, Michael Green has provided a helpful biblical study, *I Believe in Satan's Downfall.* Satan's work is seen in individuals and in societal structures. The limits to his work are also clear. Green's volume is nontechnical and maintains clear theological thinking. Also helpful on this topic is Dietrich Bonhoeffer's *Creation and Fall.*

Concerning God's sovereignty, predestination, and free will, two recent volumes look promising. D. A. Carson's *Divine Sovereignty and Human Responsibility,* focusing on the Old Testament and on the Gospel of John, argues that these beliefs are not contradictory. His understanding of free will appears to lack sufficient development, however. James Daane's *The Freedom of God,* subtitled *A Study of Election and Pulpit,* presents a good case for clear preaching on this subject. Daane avoids the scholastic pitfalls, offering a development of the theme of election as it relates to Israel, Jesus Christ, and the church.

Bonhoeffer, Dietrich. *Creation and Fall.** MCP, 1965.
Carson, D. A. *Divine Sovereignty and Human Responsibility.**
    JKP, 1981.

Daane, James. *The Freedom of God.** WBE, 1973.

France, R. T. *The Living God.**† IVP, 1970.

Frost, Robert. *Our Heavenly Father.*† Logos, 1978. Good popular development, with comments about differentiating from one's earthly father.

Green, Michael. *I Believe in Satan's Downfall.** WBE, 1981.

Houston, James. *I Believe in the Creator.** WBE, 1980.

Küng, Hans. *Does God Exist?** DC, 1978.

Lewis, C. S. *The Problem of Pain.**† McP, 1962.

Motyer, J. A. *The Revelation of the Divine Name.* TH, 1959. Concise, scholarly.

Murphy, Jon Tal. *A Loving God and a Suffering World.*† IVP, 1981. A helpful introduction to the problem of evil.

Packer, J. I. *Knowing God.**† IVP, 1973.

Ramm, Bernard. *The Pattern of Religious Authority.* WBE, 1957. Problems of individualism and anarchism as well as communism and "statism" indicate that we need a better grasp of the relationship between liberty and authority; explores different types of authority and its link with power, then shows how the church is to function under God's authority. Very helpful topical study.

Schaeffer, Francis. *The God Who Is There.* IVP, 1968. *He Is There and He Is Not Silent.* TH, 1972. Based on presuppositional apologetics, Schaeffer addresses contemporary philosophical and theological issues. Though a good evangelist, Schaeffer does not generally understand scholarly works. Most notable, he misses Kierkegaard and Barth.

Smail, Thomas A. *The Forgotten Father.** WBE, 1980.

Spittler, Russell. *God the Father.* Gospel Publishing House, 1976. Very popular, basic development.

Suenens, Leon Joseph, Cardinal. *Your God?* Seabury, 1978. Excellent devotional statement by a Roman Catholic scholar and pastor.

Torrance, T. F. *The Ground and Grammar of Theology.* University Press of Virginia, 1980. Contains a good statement on the Trinity.

Wenham, John W. *The Goodness of God.** IVP, 1974.

JESUS CHRIST

The topic of christology focuses on the nature and relationship of Jesus Christ's dual nature (divine and human), a topic directly related to the theological term "incarnation," and often attempts to separate the "historical Jesus" (who occupied a certain geographical setting during particular years) from "the Christ of faith" (worshiped by the New Testament church and by Christians today).

Jürgen Moltmann's *The Crucified God* is among the best contemporary statements. He dialogues extensively with other viewpoints and develops a theology close to classical Christianity. Unlike many conservative christologists, Moltmann understands and develops the social implications of Jesus' life, death, and resurrection. Another excellent recent volume is that by Wolfhart Pannenberg entitled *Jesus—God and Man*. Pannenberg focuses on the resurrection as the starting point for understanding Jesus, thereby missing the significance of Jesus' miracles, compassion, and concern for justice in understanding the incarnation.

Helmut Thielicke's *The Silence of God* expounds on the themes of Jesus' incarnation, crucifixion, and resurrection, and their implications for Christians. *The Lord from Heaven*, by Leon Morris, and *I Came to Set the Earth on Fire*, by R. T. France, are the best concise introductions to christology.

A flurry of discussion in England followed the recent publication of *The Myth of God Incarnate*, edited by John Hick. In that short volume several theologians challenged traditional beliefs about Jesus Christ. In response, Michael Green edited *The Truth of God Incarnate*, and a later collection, Michael Goulder's *Incarnation and Myth: The Debate Continued*, in which evangelical contributions were notable by their absence, soon followed. Probably the most beneficial result was a very worthwhile contribution by C. F. D. Moule, *The Origin of Christology*.

Another volume that received earlier mention, John Howard Yoder's *Politics of Jesus*, is an essential volume for understanding the relationship between christology and sociopolitical issues. *Jesus Christ Liberator*, written by Brazilian priest Leonardo Boff, draws on the work of Moltmann. It aids in understanding how christological issues are being developed outside the European–North American setting.

Baillie, Donald M. *God Was in Christ*. Scribners, 1948. One of the best older statements.

Berkhof, Hendrikus. *Christ, the Meaning of History.* BBH, 1979. A good Dutch Reformed work.

Berkouwer, G. C. *The Person of Christ.* WBE, 1952. Focuses on the two natures of Christ as stated in early creeds.

Boff, Leonardo. *Jesus Christ Liberator.** OB, 1978.

Cullmann, Oscar. *Christ and Time.* WP, 1962. Following a German approach that attempts to separate history into two strands, thereby studying "salvation history" apart from other more accessible history; creative, thoughtful scholarship.

France, R. T. *I Came to Set the Earth on Fire.*† IVP, 1975.

Goulder, Michael, ed. *Incarnation and Myth: The Debate Continued.** WBE, 1979.

Green, Michael, ed. *The Truth of God Incarnate.** WBE, 1977.

Henry, Carl F. H. *Jesus of Nazareth: Savior and Lord.* WBE, 1966. Leading evangelical scholars contribute essays on questions of history, theology, miracles, and recent scholarly debates.

Hick, John, ed. *The Myth of God Incarnate.** WP, 1978.

Kasper, Walter. *Jesus the Christ.* PP, 1976. Roman Catholic.

Ladd, George. *I Believe in the Resurrection.* WBE, 1975. Very good on both historicity and the theological theme of resurrection.

Marshall, I. Howard. *Work of Christ.* ZC, 1970. Sees the cross as the center of christology.

Moltmann, Jürgen. *The Crucified God.** WP, 1974.

Morris, Leon. *The Lord from Heaven.*† IVP, 1974.

Moule, C. F. D. *The Origin of Christology.** Cambridge University Press, 1977.

O'Collins, Gerald S. J. *What Are They Saying About Jesus?* PP, 1977. An informative, brief survey of modern approaches to christology, especially Küng, Pannenberg, Kasper, and Schillebeeckx; shows the link between historical-critical studies and theological formulations.

Pannenberg, Wolfhart. *Jesus—God and Man.** WP, 1977.

Sobrino, Jon. *Christology at the Crossroads.* Orbis, 1978. Draws on Moltmann, speaks to a Latin American context.

Thielicke, Helmut. *The Silence of God.*† WBE, 1962.

Thompson, John. *Christ in Perspective: Christological Perspectives in the Theology of Karl Barth.* WBE, 1978. Mainly an exposition on Barth.

Toon, Peter. *Jesus Christ Is Lord.* Judson, 1978. Introductory
lectures on Jesus as Lord of nations, the church, the universe, and the Christian's life; counters modern challenges
to the role and relevance of Jesus.

Yoder, John Howard. *Politics of Jesus.** WBE, 1972.

SEE ALSO the items on christology under Biblical Theology.

THE HOLY SPIRIT

There are a multitude of issues revolving around the doctrine
of the Holy Spirit. The *filioque* clause added to the Nicene
Creed, "who proceeds from the Father *and the Son,*" remains
today as a theological barrier between Eastern and Western
churches. The Eastern Church believes that this "restriction"
diminishes the role and significance of the Holy Spirit. The relationship of Jesus' spirit to the Holy Spirit, as well as differing
theologies concerning sanctification, "spiritual gifts," the "baptism of the Spirit," the "fullness of the Holy Spirit," and certain
"charismatic gifts," continue to provide topics for an abundance
of books. The various church traditions, especially Holiness,
Pentecostal, and charismatic, define themselves largely by their
concept of the role of the Holy Spirit.

The best introduction to the Holy Spirit is *I Believe in the
Holy Spirit,* by Michael Green, an Anglican minister involved
in church renewal. In this book Green ably demonstrates his
abilities as both a scholar and a pastor. C. F. D. Moule's *The
Holy Spirit* addresses the relationship of Jesus to the Holy Spirit, the Spirit's role in the church, and such contemporary issues
as charismatic renewal. Leon Morris's *Spirit of the Living God*
is another fine nontechnical introduction by an Australian New
Testament scholar.

Russell Spittler has edited a collection of essays under the title
Perspectives on the New Pentecostalism. Contributors include
Harvard's Krister Stendahl, Reformed theologian Rodman Williams, Canadian Baptist Clark Pinnock, Episcopalian Morton
Kelsey, Benedictine Kilian McDonnell, and thirteen others.
Biblical, theological, and practical issues receive valuable attention. Thomas Smail's *Reflected Glory* is a helpful theological
statement on contemporary charismatic thinking. Robert Culpepper offers an insightful appraisal of this renewal in *Evaluating the Charismatic Movement.* In addition to biblical, theologi-

cal, and historical discussions, he notes that there is a healthy tendency inside the movement toward appropriate self-criticism and an increasing appreciation voiced by outsiders. A bibliography follows his summary of the movement's strengths and weaknesses.

From the European scene, Heribert Muhler offers *A Charismatic Theology: Initiation in the Spirit.* Various study groups assembled the materials for this textbook. A biblical and theological critique of charismatic theology and practice is provided by Frederick D. Bruner in *A Theology of the Holy Spirit.* It appears that particular Reformed viewpoints influenced Bruner's biblical studies, thereby restricting his understanding of the contemporary movement. Another articulate critic is Anthony Hoekema. Two earlier books, *What About Tongue-Speaking?* and *Holy Spirit Baptism* have recently been combined into *Tongues and Spirit-Baptism.*

An enlightening contribution on the Holy Spirit from the Wesleyan tradition is that by Laurence Wood, *Pentecostal Grace.* Such biblical events as the Exodus and conquest are related to the resurrection and Pentecost. The theology of the Holy Spirit proceeds, linking the Wesleyan concept of perfection, the Pentecostal understanding of the infilling of the Holy Spirit, and the Roman Catholic and Anglican rite of confirmation.

Berkhof, Hendrikus. *The Doctrine of the Holy Spirit.* JKP, 1964. Good development of themes as they relate to the Holy Spirit, including Christ, the church, missions, consummation. Appears to be modalist.

Bittlinger, Arnold. *Gifts and Graces.* WBE, 1967. *Gifts and Ministries.* WBE, 1973. German charismatic, very good.

Bridge, Donald, and David Phypers. *Spiritual Gifts and the Church.*† IVP, 1973. Good basic introduction, especially the mediating comments on tongues and on apostleship.

Bruner, Frederick D. *A Theology of the Holy Spirit.** WBE, 1970.

Culpepper, Robert. *Evaluating the Charismatic Movement.** Judson, 1977.

Duncan, George G. *The Person and Work of the Holy Spirit in the Life of the Believer.* JKP, 1973. Good introduction for laypersons; develops various terms along classical lines.

Gelpi, Donald. *Pentecostalism: A Theological Viewpoint.* PP, 1971. Insightful Roman Catholic work. Sympathetic with Pentecostalism.

Graham, Billy. *The Holy Spirit.*† Warner, 1978. Most theologically aware of Graham's books.

Green, Michael. *I Believe in the Holy Spirit.**† WBE, 1975.

Hoekema, Anthony. *Tongues and Spirit-Baptism.** BBH, 1981.

Howard, David M. *By the Power of the Holy Spirit.* IVP, 1973. A nontechnical introduction to the role and work of the Holy Spirit in the life of the believer and in the church, with a focus on outreach; includes a cautious appreciation for charismatic teachings.

Hummel, Charles. *Fire in the Fireplace: Contemporary Charismatic Renewal.* IVP, 1978. Appreciative overview of historical developments, biblical passages, and prospective outlook.

Jones, James. *The Spirit and the World.* Hawthorne, 1975. A helpful academic presentation of the historical and theological issues; offers the hope that the charismatic renewal will have a powerful influence on the world beyond cloistered communities.

Kelsey, Morton. *Tongue-Speaking.* DC, 1964. *Healing and Christianity.* HR, 1973. Positive comments on the strengths and healthiness of renewal.

McDonnell, Kilian. *Charismatic Renewal of the Churches.* Seabury, 1976. Surveys various sociological and psychological studies made on charismatic happenings, critiquing the presuppositional biases evident in those explorations.

————. *The Charismatic Renewal and Ecumenism.* PP, 1978. A thorough, sympathetic evaluation of international links gaining strength within the movement.

Moody, Dale. *Spirit of the Living God.* WP, 1968. Valuable biblical, theological study.

Morris, Leon. *Spirit of the Living God.**† IVP, 1960.

Moule, C. F. D. *The Holy Spirit.** WBE, 1979.

Muhler, Heribert. *A Charismatic Theology—Initiation in the Spirit.** PP, 1978.

Ramm, Bernard. *The Witness of the Spirit.* WBE, 1959. Helpful biblical and theological study concerning the internal witness of the Spirit to truth and personal assurance.

_____. *Questions About the Spirit.* WB, 1974. Good biblical, theological survey of numerous issues; suitable for laypersons.

Ramsey, A. Michael. *Holy Spirit: A Biblical Study.* WBE, 1977. Scholarly and pastoral; presents theological issues as they relate to renewal.

Smail, Thomas. *Reflected Glory.**† WBE, 1976.

Spittler, Russell, ed. *Perspectives on the New Pentecostalism.** BBH, 1976.

Stott, John R. W. *Baptism and Fullness: The Work of the Holy Spirit Today.* IVP, 1976. Discussion of different events and issues in the Christian life; differentiates between conversion and ongoing steps of sanctification.

Tuttle, Robert. *The Partakers.* AP, 1977. Concise, basic statement from a Methodist theologian, with appreciation for charismatic distinctives.

White, R. E. O. *The Answer Is the Spirit.* WP, 1979. Refreshing overview of the Spirit's work in the New Testament to solve human problems; various implications are discussed.

Wood, Laurence. *Pentecostal Grace.** Francis Asbury, 1980.

THE MEANING OF HUMANNESS

Anthropology concerns the study of humanness. It asks, How can personhood be defined? How do men and women relate to their Creator? To each other? To themselves? What is the "image of God" in which humans were created? How has sin affected the core of humanness?

G. C. Berkouwer's two volumes, *Man, the Image of God* and *Sin,* are the most substantial recent treatments of anthropology. The first discusses God's image, the corruption of that image, and human freedom. Berkouwer is conversant with various currents in contemporary thought, including biblical, theological, sociological, psychological, existential, and the discoveries of modern science. Both volumes are faithful to the classical Reformed faith, and are fresh, contemporary contributions able to perceive the subtle nuances of numerous modern issues. *Death and Life,* by the German Lutheran theologian and preacher Helmut Thielicke, is a brilliant, thorough, biblical exploration into death, which leads into a clearer understanding of life.

Philosophical, anthropological, and psychological studies are the basis for Thielicke's study.

George Carey's *I Believe in Man* provides a thoughtful but not overly technical theological perspective. The uniqueness of humans in creation, issues of brokenness and redemption, the relationship between man and woman, and human destiny are among the topics discussed, with helpful scriptural references and interaction with human sciences.

Paul Tournier incorporates his experiences and scholarly pursuits as a Swiss psychiatrist in *The Meaning of Persons.* He contrasts the *person* (the "real person") with the *personage* (the "image or appearance" projected to others, which both reveals and conceals the person). These facets are intertwined in a way that prevents total distinction, yet the approach offers insights beyond those studies that deal mainly with theology. Tournier's integration of Christianity with his psychological pursuits is a model of excellence for other professionals.

A particular area of study receiving wider attention currently is that of male/female distinctions and similarities. Paul Jewett's *Man as Male and Female* offers one of the best biblical, theological studies which also investigates historical theology and needs for the modern church. *All We're Meant to Be,* by Letha Scanzoni and Nancy Hardesty, is probably the best overall biblical study. Recently Stephen Clark attempted to counter these studies with *Man and Woman in Christ.* Clark defends a clearer role differentiation that calls on men to be more aggressive and decisive and women to be submissive and gentle. This is by far the most massive and erudite presentation from this viewpoint and will invite a continuation of the discussion.

Berkhof, Hendrikus. *Man in Transition.* Key Publications, 1971. A helpful theological statement by a Dutch Reformed scholar.

Berkouwer, G. C. *Man, the Image of God.** WBE, 1952. *Sin.** WBE, 1952.

Carey, George. *I Believe in Man.**† WBE, 1977.

Clark, Stephen B. *Man and Woman in Christ.** Servant, 1980.

Eller, Vernard. *The Language of Canaan and the Grammar of Feminism.* WBE, 1982. A critical analysis that challenges the use of nonsexist language.

Gelpi, Donald L. *Experiencing God: A Theology of Human Emergence.* PP, 1978. A Roman Catholic scholar develops an anthropological basis for spiritual growth.

Gundry, Patricia. *Woman, Be Free.*† ZC, 1979. An insightful biblical study favoring egalitarianism.

Jewett, Paul K. *Man as Male and Female.** WBE, 1975.

Macaulay, Ronald, and Jerram Barrs. *Being Human: The Nature of Spiritual Experience.* IVP, 1978. A good study that works with input from theology and social sciences.

Martin, Charles. *How Human Can You Get?* IVP, 1973. Though written for a wide audience, this is a fairly scholarly attempt to untangle syntax problems concerning how secularists and Christians agree or disagree on the meaning of humanness.

McDonald, H. D. *The Christian View of Man.* Crossway Books, 1981. An introductory guide to biblical foundations, historical theology, and contemporary issues; modern thought on origins, issues of existentialism, and humanism; social sciences are viewed in light of Christian theology; approaches some corporate issues but fails to deal significantly with social ethics.

Middleman, Udo. *Pro-Existence.* IVP, 1974. Brief statement on how humans relate to the reality around them, especially in regard to work.

Míguez Bonino, José. *Room to Be People.* FP, 1979. The meaning of humanness, both personal and corporate, is explored with insights into biblical teachings and modern society; sin is the abandonment of responsibility, idolatry is comfort without involvement—God's love consoles and challenges.

Mollenkott, Virginia. *Women, Men and the Bible.* AP, 1977. A brief, helpful introduction to biblical, theological, and practical issues on human equality.

Scanzoni, Letha, and Nancy Hardesty. *All We're Meant to Be.**† WB, 1974.

Thielicke, Helmut. *Death and Life.** FP, 1970.

Tournier, Paul. *The Meaning of Persons.** HR, 1957.

————. *The Whole Person in a Broken World.* HR, 1964. Works at the relationship of human healthiness in the surroundings of pervasive evil and pain; excellent.

Verduin, Leonard. *Somewhat Less than God: The Biblical View of Man*. WBE, 1970. The title is fitting for this good introduction to anthropology.

SEE ALSO What Christians Believe: Salvation and The Christian Church: Missions and Evangelism.

REVELATION AND INSPIRATION

The evangelical faith claims to be distinctive in the authority and trustworthiness it believes to be resident in Holy Scripture. It affirms the doctrine of revelation—how and what God has expressed to humankind in various ways (acts in history, speeches through prophets, Scripture, and most completely in the incarnation)—and the doctrine of inspiration, which focuses on God's project of providing us with a holy "reader" or collection of writings. Several issues surround what Christians believe about the Bible: its authority, accuracy, purpose, uniqueness, power, normativeness, and the many terms used to describe and define those topics. The Bible contains an array of writings—histories, poetry, letters, parables, ceremonial liturgies and hymns, prophecies, apocalyptic compositions—each to be received as God's gracious self-revelation.

G. C. Berkouwer's *Holy Scripture* sets out the modern discussion in brilliant form. The interrelationship of the human and divine elements in Scripture tends to be one of the key issues. Berkouwer is conversant with the spectrum of beliefs on this issue, from American fundamentalists to European and North American radical critics. He develops an understanding of the canon which views it as reliable, clear, and sufficient. The "servant form" of Scripture receives careful comments. Berkouwer believes that, because Scripture comes to us in a "human channel," it is to be analyzed like other such writings. Yet there is a difference. The biblical scholar must remember that he or she is working with a text that has God's Spirit behind it, and the critical work must not infringe on the Spirit's message or authority. As is true in other doctrinal areas, Berkouwer's contribution is first-rate.

Carl F. H. Henry's *God, Revelation, and Authority: God Who Speaks and Shows* is an important and lucid contribution on revelation and inspiration. *The Divine Inspiration of Holy Scripture,* by William J. Abrahams, presents a Wesleyan perspective. Countering the work of B. B. Warfield and other Reformed conservatives, Abrahams concentrates on various models which can help us understand the concept of inspiration. Paul J. Achtemeier is working on a middle ground between the older liberal-conservative paradigms. In *The Inspiration of Scripture: Problems, and Proposals,* he presents a well-researched textbook which affirms God's work in producing and collecting the biblical documents. His hopefulness should encourage further dialogue across old barriers.

The recent debates within the evangelical subculture surrounding the term "inerrancy" may eventually offer some positive contributions to the doctrine of inspiration. Following the release of Harold Lindsell's *The Battle for the Bible* in 1976, many books, articles, conferences, and rallies have focused attention on this particular formulation concerning biblical accuracy and truthfulness. To advance the inerrancy cause, the International Council on Biblical Inerrancy was formed to provide guidance on formulating the required biblical, historical, doctrinal, and practical statements. *The Foundation of Biblical Authority,* edited by James Boice, presents several essays on relevant issues. Other authors to look for on this issue include Norman Geisler and R. C. Sproul.

Evangelicals who disagree with these views are attempting to clarify terms and advance theological positions that, though not espousing inerrancy, still maintain faithful views of scriptural truthfulness and authority. *The Debate About the Bible,* by Stephen Davis, and *The Authority and Interpretation of the Bible,* by Jack Rogers and Donald McKim, are among the most helpful books in this subject. The latter concentrates on the historical development of such terms as infallibility and inerrancy.

Abrahams, William J. *The Divine Inspiration of Holy Scripture.** OUP, 1981.

Achtemeier, Paul J. *The Inspiration of Scripture: Problems and Proposals.** WP, 1980.

Berkouwer, G. C. *Holy Scripture.** WBE, 1975.

Boice, James M., ed. *The Foundation of Biblical Authority.** ZC, 1978.

Davis, Stephen T. *The Debate About the Bible.** WP, 1977.

Demarest, Bruce A. *General Revelation.* ZC, 1982. Just re-

[115]

leased; surveys historical theology and interacts with current nonevangelical and syncretistic directions; offers a thorough, conservative approach.

Gasque, W. W., and W. S. LaSor, eds. *Scripture, Tradition, and Inspiration.* WBE, 1978. A valuable collection of essays honoring E. F. Harrison; includes G. Bromiley, R. Mounce, C. Carlston, D. Fuller, and others on the nature and purpose of the Bible and principles of interpretation.

Geisler, Norman, ed. *Biblical Errancy—An Analysis of Its Philosophical Roots.* ZC, 1981. Eight essays on the historical study of philosophy as it relates to this contemporary debate.

————. *Summit Papers.* International Council on Biblical Inerrancy, n.d. The proceedings of an early ICBI conference.

Henry, Carl F. H. *God, Revelation, and Authority: God Who Speaks and Shows.** 4 vols. WB, 1976.

Kistemacher, Simon J., ed. *Interpreting God's Word Today.* BBH, 1970. Conservative introduction to doctrine and practice.

Lindsell, Harold. *The Battle for the Bible.** ZC, 1976.

Nicole, Roger, and J. Ramsey Michaels, eds. *Inerrancy and Common Sense.* BBH, 1980. Includes essays by J. J. Davis, J. I. Packer, R. Lovelace, and others.

Pinnock, Clark. *Biblical Revelation.* MP, 1971. Defends conservative doctrines on revelation and inspiration in light of modern radical theories. Positive statement concerning the Reformed *sola scriptura* theology.

————. *A Defense of Biblical Infallibility.* Presbyterian and Reformed, 1975. A brief pamphlet, concise and helpful.

Ramm, Bernard. *Special Revelation and the Word of God.* WBE, 1971. One of the more helpful evangelical statements, tying these two theological issues together.

Ridderbos, Herman. *Studies in Scripture and Its Authority.* WBE, 1978. The first essay in this helpful volume develops a view of authority as it relates to the biblical message and purpose; other essays concern Jesus, the Kingdom of God, and the future.

Rogers, Jack, ed. *Biblical Authority.* WB, 1977. Includes essays by B. Ramm, C. Pinnock, D. Hubbard, and others in response to the Lindsell book.

Rogers, Jack, and Donald McKim. *The Authority and Interpretation of the Bible.** HR, 1979.

THE KINGDOM OF GOD

Christian expectations for the future are the subject of eschatology, the study of "last things." In recent scholarship, a cluster of theological topics surrounding the term *Kingdom of God* is closely intertwined with eschatology. Jesus—his life, death, resurrection, and ascension—is seen as the decisive event of history. Years following that event must be discussed in light of biblical teachings about "last things," or events that follow that historical event. Jesus proclaimed the Kingdom to those who follow him. In what way is that Kingdom present now? How does it relate to the future? What is the relationship between the church and the Kingdom? What prophecies in the New Testament were fulfilled during the first century of Christianity? What events are still future? What can we know about that future?

John Bright's *The Kingdom of God* is a durable, lucid statement, scholarly yet not too technical for use as an introduction. Bright traces the idea of God's Kingdom from the Old Testament (including germane comments about Israel) through the New (including interaction between Jesus and the apostolic church). He rejects any approach that drives a wedge between the Old Covenant and the work of Jesus, choosing rather to show the consistency of God's work. Jesus is the Servant Messiah of the Kingdom, and cannot be reduced to a liberal view that limits his domain to that of moral teachings intended to make humans behave more ethically. Bright's work is a pacesetter, demonstrating the benefits of solid biblical exegesis, thorough theological reflection, and a passion for preachable Christianity.

George E. Ladd is another front-runner in adding scholarly, creative, insightful studies on the Kingdom. *The Presence of the Future* is the apt title for his discussion of the promises and fulfillment of Jesus' Kingdom. Ladd clarifies many issues concerning future events that continually incite debate within Christian circles. The Kingdom of God is here now, and has been present since Jesus first proclaimed its arrival. Yet the Kingdom is still in the future. To put it another way, the future Kingdom of Christ's rule has invaded the present age, and people are called to live in that new domain. Isaac Rottenberg's *The Promise and the Presence* provides another lucid exposition on this concept of living in two ages. In the power of the Holy Spirit, we are currently living as members of the Kingdom, while the full consummation of the Kingdom is still in the future. Rottenberg discusses current positions of other scholars and the resulting impact of those theologies on the church's work in the world (evangelism, development, organizations). *And Then Comes the End*, by David Ewert, is the best overall introduction to these issues. He clearly explains various current positions, discusses relevant biblical passages, and develops an eschatology that is centered in christology. This is usually an area of strength in Anabaptist/Mennonite theology, and Ewert does not disappoint his readers.

Books that focus more specifically on prophecy and the future can also help clarify the confusion that has existed since Hal Lindsey's volumes began appearing. *Handbook of Biblical Prophecy,* edited by Carl Armerding and Ward Gasque, is a collection of fourteen essays by evangelical authors, including F. F. Bruce, George Ladd, Richard Longenecker, and many others. The role of prophecy in biblical writings and its purpose for the church today is developed in clear, nontechnical chapters. Written more directly to challenge the Lindsey era is Dewey Beegle's *Prophecy and Prediction*. Beegle's excellent biblical and theological work is apparent in this volume, which deserves a wide readership.

Armerding, Carl E., and W. Ward Gasque, eds. *Handbook of Biblical Prophecy.**† BBH, 1977. Formerly titled *Dreams, Visions and Oracles.*

Beegle, Dewey. *Prophecy and Prediction.** Pryor Pettengil, 1978.

Berkouwer, G. C. *The Return of Christ.* WBE, 1972. The Dutch Reformed theologian covers an array of topics including what happens to Christians at death, the place of Israel in the future, the millennium, judgment, and bodily resurrection.

Bright, John. *The Kingdom of God.** AP, 1953.

Clouse, Robert G., ed. *The Meaning of the Millennium.* IVP, 1977. Four different theologians write introductory essays on their views of the millennium: Ladd defends the historical premillennial position, Hoyt writes on the dispensational view, Boettner defends a postmillennium, and Hoekema asserts an amillennial belief; each writer responds to the views of the others.

Ewert, David. *And Then Comes the End.**† HP, 1980.

Fackre, Gabriel. *The Rainbow Sign.* WBE, 1969. A very good introduction to the theology of hope.

Gundry, Robert H. *The Church and the Tribulation.* ZC, 1973. Based on sound exegetical and theological work, Gundry counters those who assert that a "rapture" will remove the church from the earth before the "great tribulation" occurs.

Hoekema, Anthony. *The Bible and the Future.* WBE, 1979. Covering the full range of eschatological issues, Hoekema concludes with an amillennial view of the future; good biblical and theological work, clear presentation.

Ladd, George. *The Blessed Hope.* WBE, 1956. Believing that the "pretribulation rapture" position is inaccurate and harmful for the church, Ladd clearly sets out biblical evidence against it.

————. *The Last Things.*† WBE, 1978. A helpful, brief, nontechnical presentation on the relationship of Old Testament prophecies, New Testament fulfillments, and what we know about events still in the future; an appropriate starting place for laypersons.

————. *The Presence of the Future.** WBE, 1974. Formerly *Jesus and the Kingdom.*

————. *Crucial Questions About the Kingdom of God.* WBE, 1952. Introductory lectures on various interpretations, with Ladd's skillful presentation of theological and biblical issues; focuses on Jesus' teachings.

Limburg, J. *The Prophets and the Powerless.* JKP, 1977. Explicitly countering Hal Lindsey's view and interpretation of prophecy, Limburg offers a biblical and historical view of prophets and their messages for our time.

Lindsey, Hal. *The Late Great Planet Earth.* ZC, 1970. A pacesetting best-seller; valuable only to demonstrate how bad Bible interpretation can be.

Moltmann, Jürgen. *The Experiment Hope.* FP, 1975. Following his earlier volumes, *Theology of Hope* and *Crucified God,* these essays provide a good introduction to a theologian whose work centers around our anticipations of God's active work in history; Moltmann moves closer to classical trinitarianism in this volume.

Morris, Leon. *The Biblical Doctrine of Judgment.* IVP, 1960. A brief study of Old Testament and New Testament teachings about judgment.

Pannenberg, Wolfhart. *Theology and the Kingdom of God.* WP, 1969. A rigorous, biblical presentation developing the relationship of the Kingdom to the church, ethics, and the future.

Peters, Ted. *Futures Human and Divine.* JKP, 1978. Compares and contrasts secularist and Christian views of the future, asserting that Christianity offers the framework in which to deal with evil and failure; focuses on the values of peace, life, nature, and equality.

Ridderbos, Herman. *The Coming of the Kingdom.* Presbyterian and Reformed, 1962. A theological development within the Reformed tradition; concise, helpful.

Rottenberg, Isaac C. *The Promise and the Presence.** WBE, 1980.

Toon, Peter. *God's Kingdom for Today.*† Crossway Books, 1980. A noteworthy introduction to biblical studies (Old Testament, Jesus, early church) and appropriate modern applications of those teachings for the church, personal ethics, social ethics, and our hope for the future.

Walvoord, John F. *The Blessed Hope and the Tribulation.* ZC, 1976. Dispensationalists anticipate the Second Coming after a seven-year tribulation, preceding which all Christians will be "raptured" off the earth; needs Ladd's response.

SEE ALSO What Christians Believe: Jesus Christ and The Christian Church: Introduction; Missions and Evangelism.

SALVATION

Soteriology concerns the work of salvation. The means, steps, ingredients, results, extent, and duration of salvation enter into the discussion. Such terms as *born again, saved, repentance, confession,* and *atonement* are part of this study. How one formulates this doctrine has a direct impact on how one goes about the work of the church in evangelism and mission.

Hans Kasdorf has produced an excellent theological introduction entitled *Christian Conversion in Context.* He provides biblical exposition on such key terms as sin, salvation, and repentance and proceeds to introduce the reader to ethnotheology. This exciting field draws together the array of topics which must be included in a fuller understanding of salvation: biblical theology, systematic theology, missions, ethnic (culture) studies, psychology, and the role of the church.

Authors working within the Wesleyan-Armenian traditions have contributed several volumes. The first book in a series titled "Wesleyan Theological Perspectives" introduces us to the most recent scholarship following the directions of John Wesley. *An Inquiry into Soteriology from a Biblical Theological Perspective,* edited by John Hartley and R. L. Shelton, surveys various sections of biblical material, with special care provided for Pauline theology. This is an excellent study.

Kept by the Power of God, by I. Howard Marshall, compares the Calvinist and Armenian positions on "perseverance" and "falling away," concluding that those who cling to a doctrine of "eternal security" in order to avoid discipleship are probably in danger. Marshall's exegetical work is thorough and his understanding of the various positions is accurate. *Grace Unlimited,* edited by Clark Pinnock, brings together essays by ten scholars to challenge the Calvinistic doctrine of "limited atonement." Vernon Grounds, I. Howard Marshall, Grant Osborne, A. Skevington Wood, and David Clines are among those who examine Calvin's tradition in light of biblical exegesis. All of the essays are of high quality and make significant contributions to the study of salvation.

G. C. Berkouwer, a Dutch Reformed theologian, has written three volumes relevant to soteriology. *Faith and Justification, Faith and Sanctification,* and *Faith and Perseverance* provide thorough, biblical treatment of those related topics. Oscar Cullmann has developed a complete theological system with salvation as the central issue. *Salvation in History* and *Christ in Time* provide a statement and defense of his theological method. His thoughtful, scholarly presentation has been the focus of lively discussions in Europe and will continue to contribute significant material for reflection in soteriological formulations.

Berkouwer, G. C. *Faith and Justification.** WBE, 1952. *Faith and Sanctification.** WBE, 1952. *Faith and Perseverance.** WBE, 1952.

Bloesch, Donald. *Jesus Is Victor! Karl Barth's Doctrine of Salvation*. AP, 1976. An appropriate introduction to the thought of Barth. Jesus' powerful, thorough work on the cross is seen as a complete victory over sin and its consequences.

Burkhardt, Helmut. *The Biblical Doctrine of Regeneration*. IVP, 1980. This World Evangelical Fellowship publication provides a brief introduction into Reformed, liberal, and dialectic positions.

Cullmann, Oscar. *Christ in Time*.* WP, 1962. *Salvation in History*.* HR, 1967.

Fuller, Daniel P. *Gospel and Law—Contrast or Continuum?* WBE, 1980. Challenges both dispensational and covenantal theology concerning the OT and NT teachings on law and grace; disagrees with the Lutheran and Calvinistic dichotomy between the two concepts and sees "obedience of faith" as a key phrase—provocative and helpful in questioning some commonly misunderstood topics.

Hartley, John E., and R. L. Shelton, eds. *An Inquiry into Soteriology from a Biblical Theological Perspective*.* Warner Press, 1981.

Humphreys, Fisher. *The Death of Christ*. Broadmans, 1978. Surveys historical theology and new theories, offering insights into the development of propitiation and substitution as nuanced positions.

Kasdorf, Hans. *Christian Conversion in Context*.* HP, 1980.

Küng, Hans. *Justification: The Doctrine of Karl Barth and a Catholic Reflection*. Lucid exposition of Barth's theology and an equally clear and thorough response by a Roman Catholic theologian; all the related topics receive attention, and Jesus' resurrection is seen as the necessary center.

Lewis, C. S. *The Great Divorce*. MCP, 1973. A provocative novel about residents of hell who have an opportunity to visit heaven and reconsider their choice of abode; most, unable to shirk their personal sinfulness, return to hell.

Marshall, I. Howard. *Kept by the Power of God*.* Bethany, 1969.

Pinnock, Clark, ed. *Grace Unlimited*.* Bethany, 1975.

Smedes, Lewis. *All Things Made New*. WBE, 1970. Develops the consequences on the Christian being "in Christ"; interacts with pantheism and mysticism, concluding with a clear exposition of Pauline theology.

Wells, David F. *Search for Salvation*. IVP, 1978. Examines conservative, neo-orthodox, existential, "God is dead," liberal, and Roman Catholic theologies; especially weak on neo-orthodoxy, good basic introduction on the others.

SEE ALSO What Christians Believe: Jesus Christ; The Kingdom of God and The Christian Church.

FAVORITE BOOKS

MARTIN E. MARTY

Personal/Professional

City of God, by Saint Augustine
Letters and Papers from Prison, by Dietrich Bonhoeffer
Reflections on History, by Jacob Burckhardt
Four Quartets, by T. S. Eliot
The Large Catechism of Martin Luther
Creative Fidelity, by Gabriel Marcel
The Lively Experiment: The Shaping of Christianity in
   America, by Sidney Mead
Christ and Culture, by H. Richard Niebuhr
Pensées, by Blaise Pascal
The Christian Future, by Eugen Rosenstock-Huessy

KEITH MILLER

Personal

The Confessions of Saint Augustine
Holy Scriptures: A Survey, by Robert Dentan
The Meaning of Persons, by Paul Tournier
Mere Christianity, by C. S. Lewis
My Utmost for His Highest, by Oswald Chambers

Professional

Introductory Lectures on Psychoanalysis, by Sigmund Freud
The Varieties of Religious Experience, by William James
On Becoming a Person, by Carl Rogers
The Imitation of Christ, by Thomas à Kempis
The Writing of Non, by Walter Campbell

David O. Moberg

Personal

The New Bible Commentary, edited by Donald Guthrie et al.
Commentaries on the New Testament Books, by Charles R. Erdman
The Uneasy Conscience of Modern Fundamentalism, by Carl F. H. Henry
Christianity and the Social Crisis, by Walter Rauschenbusch
Your Other Vocation, by Elton Trueblood

Professional

The Protestant Church as a Social Institution, by H. Paul Douglass and Edmund Brunner
Older People and the Church, by Paul B. Maves and J. Lennart Cedarleaf
The Social Sources of Denominationalism, by H. Richard Niebuhr
Revivalism and Social Reform, by Timothy L. Smith
The True Life: Sociology of the Supernatural, by Luigi Sturzo

Virginia Ramey Mollenkott

Personal

The complete works of John Milton
The poems and plays of T. S. Eliot
Beyond God the Father, by Mary Daly
The New Man, by Thomas Merton

Professional

Ideas and Men: The Story of Western Thought, by Crane Brinton
Works of George Herbert, edited by F. E. Hutchinson
The Politics of Women's Spirituality, edited by Charlene Spietnak
The Church and the Homosexual, by John McNeil
God's Word to Women, by Katherine C. Bushnell

Stephen Mott

Personal

Christianity and the Social Crisis, by Walter Rauschenbusch
An Interpretation of Christian Ethics, by Reinhold Niebuhr
The Destiny of Man, by Nicholas Berdyaev
The Sane Society, by Erich Fromm
The Affluent Society, by John Kenneth Galbraith

Professional

The Social Teaching of the Christian Churches, by Ernst Troeltsch
Agape: An Ethical Analysis, by Gene Outka
Reinhold Niebuhr on Politics, edited by Harry R. Davis and Robert C. Good
Karl Marx, Early Writings, edited by T. B. Bottomore
The Christian Witness to the State, by John Howard Yoder

Richard J. Mouw

Personal

Sermons, by Charles Spurgeon
Institutes of the Christian Religion, by John Calvin
To Be Near Unto God, by Abraham Kuyper
The Autobiography of Malcolm X
Testament of Vision, by Henry Zylstra

Professional

Lectures on Calvinism, by Abraham Kuyper
The Politics of Jesus, by John Howard Yoder
Christ and Culture, by H. Richard Niebuhr
Man—The Image of God, by G. C. Berkouwer
The Calvinistic Concept of Culture, by Henry Van Til

Harold Myra

Personal

Daily Thoughts for Disciples, by Oswald Chambers
The Space Trilogy, by C. S. Lewis
The Meaning of Persons, by Paul Tournier

The Waiting Father, by Helmut Thielicke
Anna Karenina, by Leo Tolstoy

Professional

The Brothers Karamazov, by Fyodor Dostoyevsky
Cry, the Beloved Country, by Alan Paton
Christian Letters to a Post-Christian World, by Dorothy L.
  Sayers
The Genesee Diary, by Henri Nouwen
Our Heavenly Father, by Helmut Thielicke

ROGER NICOLE

Personal

Theopneustia, by L. Gaussen
Institutes of the Christian Religion, by John Calvin
Saved and Kept, by F. B. Meyer
The Secret of the Universe, by N. R. Wood
Le Mystère de la Foi, by R. Saillens

Professional

Gereformeerde Dogmatiek, by Herman Bavinck
Systematic Theology, by Louis Berkhof
Revelation and Inspiration, by B. B. Warfield
The Apostolic Preaching of the Cross, by Leon Morris
The Death of Death in the Death of Christ, by John Owen

CHRISTIAN ETHICS

INTRODUCTION

The behavior of any person is based upon the elements which
that individual values. A Christian, for example, usually acts in
accordance with signals received from the Bible, the church, the
surrounding culture, and his or her own conscience. Such input
and the sorting process that precedes an action often occur sub-
consciously rather than according to a planned system of behavior. Thus efforts at consistency, faithfulness, and evangelism
will lead the Christian toward more thoughtful approaches to
such decision-making. Consistency is needed in order to avoid
working against oneself; faithfulness deals with how a Christian

lives in light of God's values; and evangelism promotes communication of the gospel to others (and demands, for credibility, that one's behavior not contradict one's words—again, consistency).

Ethics concern both personal and institutional relationships, both an individual's relationship with a group of people and the relationship between groups. The term "theological ethics" implies that a person's efforts toward ethical behavior are based upon individual theological understandings about God, the creation, sin, Jesus Christ, the Holy Spirit, the Church, and other theological topics.

Politics and the Biblical Drama, by Richard Mouw, concerns the scope and role of political theology. Since the image of God is present in human society, and sin has also made its mark, the church is involved in redeeming that society. Issues of oppression, hunger, and injustice are to be met with the gospel of liberation, food, and justice. This is one of the best introductions to this complex area of Christian study and responsibility.

Lay theologian Jacques Ellul, in *The Presence of the Kingdom,* provides an introduction to the Christian's dilemma of being *in* the world but not *of* the world. Christians as light, salt, and sheep among wolves are to be fulfilling God's purposes on earth. Caught not only in personal sin, but also tainted by involvement in corporate (institutional) evils, the Christian lives between the Kingdom of God and this world. Ellul's analysis, offering penetrating criticism of our society and a prophetic call to the church, provides a biblical framework for Christian thought and action.

William Stringfellow, whose works often build on the motif of death and resurrection, can be introduced through his book *Instead of Death.* In loneliness, sexuality, and work, death easily gains an upper hand. Stringfellow illuminates our society and its values through a biblical critique. Often controversial, his conclusions and suggestions provide valuable material for ethical deliberations.

Helmut Thielicke, a German pastor-theologian, has authored a three-volume set entitled *Theological Ethics.* Volume I, *Foundations,* considers secular humanism, the relationship between theology and ethics, and several general essays on Christians and the world, compromise, and "borderline" ethical decisions.

Volume II, *Politics,* concerns the nature of the state, church-state relations, resistance to authority, revolution, the military, nuclear war, and conscientious objectors. Volume III, *Sex,* covers topics regarding eros, agape, marriage, divorce, remarriage, equality, homosexuality, abortion, and artificial insemination. Thielicke is a Lutheran theologian, and these compendiums on ethics are consistent with that persuasion. Although this bias will not receive unanimous approval, few have provided such a thorough, insightful treatise attempting to meet the modern world with biblical faithfulness.

John Howard Yoder's *The Politics of Jesus* offers Jesus as the paradigm. This Anabaptist-Mennonite approach, which has gained increasing influence among evangelicals during the last decade, indicates the ethical implications of Jesus as Messiah, touching on Old Testament concerns, the meaning of justification, the meaning of power, and the place of subordination. Yoder's work will continue to be the central exposition of this approach. Vernard Eller, in a more conversational mode, wrote *The Promise: Ethics in the Kingdom of God.* The emphasis on radical discipleship, relating one's behavior to the priorities evident in Jesus' life, is illuminated by his treatment of the Anabaptist contributions and by Søren Kierkegaard.

Anderson, Norman. *Issues of Life and Death.* IVP, 1977. Topical discussion of ethical issues; includes genetic engineering, euthanasia, capital punishment, violence.

––––––. *Morality, Law, and Grace.* IVP, 1972. Discusses the relationship between morality and determinism, permissiveness, law, grace; calls Christians to work for social justice out of biblical obedience and as a witness to a gracious God.

Barth, Karl. *Against the Stream.* New York Philosophical Library, 1954. A brief, introductory guide to Christian ethics as compared to philosophical ethics.

––––––. *The Christian Life—Church Dogmatics, Vol. IV, Part 4.* WBE, 1981. Rewarding study on the relationship between ethics and reconciliation; includes discussions of God's goodness in relation to human goodness, God's covenant of grace, and the meaning of "zeal for God's Kingdom."

Birch, Bruce C., and Larry L. Rasmussen. *Bible and Ethics in the Christian Life.* JKP, 1979. Discusses methodological questions concerning the Bible and contemporary ethics, the relationship of being (character) and doing (behavior); calls for the church to develop character and to provide ground for moral deliberations.

Cothan, Perry C., ed. *Christian Social Ethics.* BBH, 1979. Moberg, Pierard, and others provide insightful, introductory essays on topics like OT foundations for law, the family, electronic media.

Eller, Vernard. *The Promise: Ethics in the Kingdom of God.** DC, 1970.

Ellul, Jacques. *The Ethics of Freedom.* WBE, 1976. Hope is a creative human response to what God has done for us, while freedom is an ethical aspect of hope expressed in obedience; issues in politics, revolution, money, sex, and violence receive comments.

————. *The Presence of the Kingdom.** Seabury, 1967.

Geisler, Norman. *Ethics: Alternatives and Issues.* ZC, 1976. *The Christian Ethic of Love.* ZC, 1973. *Options in Contemporary Christian Ethics.* BBH, 1981. Fairly popular presentations of theories, case studies, and his own—at times eccentric—views; develops a system for rating absolutes so contradictions between biblical norms can be appraised.

Hauerwas, Stanley. *A Community of Character: Toward Constructive Christian Social Ethic.* Notre Dame Press, 1981. Places an emphasis on the church as a separate community, living under scriptural authority, which must produce people of virtue; criticizes liberal social systems and shows the role of narrative in the Christian community.

Henry, Carl F. H. *Baker's Dictionary of Christian Ethics.* BBH, 1973. Too few of the contributors understand methodologies in ethical thinking, thus the many items included are of varying value; still the only evangelical resource of its kind.

————. *Christian Personal Ethics.* Reprint. BBH, 1977. *Aspects of Christian Social Ethics.* Reprint. BBH, 1980. Working with a philosophical ethics approach, outlines the basics of Reformed thinking; helpful introductions.

Hubbard, David Allan. *Right Living in a World Gone Wrong.*†

IVP, 1981. Basic, introductory studies on sexuality, justice, ecology, consumerism.

Hunsinger, George, ed. *Karl Barth and Radical Politics.* WP, 1976. Seeing Barth's early social and political activities as possibly the beginning framework for his later theological volumes, several European theologians debate the role of Barth's theology in the modern bourgeois church; provocative and relevant.

Mouw, Richard J. *Politics and the Biblical Drama.**† WBE, 1976.

Murray, John. *Principles of Conduct.* WBE, 1967. A helpful introduction to Reformed ethics; includes personal and social, biblical and anthropological.

Ramm, Bernard L. *The Right, the Good and the Happy.* WB, 1971. An array of contemporary ethical issues receive very brief comments; helpful as introduction.

Richardson, Peter. *Paul's Ethic of Freedom.* WP, 1979. Focuses on Paul's role as pastor, responding to specific issues as they arise; sees an emphasis on reconciling relationships, with many particulars to be worked out according to the church's local setting; valuable study.

Rudnick, Milton L. *Christian Ethics for Today: An Evangelical Approach.* BBH, 1979. Discusses the role of the Bible, reason, context, conscience, failure in making ethical decisions; helpful introductory text.

Smedes, Lewis B. *Love Within Limits—A Realist's View of I Corinthians 13.* WBE, 1978. Real love is a powerful force for change; it enables before it obligates and must be practical for ordinary people; Reformed viewpoint, fairly basic.

Stringfellow, William. *An Ethic for Christians and Other Aliens in a Strange Land.* WB, 1976. Written as a meandering tour through Revelation, parallels John's description of Babylon with modern U.S.; penetrating analysis of evil in society and the church's role.

————. *Instead of Death.** 2d ed. Seabury, 1976.

Thielicke, Helmut. *Theological Ethics, Vol. I, Foundations; Vol. II, Politics; Vol. III, Sex.** Reprint. WBE, 1979.

Walter, J. A. *Sacred Cows: Exploring Contemporary Idolatry.*† ZC, 1979. Society is not becoming less religious. A person's sense of homelessness, finitude, and mortality usually causes that person to create structures (economic, class, race) in ways that eventually demand loyalty, thus causing idolatry. Discusses problems with the nuclear family, individualism, religion's partnership with culture; complex themes receive perceptive, clear explanations.

White, R. E. O. *Biblical Ethics.* JKP, 1979. Seeks to explore ethical issues in Scripture; weak in the OT, better on Jesus.

Winter, Rebecca J. *The Night Cometh.* WCL, 1977. Two established businessmen of the nineteenth century face difficult ethical decisions, respond faithfully, receive wrath of their community; a noteworthy historical sketch.

Yoder, John Howard. *The Politics of Jesus.** WBE, 1972.

THE CHURCH IN SOCIETY

A specific concern of theological ethics is that of the relationship between the Christian (or the church) and society (including governments, corporations, and other social institutions). In *The Secular Saint: A Case for Evangelical Responsibility,* Robert Webber outlines three styles of church-state relations: they can be carefully separated; they can be identified with each other; or the church can be seen as an agency that transforms culture. Building upon biblical and historical precedents, Webber explores the history of church-state relations in the United States. Such theological themes as creation, sin, evil, and redemption are carefully explained. Webber concludes that all three models are needed, and values increasing cooperation among those who hold the various positions.

Hendrik Berkhof, in *Christ and the Powers,* explores the Pauline concept of "principalities and powers," indicates how this concerns Jesus' agenda for his church in the world, and thereby offers a conceptual framework for the relationship between Christians and social institutions. This approach, challenging many American misconceptions about God's relationship with the government, provides a clear, biblical corrective. Similarly, William Stringfellow, in *Conscience and Obedience,* contrasts two seemingly contradictory views of government offered in the New Testament. Romans 13 appears to vindicate governmental authority and activities, while Revelation 13 indicates that the government is the personification of evil. Stringfellow's discerning comments offer direction for the confusion in the American church concerning this issue. Richard Pierard questions the affinity of conservative Christians with conservative politics in *The Unequal Yoke*. Though written over a decade ago, this warning is needed more now than ever. Quests for success, the lure of nationalism, and inappropriate alignment with various power structures easily cause the church to lose its biblical foundation.

More hopeful trajectories in the evangelical milieu found adherents during the 1970s. In *The Chicago Declaration,* editor Ronald Sider is joined by others in commenting on the convention statement by that name. A concern for biblical values—caring for the poor, seeking justice for disenfranchised persons, peacemaking—has caused many Christians to re-examine priorities. One of the results of that gathering was the founding of Evangelicals for Social Action, an organization working alongside churches to encourage biblical faithfulness concerning these issues. Also, at the 1976 Lausanne Congress on World Evangelization, a final statement issued at the close of the activities indicated that social ethics are directly relevant to evangelism. In *Evangelicals and Social Ethics,* Klaus Bockmuehl offers an exposition of Article 5, concerning justice, reconciliation, liberation, and the topics of servanthood and righteousness. Although there will continue to be attempts to dismantle these efforts, it is hoped that the priorities of Scripture and especially of Jesus' own life will gain more influence.

Written specifically for the Christian layperson, *Called to Holy Worldliness,* by Richard Mouw, offers a lucid guide for understanding the world and its systems. Convinced that laypeople are on the front lines of the work of the Kingdom, Mouw sketches how one can better understand issues in business, economics, politics, and other realms where Christians are seeking to represent biblical priorities. While most Christian business executives are convinced of the need for prayer and silence as occasional escapes from the chaos, does Jesus also have something *for* the chaos? Mouw dismisses the possibility that individuals can choose to avoid sensitive, difficult issues because they are not "into social action." Biblical doctrines about creation and the church require that laity deal with issues of racism, energy, food, Marxism, right-wing politics, and other challenging concerns. A person cannot develop a life of piety that is separated from the life and words of Jesus. In the same series of books, Mark Gibbs has written *Christians with Secular Power*. Displaying a deep concern for and identity with other laypersons, Gibbs approaches the use of power by various modern structures: government, business, unions, police, military, and media.

Between a Rock and a Hard Place presents the struggles, thoughts, and hopes of Senator Mark Hatfield. He discovered that a whole new set of values and priorities arose out of a commitment to Jesus. Issues like war, economics, and power are discussed in light of Christian concerns for servanthood, the cross, and stewardship. Hatfield includes not only a factual account of his political career, but also allows us close enough to feel the emotions and tensions of such involvement. Highly recommended.

Berkhof, Hendrik. *Christ and the Powers.** HP, 1962.

Bockmuehl, Klaus. *The Challenge of Marxism: A Christian Response*. IVP, 1980. Helpfully clarifies terms, evaluates Marxist critique of religion, and offers Christian response, with a focus on the varying views of the "New Man"; while explicitly agreeing with Marxist critique of liberal theologies, shies away from equally deficient evangelical tendencies toward subjectivism and individualism.

————. *Evangelicals and Social Ethics.** IVP, 1979.

Bonkovsky, Frederick O. *International Norms and National Policy*. WBE, 1980. Discusses the just war theory, from classical beginnings to the present, then builds toward norms for international relationships; attempts to work without transcendent dimensions with limited success.

Clouse, Robert et al., eds. *The Cross and the Flag*. Creation House, 1972. Several evangelical educators offer insightful introductory essays on crucial topics like the military, poverty, racism, ecology, sexism.

Eels, Robert, and Bartell Nyberg. *The Life of Senator Mark Hatfield*. Christian Herald, 1979. Thoughtful, revealing account of history, politics, personal stories, thinking, and hopes of a Christian politician; Hatfield's life and thought deserve continued expositions.

Ellul, Jacques. *The Meaning of the City*. WBE, 1979. A biblical study of the city from the time of Cain to the New Jerusalem, with incisive comments on modern society and the factors that make up today's cities; as humanity's greatest achievement, cities also represent, therefore, a rejection of God; required reading for spiritual and social renewal in our urban settings.

Gibbs, Mark. *Christians with Secular Power.**† FP, 1981.

Grounds, Vernon. *Revolution and the Christian Faith.* Lippincott, 1971. A thoughtful introductory work on the revolutionary character of Christianity; social change is valued through nonviolent methods.

Hatfield, Mark. *Between a Rock and a Hard Place.**† WB, 1976.

Holmes, Lionel, ed. *Church and Nationhood.* World Evangelical Fellowship, 1978. From a 1976 symposium, explores the church's responsibilities and means in promoting justice and morality; Bible studies, theological questions, contemporary political and economic problems weave through this informative presentation.

Kaye, Bruce, and Gordon Wenham, eds. *Law, Morality and the Bible.* IVP, 1978. Discussion of relativism and absolutism in ethics, surveying biblical themes of grace, freedom, and law, for Christians who seek both theory and practical applications; includes Norman Anderson, J. I. Packer, Gordon Wenham.

Lesick, Lawrence Thomas. *The Lane Rebels: Evangelicalism and Antislavery in Antebellum America.* Scarecrow, 1980. An insightful case study in theology and social change; seventy-five Lane Seminary students, influenced by Finney in the second quarter of the nineteenth century, work to end slavery.

Linder, Robert D., and Richard V. Pierard. *Twilight of the Saints: Biblical Christianity and Civil Religion in America.* IVP, 1978. Two historians explore the entanglement of conservative Christianity with American civil religion, asking if we are witnessing dawn or twilight concerning biblical faithfulness.

Monsma, Stephen V. *The Unraveling of America.* IVP, 1974. Discusses the purpose of politics, the role of Christian values, and relevant biblical themes; though a decade old, this introduction is still valuable.

Mouw, Richard. *Called to Holy Worldliness.**† FP, 1980.

Pierard, Richard V. *The Unequal Yoke.**† Lippincott, 1970.

Schaeffer, Francis. *A Christian Manifesto.* Crossway Books, 1981. Argues that secular humanism is itself a religion, subtly taking over society. Civil disobedience may be a necessary response for Christians.

Sider, Ronald, ed. *The Chicago Declaration.**† Creation House, 1974.

Stringfellow, William. *Conscience and Obedience.** WP, 1977.

Verduin, Leonard. *The Anatomy of a Hybrid: A Study in Church-State Relationships.* WBE, 1976. This historical survey offers insights drawn from Jesus and the Sanhedrin, the era of Constantine, Calvin's Geneva, and the colonial Puritans.

Webber, Robert E. *The Secular Saint: A Case for Evangelical Responsibility.**† ZC, 1979.

SEE ALSO The Christian Church: Missions and Evangelism and The Christian in the World.

PEACE AND VIOLENCE

Throughout the history of the church, Christians have responded in various ways to warfare and other types of violence. During the early centuries, Christians held predominantly to pacifist behavior, based on the teachings of Jesus. During the Crusades, however, Christian armies tried to free the Holy Land from Muslims in a "holy war." Gradually, a just war theory developed, which specified circumstances and strategies that could justify the active fighting of Christians. As various viewpoints are developed, warfare in the Old Testament is often studied. Millard Lind, in *Yahweh Is a Warrior—The Theology of Warfare in Ancient Israel,* challenges just war theories. As he surveys Old Testament accounts, Lind focuses on the miraculous works of God in every victory. Military preparedness is, in fact, denounced by God. He is especially against military alliances, because they express unbelief. Thus Lind finds consistency between the Old Testament and the teachings of Jesus.

War and Peace—From Genesis to Revelation, by Vernard Eller, posits the same unity of the testaments. Security is to be received from God. In his usual conversational and insightful manner, Eller challenges both the defenders of warfare and the peace movement, though expressing more sympathies with the latter. Both Lind and Eller offer significant, thoughtful comments on this complex issue.

Clouse, Robert G., ed. *War: Four Christian Views.*† IVP, 1981. Nonresistance, pacifism, just war, and preventative war views are presented, then critiqued by each of the other contributors; helpful overview of the issues, good bibliography.

Craigie, Peter C. *The Problem of War in the Old Testament.* WBE, 1978. Not only a reflection on the OT, but also on philosophy, history, sociology, and comparative religion; the Christian is seen as living between pacifism (ideal) and just war (reality), unable to avoid involvement in a sinful state that is to be perpetuated; needs to be corrected by Lind.

Eller, Vernard. *War and Peace—From Genesis to Revelation.**† 2d ed. HP, 1981.

Hornus, Jean-Michel. *It Is Not Lawful for Me to Fight.* HP, 1980. Early Christians maintained a pacifist stance until the cultural accommodation of the fourth century; excellent documentation and bibliography.

Keeney, William. *Lordship as Servanthood.* Faith and Life, 1975. An introductory Bible study on peacemaking; challenging.

Lind, Millard C. *Yahweh Is a Warrior—The Theology of Warfare in Ancient Israel.** HP, 1980.

Sider, Ronald J. *Christ and Violence.* HP, 1979. Spiritual commitments have social implications; Sider's introduction explores types of violence and relevant questions for the Christian.

Sider, Ronald J., and Richard Taylor. *The Bomb and the Cross* (tentative title). IVP and PP, 1982. Expected soon; analysis of the dangers present in the nuclear threat, historical development of just war and pacifist positions, application of those theories to nuclear armaments, practical suggestions for individuals and churches, and an insightful case for a civilian-based defense.

Yoder, John H. *Karl Barth and the Problem of War.* AP, 1970.

Challenges the recent theologies which lack social ethics; expounds Barth's "chastened nonpacifism" and offers comments that contrast Barth's position with Barth's own theology; provocative, scholarly.

POVERTY AND HUNGER

Evangelicals have always been involved in feeding people at home and abroad. The social gospel debate, however, led some to focus on a segmented "gospel" that somehow forgot biblical teachings concerning human needs. The last decade has brought a much-needed revival of biblically-informed involvement in the issues of poverty and hunger.

Ronald Sider's *Rich Christians in an Age of Hunger* deserves and has received wide attention. Providing a survey of the world's neediness, insightful Bible studies, and practical suggestions, this volume helped raise the consciousness and change the behavior of Christians. Sider is more of a biblical ethicist than an economist, which leads some to criticize him as a naive idealist; yet others, recognizing the validity of Sider's case, attempt to provide more thorough case studies and economic theories to help Christians move ahead to change not only personal lives but institutional structures as well.

Stanley Mooneyham's *What Do You Say to a Hungry World?* challenges the widely held belief that "it can't be done." The reader is given a personal encounter with Mooneyham's world—one of individual men and women, with families, sorrows, joys, labor, hopelessness, gratefulness, love. The technical aspects of need can be met, but personal and political will is lacking. Hunger and death are emotional issues, and those emotions are not omitted from this account. But the emotions do not hamper clear thinking, and thus Mooneyham offers comments on all the relevant issues—population growth and shifts, production of food, consumption patterns in developed and developing nations, and economic systems which are intertwined governmental and corporation creations. A penetrating, lucid chapter of questions and answers offers many insights.

Arthur Simon in *Bread for the World* writes that personal adjustments in finances and food may not have any impact on world hunger unless public policies are changed. Food distribution, international trade, foreign aid, the arms race, and many other issues must be studied and reworked if world hunger is to be lessened. United States government policies have often been destructive. The ultimate value of profit in international corporations saps the resources of other countries. Simon offers not only an insightful analysis but also a studied, hopeful procedure for change. The organization by the same name as his book has already won the praise of people in government and industry for its successful efforts in making an impact on United States governmental legislation.

Beckmann, David M. *Where Faith and Economics Meet*. AG, 1981. A World Bank economist asks questions about Christian values and the world's economic cultures; the one world of rich and poor can find direction in Christianity's "spiritual core."

Birch, Bruce C., and Larry L. Rasmussen. *The Predicament of the Prosperous*. WP, 1978. A helpful volume that faces biblical concerns without ignoring the complexities of American economic life.

Eller, Vernard. *The Simple Life: A Christian Stance Toward Possessions*. WBE, 1973. Personal glimpses of Jesus, Paul Diognetus, and Kierkegaard concerning the lure of earthly treasures and the grace of God's Kingdom; demonstrates the inherent link between a person's inner life with God and relationship to things.

Jegen, Mary Evelyn, and Charles K. Wilber, eds. *Growth with Equity: Strategies for Meeting Human Needs*. PP, 1979. Economists, ethicists, policymakers, sponsored by Bread for the World and Notre Dame, present lectures and responses on hunger, agriculture, employment, international institutions; includes two helpful lectures from John Howard Yoder; an insightful symposium.

Mooneyham, Stanley W. *What Do You Say to a Hungry World?**† WB, 1975.

Rasmussen, Larry L. *Economic Anxiety and Christian Faith*. AG, 1981. A brief, introductory overview of biblical issues and the current economic scene.

Sider, Ronald J. *Rich Christians in an Age of Hunger*.*† IVP, 1977.

Sider, Ronald, ed. *Cry Justice.* PP and IVP, 1980. A useful collection of an overwhelming number of Bible passages on topics like poverty and oppression; sketchy comments occasionally help establish historical setting.

————. *Living More Simply: Biblical Principles and Practical Models.* IVP, 1980. A collection of papers from the U.S. Consultation of Simple Lifestyle; includes Pannell, Haynes, Gish, Monsma, biblical foundations, contemporary economics for churches, and individual testimonies.

Simon, Arthur. *Bread for the World.**† PP and WBE, 1975.

Taylor, John V. *Enough Is Enough: A Biblical Call for Moderation in a Consumer-Oriented Society.* AG, 1975. An analysis of the current situation, a theology for decision making, and suggested responses; "The Cheerful Revolution" encourages responsible, practical changes.

White, John. *The Golden Cow: Materialism in the Twentieth-Century Church.*† IVP, 1979.

RACISM

Evangelicals have been slow in producing much-needed volumes concerning racial issues. In this post–Martin Luther King, Jr., era many events indicate an increase in racial discrimination and an unwillingness on the part of many church people to work seriously against such prejudice. As nonwhites continue to increase in number and percentage of the population, thoughtful, biblical books can help the church lead the way toward a racially pluralistic society.

What Color Is Your God? Black Consciousness and the Christian Faith approaches the sensitive issues of the church's role in oppression and the resulting distortion of the gospel. Authors Columbus Salley and Ronald Behm have written separate chapters to whites and blacks, not only suggesting the appropriateness and validity of Christianity for blacks, but offering practical measures of repentance and action for whites. Now we need similar books concerning Asian Americans, Hispanics, Amerindians and others.

Pannell, William E. *My Friend, the Enemy.* WP, 1968. A personal, provocative account of a black Christian growing up in white America which lacks the ability or desire to teach the black youth about black culture; response to fundamentalism and to white responses to black causes.

Salley, Columbus, and Ronald Behm. *What Color Is Your God? Black Consciousness and the Christian Faith.**† IVP, 1981.

Skinner, Tom. *How Black Is the Gospel?* Lippincott, 1970. *Black and Free.* ZC, 1970. A black evangelist interacts with black history, theology, culture, and biblical concerns for conversion, the church, power, and obedience.

Verkuyl, Johannes. *Break Down the Walls: A Christian Cry for Racial Justice.* WBE, 1973. A study in human nature, seeing sin as the cause of brokenness and disunity which leads to imperialism and expansionism; helpful introduction.

THE ENVIRONMENT

It is hard for some to believe that our natural resources are in fact being depleted. After centuries of seemingly unlimited raw materials, prophets of woe now speak of the devastation humans have wrought, prophets more accurate than we care to admit. An abundance of biblical guidelines are also available and should be heeded.

Loren Wilkinson's *Earth Keeping: Christian Stewardship of Natural Resources* offers the writings of seven contributors on the environment, engineering, philosophy, economics, and history. As the planet's resources are surveyed, appropriate questions are raised about distribution. A study of history reveals various approaches taken by humans as they interact with natural resources. Biblical studies indicate that "the earth is the Lord's" and has been given to humans for wise use and enjoyment. However, that delegation of authority carries with it an accountability to God for actions taken. Finally, guidelines are offered for individuals, churches, corporations, and the government.

Barnette, Healee H. *The Church and the Ecological Crisis.* WBE, 1972. Understands ecological problems as religious and moral, not just scientific and economic; includes suggestions for individuals and for groups, such as churches.

Elsdon, Ron. *Bent World: A Christian Response to the Environmental Crisis.*† IVP, 1981. A readable, informed, serious look at worldwide problems concerning resources; biblical perspectives are offered and practical suggestions for involvement are promoted.

Moule, C. F. D. *Man and Nature in the New Testament.* FP, 1967. A twenty-six-page essay on ecological implications from Jesus' teachings about the world as God's creation and humans as sinful and responsible.

Schaeffer, Francis. *Pollution and the Death of Man: The Christian View of Ecology.* TH, 1970. This is a lament, recounting the inadequacy of secularism, pantheism, and other world views in providing bases for stewardship and ecological healing; sets forth Christian responsibilities.

Wilkinson, Loren, ed. *Earth Keeping: Christian Stewardship of Natural Resources.** WBE, 1980.

FAVORITE BOOKS

ELIZABETH O'CONNOR

Personal

Life Together, by Dietrich Bonhoeffer
Letters and Papers from Prison, by Dietrich Bonhoeffer
Prison Meditations of Father Delp, by Alfred Delp
The Cloud of Unknowing, edited by Ira Progoff
New Seeds of Contemplation, by Thomas Merton

Professional

Pedagogy of the Oppressed, by Paulo Freire
Purity of Heart, by Søren Kierkegaard
Martin Buber: The Life of Dialogue, by Maurice Friedman
Collected Works of Carl G. Jung, Vol. 17
Spirituality of Meister Eckhart, by Matthew Fox

LLOYD OGILVIE

Personal

A Man in Christ, by James S. Stewart
A Diary of Private Prayer, by John Baillie
The Acts of the Apostles, by G. Campbell Morgan
Prayer, by George Buttrick
Space, Time, and Incarnation, by Thomas Torrance

Professional

An All-Round Ministry, by C. H. Spurgeon
The Word of God and the Word of Man, by Karl Barth
Expositions of Holy Scripture, by Alexander McLaren

ALBERT C. OUTLER

Personal

The Confessions of Saint Augustine
Enchiridion, by Saint Augustine
The Three Treatises, by Martin Luther
Sermons on Several Occasions, by John Wesley
Epistle to the Romans, by Reinhold Niebuhr
The Nature and Destiny of Man, by Reinhold Niebuhr

Professional

Textbook of the History of Doctrines, by Reinhold Seebert
Christianity and Classical Culture, by Charles Norris Cochrane
The Ecumenical Councils, in the Library of Post-Nicene Fathers, Vol. XV
Nature, Man, and God, by William Temple
The Constitution on the Church, from the Vatican Council II

EARL PALMER

Personal

Pensées, by Blaise Pascal
The Screwtape Letters, by C. S. Lewis
Crime and Punishment, by Fyodor Dostoyevsky
Various works by T. S. Eliot
Orthodoxy, by G. K. Chesterton

Professional

Dogmatics in Outline, by Karl Barth
The Institutes of the Christian Religion, by John Calvin
Letters and Papers from Prison, by Dietrich Bonhoeffer
Christian Letters to a Post-Christian World, by Dorothy L. Sayers
Romans, by Martin Luther

Ben Patterson

Personal

Pensées, by Blaise Pascal
Prayers of Kierkegaard, edited by Perry D. LeFevre
Pilgrim at Tinker Creek, by Annie Dillard
Brother to a Dragonfly, by Will D. Campbell
The Screwtape Letters, by C. S. Lewis

Professional

Wishful Thinking, by Frederick Buechner
The Waiting Father, by Helmut Thielicke
Freedom for Ministry, by Richard John Neuhaus
Love Within Limits, by Lewis Smedes
The Dust of Death, by Os Guinness

Clark H. Pinnock

Personal

Dynamics of Spiritual Life, by Richard F. Lovelace
Preacher's Portrait in the New Testament, by John Stott
Celebration of Discipline, by Richard J. Foster
Prayer, by O. Hallesby
Daily Light

Professional

The Inspiration and Authority of the Bible, by B. B. Warfield
Essentials of Evangelical Theology, by Donald G. Bloesch
The God Who Is There, by Francis A. Schaeffer
Remaking the Modern Mind, by Carl F. H. Henry
Church Dogmatics, by Karl Barth

Richard Quebedeaux

Personal

The Cost of Discipleship, by Dietrich Bonhoeffer
The Confessions of Saint Augustine
Mere Christianity, by C. S. Lewis
The Art of Loving, by Erich Fromm
The Catcher in the Rye, by J. D. Salinger

Professional

The Spirit Bade Me Go, by David J. DuPlessis
What Color Is Your Parachute? by Richard Bolles
Religion in America, by Winthrop S. Hudson
Christ and Culture, by H. Richard Niebuhr
The Social Impact of New Religious Movements, edited by
    Bryan Wilson

PAT ROBERTSON

Personal

Rees Howells: Intercessor, by Norman P. Grubb
Touching the Invisible, by Norman P. Grubb
The Works of John Wesley: Letters
Autobiography of Charles Finney
Revival Lectures, by Charles Finney

Professional

Methodical Bible Study, by Robert Traina
Six Heads of Dogma, by J. Edwin Orr

THE CHRISTIAN CHURCH

INTRODUCTION

The major streams of church history (such as Roman Catholic, Anglican, Lutheran, Reformed, Anabaptist, Wesleyan) have produced their own works on the doctrine of the church. Such writings appropriately indicate the biblical basis for their foundations, and proceed to explain their structures and ministry in that light. The major themes of such theology include God's intentions for the church, its relationship with the Kingdom of God, the work of the Holy Spirit in its formation, inner life, and ministries, and its relationship with the world.

Howard Snyder's two volumes, *The Community of the King* and *The Problem of Wineskins,* provide a challenging, thoughtful discussion of the church's purposes and appropriate structures from a Wesleyan perspective. The church is understood as the "agent" of the Kingdom of God. As Jesus came to reconcile the world to God, the church is now the visible, active agent in reconciliation. This terminology goes beyond the often heard separation of evangelism as spoken truths and social action as demonstrated truths. The work of the Kingdom is to confront sin and evil in whatever forms it may have taken, whether in individual human lives, in society, or in relationship to ecology. Snyder's emphasis is on the church as a charismatic (gifted) community of believers living out and verbally witnessing to this "new age." Too often the church is merely reflective of the world's structures and causes. Warm, vital, personal relationships with God are turned into cool, programmed corporations. Both books explore biblical themes and early churches, studying the nature of leadership, the unique relationship with the poor, and the necessary, visible differences between the church and the surrounding society. Snyder's biblical work, discerning comments on contemporary church forms, and suggestions for change deserve serious consideration.

The Church, by Hans Küng, offers a more academic though still applicable study of biblical, historical, and modern issues. Küng is a Roman Catholic theologian, but his work here will be appreciated and helpful to Protestants as well. He discerns the differences between permanent and passing features of the church, asserting that we can neither conform to the present nor totally adopt the ways of the past. The various forms of the church in the New Testament offer not only useful insights into God's purposes, but also instructive occasions of tensions and mistakes. Küng's presentation—he offers a succinct statement followed by thorough defense and commentary—makes it easy for readers to select those issues relevant to their needs. His own focus often falls on themes concerning the work of the Holy Spirit in gathering people to the church, gifting them, sanctifying them, and providing through them a witness to the world.

From the Anabaptist tradition, Arthur Gish offers *Living in Christian Community.* Far more than a breezy look at Christian fellowship, this a perceptive, relevant, articulate presentation of a theological foundation for the church. Biblical terms—"people of God," "new humanity," "fellowship," "body of Christ," and others—receive attention. In the Reformed and Lutheran traditions, the church is seen as the place where the word of God is rightly proclaimed and the sacraments rightly administered; but the Anabaptists present the equally needed dimension of fellowship. The church is to be a local expression of God's work. Salvation is embodied in the church which, though always imperfect, is itself part of the message of the inbreaking Kingdom of God. The Christian's need for support, accountability, instruction, and partnership in witnessing requires a local church. While there are benefits to understanding the church as a worldwide body, the visible local gathering must be central in a Christian's life. Gish warns against false expectations of ease or utopia. The need for both self-surrender and healthy assertiveness is explained. Gish is sensitive to our modern society in which lonely people live in crowds, and our fears of loneliness are matched by our fears of being known. God's grace needs to be tangible, and the church is the Spirit's creation for that purpose.

For resources from other traditions, Volume III of Thielicke's *The Evangelical Faith* and Volume II of Bloesch's *Essentials of Evangelical Theology* provide Lutheran and Reformed perspectives, respectively.

A collection of theological essays on ministry, edited by Ray Anderson, offers thought-provoking, rich resources for the church. *Theological Foundations for Ministry* includes writings by Barth, Bonhoeffer, Küng, Thielicke, Torrance, and others. There is a consistency in the methodology of these theologians, providing needed reflections on the purpose, goals, methods, resources, and dynamics of God's church. Catholic, Lutheran, and Reformed authors exhibit an amazing consistency on their understandings about Christian ministry.

Anderson, Ray S., ed. *Theological Foundations for Ministry*.* WBE, 1979.

Beckwith, Roger T., and Wilfrid Stott. *The Christian Sunday*. BBH, 1978. A biblical, theological, and historical study with comments on modern concerns.

Bloesch, Donald G. *Essentials of Evangelical Theology: Vol. II Life, Ministry and Hope*.*† HR, 1979.

Gish, Arthur G. *Living in Christian Community*.*† HP, 1979.

Green, Michael. *Called to Serve: Ministry and Ministers in the Church*. WP, 1964. A brief, helpful study on the NT and church history; includes comments on modern church structures and activities.

Küng, Hans. *The Church.** Sheed & Ward, 1967.

Martin, Ralph. *The Family and the Fellowship.* WBE, 1979. Thematic comments on Jesus and Pentecost, a look at church history, and suggestions on such practical contemporary concerns as fellowship, spiritual gifts, ministry, ordinances, and unity.

Moltmann, Jürgen. *The Church in the Power of the Spirit.* HR, 1977. Volume 3 of Moltmann's systematics; theological analysis of modern society and the Kingdom, focusing on the church as the "messianic community."

Snyder, Howard A. *The Problem of Wineskins.**† IVP, 1975. *The Community of the King.**† IVP, 1978.

Thielicke, Helmut. *The Evangelical Faith,** Volume III. WBE, 1982.

Toon, Peter. *God's Church for Today.* Crossways, 1980. An introductory look at biblical images and practical implications concerning worship, mission, eternal destiny; helpful emphasis on the local parish.

See also The Christian Church: Missions and Evangelism.

Ministry, Fellowship, Worship, and Leadership

The work of the church for its own people and for the world can best be understood in light of both theology and practical models. The importance and meaning of fellowship, the interrelationship between inward and outward ministries, and the methods of leadership require attention.

The Church of the Saviour in Washington, D.C., offers welcome creative alternatives to standard church structures and ministries. Its insights, experiments, and structures have become known throughout the nation as church leaders visit its ministries and as the writings of Elizabeth O'Connor continuously attract readers. *Call to Commitment* and *The New Community* provide an early and a later tour of the ingredients, history, biblical foundations, and practical outworking of this witnessing community. The "inward journey" of personal and group life and the "outward journey" of affecting individuals and society for the redemptive work of Jesus Christ are not only explained as concepts, but warm, personal stories prevent the reader from dismissing these concepts as idealistic or utopian. Gordon Cosby, the pastor, in *Handbook for Mission Groups,* explains and illustrates the structures such as membership requirements, classes, outreach groups, spiritual disciplines, and various facilities. Sermons, class outlines, pages from personal journals, and written covenants provide not only information but also a sense of the ethos and vision that take these people into urban housing projects, ministry to decision makers in government, day-care provisions for city children, studios and outlets for artists, retreat centers, and a coffeehouse. More traditional churches are discovering that many of these ministries can be adapted into different settings, providing new life for meandering but searching church leaders.

The dangers of professionalism are challenged by Henri Nouwen in *Creative Ministry.* The tasks of teaching, preaching, counseling, organizing, and celebrating are seen as redeeming ministries requiring fresh insights and the invigorating power of the Holy Spirit. Teaching, which is too often "violent," needs to be dialogistic and congruent with the teacher's life and faithfulness. Counseling should be more than the employment of programmed skills. Organizing, rather than being simply the manipulation of structures, should express sensitivity to God and his people. These ministries, all vital to the church, need to be redeemed and empowered. Nouwen's brief book offers thoughtful, lucid biblical models for the church.

Hal Miller's *Christian Community: Biblical or Optional?* provides word studies, theological reflections, and practical suggestions on the meaning, importance, and function of fellowship. The purpose of relationships is explored from the various vantage points—creation, fall, redemption—and the church as a reflector of God's image and glory is given thorough treatment. A sense of life pervades Miller's writing. Shallow, functional understandings of fellowship are challenged. The church needs to be a genuine daily expression of God's redemption for its own sake and for the sake of the world.

Rightful, deserved, powerful authority is that which gains allegiance because the leader proves himself or herself as a trusted servant, according to Robert Greenleaf in *Servant Leadership.* The highest priority is put on the needs of others, and a society's marginalized peoples play a crucial role in evaluating how decisions are made. A "servant leader" is able to point the right direction, take risks, listen to others, provide imaginative alternatives and arrangements, offer intuition and foresight, work in and through community, deliniate both a conceptualization of the goal and steps to be taken. Servanthood for trustees, institutions, businesses, churches, governmental agencies, and social institutions receives special consideration. If leadership is to be redemptive, Greenleaf's work is required reading. Though it is appropriate for leaders in all organizations, its placement in this section is to encourage the church to be the society's model in the legitimate, necessary, exciting role of power.

Bloesch, Donald. *Wellsprings of Renewal.* WBE, 1974. Explores Christian communities with an appreciation for renewal.

Bonhoeffer, Dietrich. *Life Together.* SCM, 1949. The communal life of seminarians in Germany provides the setting for this writing; a realistic, practical, at times profound view of God's grace as mediated through human relationships, including worship, sacraments, silence, ministry, and confession.

Bromiley, Geoffrey W. *Children of Promise: The Case for Baptizing Infants.* WBE, 1979. Not primarily a polemic, but a helpful treatment for those who were baptized and later experienced significant spiritual renewal; explores OT issues on covenantal sacraments and NT teachings about baptism and sociological aspects of church and family ties; not a defense of baptismal regeneration, but sees God's activity expressed in and through the church's sacraments.

———. *Christian Ministry.* WBE, 1959. Jesus' ministry toward God on the world's behalf and toward the world (in word and deed) on God's behalf are now continued via the church; ministers provide leadership (in worship, sacraments, action, rule) in the church's service toward Jesus and ministry of reconciliation toward the world.

Bucy, Ralph D., ed. *The New Laity Between the Church and the World.* WB, 1978. A collection of papers from a 1976 conference; helpful biblical reflection, sociopolitical ethics, and delineation of clergy-laity teamwork.

Cosby, Gordon. *Handbook for Mission Groups.** Reprint. Church of the Saviour, 1980.

Goodwin, Bennie E., II. *The Effective Leader.*† IVP, 1981. Ingredients, styles, values are discussed with illustrations and a helpful focus on human growth.

Greenleaf, Robert K. *Servant Leadership: A Journey into the Nature of Legitimate Power and Greatness.** PP, 1977.

————. *Teacher as Servant: A Parable.* PP, 1979. An insightful mixture of myth and personal experiences concerning how a teacher can influence students toward servanthood; valuable for leadership training and Christian education.

Griffiths, Michael C. *God's Forgetful Pilgrims: Recalling the Church to Its Reason for Being.* WBE, 1975. Recurring apathy and despair in the church cause organizational insensitivity and impotence; biblical themes, lessons from Asian churches, and an understanding of salvation as both individual and corporate make this a valuable reminder.

Jackson, Dave and Neta. *Living Together in a World Falling Apart.* Creation House, 1974. A pilgrimage through Christian communities (from extended families to neighborhood house churches to communes) provides the setting for biblical and practical insights into leadership, economics, emotions, ministry, and vitality; not utopian, but realistically hopeful.

Jennings, Theodore W., Jr. *Life as Worship.* WBE, 1982. Expected soon; proposes that prayer and praise are central to all areas of one's life.

Jewett, Paul K. *Infant Baptism and the Covenant of Grace.* WBE, 1978. After examining OT teachings on circumcision and NT teachings on baptism, concludes that the parallels between the two are limited and do not therefore promote infant baptism; insightful biblical, historical, and theological study.

Krass, Alfred. *Beyond the Either-Or Church.* Tidings, 1973. Jesus is diminished in both liberal and conservative churches; biblical ministry of evangelism and service must be kept unified.

Lloyd-Jones, D. Martyn. *Christian Unity.* BBH, 1980. An exposition of Ephesians 4:1–16 that focuses on cooperation and truth.

Mickey, Paul A., and Robert L. Wilson. *Conflict and Resolu-*

tion: A Case-Study Approach to Handling Parish Situations. AP, 1973. Conflict, from both a theological and sociological perspective, is a means to an end, bridging chaos and reconciliation; actual situations are studied: pastor-parish, church staff, program decisions, church mergers, conflict between members—with helpful lessons in how to process such tensions.

Miller, Hal. *Christian Community: Biblical or Optional?**† Servant, 1979.

Nouwen, Henri J. M. *Creative Ministry.** DC, 1978.

O'Connor, Elizabeth. *Call to Commitment.**† HR, 1963. *The New Community.**† HR, 1976.

————. *Journey Inward, Journey Outward.* HR, 1968. The "inward" needs for personal exploration and growth, small groups, and a church's task of discovering spiritual gifts are seen in light of "outward" ministries to the spiritual and physical needs of the world; invaluable experiences from the Church of the Saviour (Washington, D.C.) highlight all of O'Connor's works.

Pattison, E. Mansell. *Pastor and Parish: A Systems Approach.* FP, 1977. The church is a system of sub-systems going about the business of being and doing; the interrelatedness of the parts must be understood if the pastor is to enable effective growth and movement; a helpful appropriation of systems theory.

Rayburn, Robert. *O Come, Let Us Worship.* BBH, 1980. Critiques modern norms in which the sermon is central and music is thrown in to prevent boredom; calls for a biblical rethinking that values repentance, seeks to interact with God, and integrates hymns and sacraments meaningfully. Critique is better than the suggestions, but it is a start.

Richards, Lawrence O., and Clyde Hoeldtke. *A Theology for Church Leadership.* ZC, 1980. Biblical reflections and practical suggestions on leadership principles; waivers between insightful and shallow.

Richards, Lawrence O., and Gib Martin. *A Theology of Personal Ministry.* ZC, 1981. Through comments on biblical concepts, contemporary church needs, questions for discussion, ample illustrations, and case studies; the identity, calling, gifts, leadership effectively expounded.

Schaeffer, Edith. *L'Abri.* TH, 1969. The story of the Schaeffer's

Swiss community provides a helpful picture of truth and love; Edith's cookies are said to have brought more into the Kingdom than Francis's apologetics.

Smart, James D. *The Rebirth of Ministry*. WP, 1960. Theological depth and a healthy rejection of the overly accommodating era of the church mark this volume; preaching, teaching, pastoring of Jesus provide direction for today's ministers.

Stott, John R. W. *What Christ Thinks of the Church*. IVP, 1958. Exposition on the Revelation 2–3 passages; Stott's usual clarity and practical insights are here.

Torrance, Thomas F. *Theology in Reconciliation*. WBE, 1976. As the church sought to take reconciliation into the world, the brokenness of the world came back into the church, and therefore ministry must include efforts toward the unity of the church; believes that better theology, appropriation of recent philosophy of science advances, and questioning of world view presuppositions can help. For the advanced student.

Trueblood, Elton. *Alternative to Futility*. WB, 1972, reprinted from 1948. Sees the decay of the West and hopes for redemptive Christian fellowships to provide hope, discipline, and purpose.

PREACHING

Preaching suffered during the sixties and seventies because of forces in both liberal and conservative churches. The loss of an authoritative Word led the liberal church to emphasize current events from the pulpit and to encourage meandering conversations in small-group discussions. The conservative church often turned the sanctuary into a moralizing-styled lecture hall, with speeches that touched neither the human soul nor the world Jesus loves. The eighties, however, promise renewed concern for preaching.

Helmut Thielicke, the German pastor-theologian, recognized the need in America for renewal. *The Trouble with the Church* is a call to authoritative preaching and to church life that authenticates that preaching. The church's escape into "liturgism," busyness, and bureaucratic centralization only served to expose the vulnerable nature of an institution that had lost its calling. Thielicke's call to faithfulness in this volume, and the many models of preaching in his other books, provide excellent resources for the church as once again proclamation in worship becomes a priority. Also, in *A Little Exercise for Young Theologians,* Thielicke writes to the student. As preparation for pastoring progresses, the student's encounters with professors, friends back home, oneself, and in prayer with God all benefit from the wisdom offered here.

Since renewal offers the opportunity for change, perhaps the rich heritage of black preaching can be a resource for the church. Henry Mitchell's *The Recovery of Preaching* develops the genius of black preaching, offering an insightful critique of the overly "cerebral" nature of white preaching. Preaching should minister to the whole being, not just the mind, and Mitchell provides explanations and guidelines toward that end.

The Reformed tradition, which has usually stressed the value of the preached word, is well served by James Daane in *Preaching with Confidence.* This not only offers a valuable theology of preaching, but also indicates how the power of God is actually efficacious in preaching, thus providing a helpful textbook on both theory and practice.

Broadus, John A. (revised version by Vernon L. Stanfield). *On the Preparation and Delivery of Sermons.* HR, 1979. This is the fourth update of a nineteenth-century Southern Baptist textbook; covers biblical basis, content, formation, delivery, types, and use of illustrations.

Daane, James. *Preaching with Confidence (A Theological Essay on the Power of the Pulpit).** WBE, 1980.

Ford, D. W. Cleverley. *The Ministry of the Word.* WBE, 1980. Offers comments on sermons found in Scripture; various themes are examined in light of unique problems and opportunities; understands that the preacher's goal is to have his or her congregation carry the message further.

Kaiser, Walter C., Jr. *Toward an Exegetical Theology.* BBH, 1981. Demonstrates a method for moving from exegesis to preaching; practical with helpful illustrations.

Lloyd-Jones, D. Martyn. *Preaching and Preachers.* ZC, 1971. Insights from his own years as one of England's finest preachers; offers comments on skills, preparation, delivery, and priorities.

Mitchell, Henry H. *The Recovery of Preaching.** HR, 1977.

Paul, Cecil R. *Passages of a Pastor: Coping with Yourself and God's People.* ZC, 1981. Early, middle, and senior years of pastoring are seen in light of various stresses: loss of inner resources, lack of supportive community, over-extension, insensitivity to own needs; oriented toward the male experiences, helpful for re-ordering priorities.

Robinson, Haddon W. *Biblical Preaching: The Development and Delivery of Expository Messages.* BBH, 1980. Helpful guidelines on expository preaching; naive on sociopolitical implications of biblical preaching.

Stott, John R. W. *Between Two Worlds.*† WBE, 1982. Expected soon from an eminent British expositor.

Thielicke, Helmut. *A Little Exercise for Young Theologians.** WBE, 1959.

_____. *Encounter with Spurgeon.* Reprint. BBH, 1975. A twentieth-century German theologian-pastor looks at a nineteenth-century Victorian Baptist pastor; the texts of Spurgeon's sermons are used to illustrate preaching that is cheerful, "worldly," biblical, and compassionate.

_____. *The Trouble with the Church.**† HR, 1965.

WOMEN IN MINISTRY

Women in ministry today are often met with skepticism, in spite of historical accounts that support such a role: Paul had women partners in ministry, frescoes of the early centuries picture women bishops, nineteenth-century evangelical and holiness churches had women pastors, and valuable, scholarly books in recent years have all indicated that Jesus redeems women and the Holy Spirit ministers through women.

Paul Jewett's *The Ordination of Women* is a lucid, precise, tightly argued case that favors formal recognition of women for ministry. After biblical explorations on the "nature of women" and the "nature of ministerial office," Jewett discusses language that indicates that God is masculine and historical circumstances that allowed the church to move from early apostles (all men) to a post-Pentecost inclusion of women in church ministry. Jewett also offers helpful comments on implementation of changes and on inclusive language.

The Evangelical Women's Caucus has often provided the settings, energy, companionship, and resources for church renewal in this area. In preparation for a conference cosponsored by Fuller Seminary, *Women and the Ministries of Christ* was assembled and edited by Roberta Hestenes and Lois Curley. Background papers, plenary lectures, Bible study notes, and seminar outlines provide both scholarly resources and practical suggestions. Contributors include Virginia Ramey Mollenkott, Becky Manley Pippert, Jack Rogers, Leon Morris, and Paul Jewett.

Clark, Stephen. *Man and Woman in Christ.* Servant, 1980. A sociological-theological survey that defends clearly delineated traditional roles.

Gundry, Patricia. *Woman, Be Free.*† ZC, 1979. An excellent introduction to key biblical issues; evangelical viewpoint that favors egalitarianism.

Hestenes, Roberta, and Lois Curley, eds. *Women and the Ministries of Christ.** Fuller Theological Seminary, 1979.

Howe, E. Margaret. *Women and Church Leadership.* ZC, 1982. Inconsistencies in modern church practices, variations in historical church traditions, and suppressed church history bring enlightening comments on questions which many churches are now facing; further helpful materials come from a study of NT leadership and other related biblical studies, and concludes with informative surveys concerning women in seminaries and in ministry. A very helpful evangelical contribution.

Hurley, James B. *Man and Woman in Biblical Perspective.* ZC, 1981. One of the more thorough biblical studies that focuses on exegetical methods; author is somewhat restricted by his own cultural biases (aren't we all?), and thus provides conservative conclusions.

Jewett, Paul K. *Man as Male and Female.* WBE, 1975. A biblical, theological study, with special attention on Barth, that aptly advances equality in the church; criticized for handling of Pauline material.

————. *The Ordination of Women: An Essay on the Office of Christian Ministry.** WBE, 1980.

Mollenkott, Virginia. *Women, Men and the Bible.* AP, 1977. A brief, helpful introduction to biblical, historical, theological, and practical concerns for equality.

Scanzoni, Letha, and Nancy Hardesty. *All We're Meant to Be.* WB, 1974. One of the pacesetters (and still most helpful), with biblical materials and practical issues.

Tetlon, Elizabeth M. *Women and Ministry in the New Testament.* PP, 1980. The historical setting of Judaic culture, the Roman Empire, and the growing NT church provide clarifying dimensions for this helpful exegetical and practical study by a Roman Catholic scholar.

Williams, Don. *The Apostle Paul and Women in the Church.* GL/R, 1977. Analyzes every Pauline passage that refers to Christian women, whether in theological teachings or in passing historical comments; offers helpful interpretation for the contemporary church.

Pastoral Care and Healing

Jesus' ministry is often summarized as preaching, healing, and casting out demons. Healing can take many forms, of course, since the brokenness of an individual's life can be physical, emotional, relational, or spiritual. As God's grace enters that person's life, healing efforts may take several different directions simultaneously. The church's role as agent of healing for those in the parish and for the world around it requires a combination of gifts, strategies, professional skills, and the Spirit's anointing.

Eugene Peterson's *Five Smooth Stones for Pastoral Work* offers a creative, biblical look at the pastoral care ministry. Old Testament books (Song of Songs, Ruth, Lamentations, Ecclesiastes, and Esther) are interpreted in light of the role they had in Israelite religion and festivities. Issues of personal identity, suffering and grief, love and prayer, guidance and discipline, and joyous community in the midst of a hostile world receive the insights of informed exposition and pastoral sensitivity. As pastors currently gain the advantages offered by contemporary human sciences, the unique wisdom and spiritual dimensions of the Scriptures too easily become sidelined. Peterson's contribution is a welcome reawakening to biblical faithfulness.

Pastoral Assertiveness, by Paul Mickey and Gary Gimble, provides an option to the overemphasized "passive/supportive" model in pastoral care. Theological misconceptions that have relegated grace to mean indulgence and redefined support as license are to be challenged. Mickey and Gimble believe that the disillusionment among clergy and the loss of direction in congregations are the result of too little sensitive, biblical assertiveness. Various concerns of the church—programs, money, personal growth, crises, evangelism—are seen in light of the gospel's call for initiative and leadership. Personal stories and biblical reflections strengthen the book's message.

Francis McNutt's *Healing,* which provides the best overview of healing ministries, is from a Catholic charismatic perspective. Guilt and forgiveness, psychological and emotional needs, physical healing, and the ministries of deliverance and exorcism are treated with theological savvy and clarity. Healing is seen in light of faith, hope, and love. Reasons for continued illness are discussed. The place of prayer, medicine, sacraments, and the Christian community receive insightful treatment. McNutt's concern for discovering the root brokenness behind illness is a helpful approach as even secular healing professions gain appreciation of this element in healing.

Few writers have contributed as much valuable wisdom and practical insights into psychological and spiritual healing as has Paul Tournier. While any of over a dozen volumes may be helpful, perhaps *A Doctor's Casebook in the Light of the Bible* is most appropriate here. Tournier's deep personal faith and professional expertise are conveyed through stories about clients, biblical reflections, and the explanation of therapeutic methods. The "meaning" of an illness is discussed, with appreciation not only for healing but for lessons learned.

Collins, Gary R. *The Christian Psychology of Paul Tournier.* BBH, 1974. A summary of the Swiss psychiatrist's life and views (psychology, theology, methods); appreciative evaluation.

Grounds, Vernon. *Emotional Problems and the Gospel.*† ZC, 1976. Fear, anxiety, anger, pride, and guilt receive biblical, psychological-perceptive comments; helpful introduction to emotional healing.

Lawrence, Roy. *Christian Healing Rediscovered: A Guide to Spiritual, Mental, Physical Wholeness.*† IVP, 1980. Christian resources of worship, the power of the resurrection, the extent of salvation, and possible sources of suffering are given insightful, biblical, practical treatment; well-balanced approach to the interrelationships of spiritual, emotional, physical health.

McNutt, Francis. *Healing*.*† Ave Maria, 1974. Bantam, 1977.

Mickey, Paul, and Gary Gimble. *Pastoral Assertiveness*.* AP, 1978.

Nouwen, Henri J. M. *The Wounded Healer: Ministry in Contemporary Society*. DC, 1972. Modern men and women suffer from loneliness, hopelessness, and rootlessness; ministers (lay or clergy) can be healers if they understand their own brokenness.

Oden, Thomas. *Pastoral Theology*. HR, 1982. Expected soon; because ministerial tasks have become separated from the primary calling as priest, correctives are needed that once again link functions with office; thoughful, practical.

Ohsberg, N. O. *Church and the Handicapped Person*. HP, 1982. An insightful, awareness-level book for churches and interested individuals.

Peterson, Eugene H. *Five Smooth Stones for Pastoral Work*.* JKP, 1980.

Scanlan, Michael, and Randall J. Cirner. *Deliverance from Evil Spirits: A Weapon for Spiritual Warfare*. Servant, 1980. Explores the existence of personal evil forces that work against individual persons, including comments on different types of deliverance; helpful case studies and practical guidelines are provided.

Thielicke, Helmut. *Out of the Depths*. WBE, 1962. Post–World War II letters and sermons indicate pastoral sensitivities, wisdom, and power; Thielicke's biblical grasp and unrelenting realism offer an enduring example.

Tournier, Paul. *A Doctor's Casebook in the Light of the Bible*.* HR, 1960.

Tweedie, Donald. *The Christian and the Couch*. BBH, 1963. An introductory explanation concerning Christianity and psychological approaches to healing.

White, John. *The Marks of Melancholy*. IVP, 1982. Primarily written for counselors; discusses causes and possible resources for depression.

See also The Christian Church: Missions and Evangelism and The Christian Life: Spirituality.

CHRISTIAN EDUCATION

Often relegated to secondary status among church professions, Christian education too long has suffered from an identity crisis. The age separation in Sunday schools, though appropriate for limited goals, perpetuates family disintegration. As parents jettison their responsibility for Christian education, they expect the church to save them and their children. Though we have an overabundance of Sunday school materials, some designed with helpful insights of education theory, most have proven to be increasingly ineffective. While many educators discuss the content or information which they hope to impart, little study is done on *why* we change. Systems for learning specified materials ignore the activities of God in human lives and in current events which should form the context for character development and the steps toward biblical faithfulness.

James Loder's *The Transforming Moment* is an exception to the norm. Loder sees his own life and the lives of others against the backdrop of God's involvement. Opportunities for growth, learning, change, and commitment take shape in the midst of such "convictional experiences." The need for appropriate responses from a person's Christian community, the necessity for language that adequately describes what is happening, and the array of situations God offers to his people for such changes are all discussed. Loder's grasp of the Holy Spirit's means and human options for response provide the reader with an exciting, mind-stretching approach to education.

In the midst of church renewal, Lawrence Richards believes that learning in the church should also receive fresh insights. *A Theology of Christian Education* and other books by Richards provide church leaders with biblical values, human sensitivities, and program suggestions that are more complete and unified than the scattered comments found in other writings.

Handbook for Bible Study, by Grant Osborne and Stephen Woodward, is a compact, yet thorough guide to personal and group Bible study. Methods for beginners and for veterans are offered. Different approaches are adequately described, demonstrated, and evaluated. Problems in biblical interpretation are

[159]

discussed, and resources are listed which will help the student move through these difficulties. Osborne and Woodward provide both instructions and encouragement for Christians who are aware that a gold mine awaits those who are willing to work.

Kristensen, Brede, and Ada Lum. *Jesus One of Us: Bible Studies on the Person of Jesus Christ.* IVP, 1976. A collection of fifty-two studies for personal or group use; includes study on the life of Jesus as well as topics like doubt and faith.

Loder, James. *The Transforming Moment.** HR, 1981.

Osborne, Grant, and Stephen Woodward. *Handbook for Bible Study.**† BBH, 1979.

Richards, Lawrence O. *A Theology of Christian Education.**† ZC, 1975.

Wolterstorff, Nicholas P. *Educating for Responsible Action.* WBE, 1980. Helpful theories and strategies for moral action.

SEE ALSO The Christian Life: Discipleship.

CHURCH RENEWAL

It is difficult to treat renewal as a topic by itself. Many books listed in other parts of the chapter are relevant to this more focused section on renewal.

Donald Bloesch, a prolific writer in the Reformed tradition, discusses both inner and outer vitality in *The Reform of the Church.* He does not miss any crucial issue—prayer, liturgy, church discipline, healing, spiritual gifts, evangelism, social concerns, church structures. Bloesch is especially concerned that the church not become secularized by losing its place between the transcendence of God and its role in the world. Offering biblical insights and perceptiveness to the current church context, Bloesch deserves a wide hearing.

Subtitled "An Evangelical Theology of Renewal," Richard Lovelace's *Dynamics of Spiritual Life* offers a survey of the periodic renewals in recent history and a thoughtful account of elements common to those chronicled events. The intersection of personal spirituality, church structures, and the church's relationship with the surrounding culture are seen as the crucial ingredients. Lovelace believes we are currently experiencing a significant revival, and he wishes to offer guidelines for its strength and purification. He discusses why some revivals fail, and especially notes the lack of either piety or engaging social involvement as deficiencies. This is a long book, well worth the effort though.

Howard Snyder's *The Radical Wesley and Patterns for Church Renewal* spells out those strengths in John Wesley which can serve the church today. Wesley is discussed as evangelist, theologian, organizer, and disciple. The fervent mixing of personal regeneration and social reform in Wesley's ministry provides us with a model worth studying. Snyder also demonstrates how the Wesleyan concerns often parallel Anabaptist emphases. Written in a lively manner with informed comments on current needs of the church, this volume offers sound theological reflection, lessons from history, and practical guidelines.

The church's rethinking of its mission has often been sparked and influenced by Jim Wallis and others who write for *Sojourners* magazine. Wallis's *The Call to Conversion* challenges the church to understand, embody, and proclaim conversion in a way that, rather than being otherworldly, is historically specific. A study of Bible passages and church history reveals that regeneration, renewal, worship, and spiritual disciplines should result in personal and corporate activities that challenge the existing trajectories in a society. Wallis believes that, in the United States today, human poverty and the nuclear arms buildup are the causes that must be confronted. The affluence of some Americans, with the resulting concern for protecting property from foreign powers, starts a chain reaction based in insecurity. The Christian's concerns for the poor and for peace, both well demonstrated by Jesus, should be lived out in practical ways, undergirded by worship and personal spiritual disciplines. Though many will disagree with Wallis's choice of issues, or perhaps with the style of life he advances, the biblically based necessity that conversion affect an individual's own life and own society must again be heard.

Bloesch, Donald G. *The Invaded Church.* WB, 1975. Welcomes contemporary renewals, calls for the reaffirmation of orthodox theology and biblical foundations (citing some pervasive problems), then calls for both personal and social changes based on the Spirit's renewal work.

————. *The Reform of the Church.**† WBE, 1970.

Engle, James F., and H. Wilbert Norton. *What's Gone Wrong with the Harvest?* ZC, 1975. Words on the dos and don'ts of communication (proclamation, witness); comments on the nature of the church and how that can be conveyed.

Gish, Arthur. *The New Left and Christian Radicalism.* WBE, 1970. The roots, values, social analysis, strategies, and goals of the New Left are compared with the modern descendants of the "left wing" of the Reformation; indicates some similarities along with critical differences; relevant for renewal in that the church's role in social change is always a key factor in widespread renewals.

Lovelace, Richard F. *Dynamics of Spiritual Life: An Evangelical Theology of Renewal.** IVP, 1979.

Mallone, George. *Furnace of Renewal.* IVP, 1981. Themes from Malachi are used to call for church renewal.

Richards, Lawrence. *A New Face for the Church.* ZC, 1970. Examines renewal as both personal and structural; includes comments on Christian experience, leadership, and organization, with an emphasis on group life.

Schaeffer, Francis A. *The Church at the End of the Twentieth Century.* IVP, 1970. Schaeffer is much stronger in these areas of personal and church renewal than when he works at scholarly issues; insights here concerning the church's approach to living in and bringing truth to society are invaluable.

Snyder, Howard A. *The Radical Wesley and Patterns for Church Renewal.**† IVP, 1980.

Trueblood, Elton. *The Company of the Committed.* HR, 1961.† The church is to be transformed internally, then to have a role in redeeming society; NT concepts, including the need for group commitments and strategies, are encouraged by Trueblood's sense of urgency.

Wallis, Jim. *Agenda for Biblical People.* HR, 1976. In calling for renewed faithfulness to Scripture, contrasts "biblical faith" and "establishment Christianity;" seeks a renewal that separates the church from its conformity to society's values (violence, racism, materialism) in favor of the teachings of Jesus.

————. *The Call to Conversion.**† HR, 1981.

MISSIONS AND EVANGELISM

Introduction

Few areas of Christian study and activity have experienced as much creative interaction in recent years as has the topic of mission. The cities in which congresses are held become household code words—Bangkok, Lausanne, Melbourne, Pattaya. The best way to follow these developments, apart from subscribing to half a dozen journals, is to read *Mission Trends,* edited by Gerald Anderson and Thomas Stransky. Five books in this series have been released, with more anticipated. The first volume includes contributions from Glasser, Newbigin, and Beyerhaus. That introductory book was followed by a second, *Evangelization,* which includes the statements from Lausanne and Bangkok. Even the minority report at Lausanne on "radical discipleship" receives attention. Also, contributions from the 1971 and 1974 Roman Catholic conferences and the 1974 Eastern Orthodox meeting in Bucharest are covered. Stott, Padilla, and Winter are included, with the latter explaining the now common terminology of "E–0, E–1, E–2, E–3" to designate the degrees of cross-cultural outreach. Volume III, *Third World Theologies,* focuses on Asia, Africa, and Latin America with contributions from Arias, Escobar, and others. *Liberation Theologies,* the fourth volume, features Wallis, Cone, Pannell, Mollenkott, Sano, and others on an array of liberation issues particularly relevant to the North American scene. *Faith Meets Faith,* Volume V, speaks to the uniqueness and universality of Jesus Christ. Newbigin, Hesselgrave, Stott, and Conn are among the contributors to this discussion about religious pluralism and interfaith dialogue. Throughout the series Anderson and Stransky have collected both original essays and the most valuable works published in other places. Such extensive, up-to-date information, presented in inexpensive paperbacks, provides a valuable service to the church.

The Integrity of Mission, by Orlando Costas, is subtitled "The Inner Life and Outreach of the Church." Chapters include proclamation, disciple making, mobilization, growth, liberation, and celebration. The unique insights of this volume are partially due to the author's viewpoint as a Latin American churchman now teaching in the United States. Mobilization of the faithful for witnessing requires motivation, recruitment, the recognition of gifts, supervision, and problem solving. Costas's brief volume shows the relationship between proclamation and disciple making, and economic, political, and social issues.

Waldron Scott's *Bring Forth Justice* works with the interrelationship of mission, discipleship, and justice. Scott sees the establishment of justice as the larger, ultimate mission of the church. God's program for establishing justice, summarized in the Great Commission, focuses on disciple making. The church's mission of rectification, or setting straight God's creation, is explained in light of biblical exposition, insights from church history, and helpful, provocative theological reflections. Jesus altered earlier limited thinking about the Kingdom of God, teaching that it included more than the Hebrew people, redefining it as a gift, and proclaiming it as a present reality. The cross is a sufficient work for countering the depth and extent of evil and sin in the world. Scott offers comments on the profile of a Christian disciple, appropriate changes in missionary strategy, and measures for countering brokenness wherever it appears. As Costas has commented, Scott may well have built the much-needed bridge between older evangelicals, younger pacesetters, third world missiologists, and North Atlantic positions. The importance of this book cannot be overstated.

Insights from church history are especially valuable when beliefs and actions can be studied together. Michael Green's *Evangelism in the Early Church* is an informed, lively account of the message and methods of early Christians. Evangelistic thrusts, problems, differing audiences, and cultural issues receive more than adequate attention. Green writes as if history is exciting and relevant, and the reader easily gets caught in the events and discovers lessons and motivation for today.

Another valuable study on the mission of the church is available in a collection of essays, *Mission and the Peace Witness,* edited by Robert Ramseyer. To meet brokenness, whether personal, local, or international in scope, the church's mission is that of shalom. The ethical content of the gospel, concerning justice and harmony, is needed to confront hate, oppression, contempt, and fear. The church is seen as the visible, concrete expression of shalom. Writers, including Yoder and Sider, provide lucid, biblical, thoughtful essays toward that end.

The "church growth" school of evangelism has been a creative, popular force in missions. Donald McGavran's *Understanding Church Growth* is the authoritative guide to presuppositions, ingredients, strategies, and results. The church, as a local expression of the faith, must be the central agent of evangelism to any given "people group." As churches grow, they should plant other churches. The tasks of discipling (calling people to Christian commitment), prefecting (bringing believers to maturity in the faith), and church planting are the cycles of church work. Evangelism is most effective when people of a social culture are able to hear the message from others of the same, homogeneous group. Thus the term "homogeneous unit principle" is often heard. The focus on the local church and on cross-cultural sensitivities is valuable. Challenges are hurled at these methodologies because numerical growth is too often stressed, and homogeneity easily leads to racial segregation. The need for dialogue between this school and others should be foremost on missiology agendas.

Many are critical of those who believe that missions must involve economic, social, and political concerns. Edward Norman, in *Christianity and the World Order,* denounces the "politicalization" of the church. As he surveys the activities of the World Council of Churches, "Marxist liberals," and those who emphasize human development, Norman calls on the church to focus on spiritual matters and issues of "correct religious belief." Often accurate in recounting the errors of reductionism which often plague the church, Norman nevertheless slices the issues incorrectly. Claiming that Christianity has a personal morality to live and teach rather than a social one, he obviously misses much of the biblical record. An overemphasis by some cannot be rightly corrected by such a corresponding overreaction. Scott and Costas (above) more faithfully develop biblical concerns and appropriate directions for the church.

Anderson, Gerald, and Thomas F. Stransky, C.S.P., eds. *Christ's Lordship and Religious Pluralism.* OB, 1981. Papers, responses, counter-replies on Christians and religious dialogue; includes four different perspectives on discipleship.

———. *Mission Trends.** 5 vols. WBE and PP, 1974–1981.

Bosch, David J. *Witness to the World: The Christian Mission in Theological Perspective.* JKP, 1980. Biblical, theological, historical surveys concerning Jesus as Lord of the church and of the cosmos; critical of reductionism in ecumenical and liberation contributions, fails to see similar weaknesses in conservative emphasis on "pure doctrine" and on personal forgiveness as the core of the gospel.

Braaten, Carl E. *The Flaming Center: A Theology of the Christian Mission.* FP, 1977. More sensitive to thinking of Christians outside North Atlantic sphere; critical of utopian humanism, American civil religion. Very worthwhile presentation.

Costas, Orlando E. *The Integrity of Mission.** HR, 1979.

Frenchak, David, and Sharrel Keyes. *Metro-Ministry.* Cook, 1979. From the Chicago-based Congress on Urban Renewal; analysis, proposals, resources.

Green, Michael. *Evangelism in the Early Church.** WBE, 1970.

———. *The Meaning of Salvation.* Hodder and Stoughton, 1965. Theological explanations that offer practical implications for evangelism; Green's usual clarity and pastoral concerns are present.

Howard, David M. *The Great Commission for Today.* IVP, 1976. Four passages on the Great Commission (each gospel and Acts) receive insightful, practical exposition.

Kraft, Charles H. *Christianity in Culture: A Study in Dynamic Biblical Theologizing in Cross-Cultural Perspective.* OB, 1979. Christianity has been dominated by Western thinking and lifestyle—the Bible is more multicultural; looks at both absolute and relative ingredients in Scripture with a concern for communicating the gospel; most thorough textbook on cross-cultural issues now available.

McGavran, Donald A. *Understanding Church Growth.** WBE, 1981.

Míguez Bonino, José. *Room to Be People.* FP, 1979. A Latin theologian shows the intertwining concerns for justice, spirituality, and love, in that sin includes abandonment of responsibility. The Christian, in partnership with God, works with issues of politics and economics as well as those of interpersonal relationships and of eternal life.

Newbigin, Lesslie. *The Open Secret.* WBE, 1978. *Sign of the Kingdom.*† WBE, 1981. Theologically astute, experienced in missions, Newbigin, a student of history, provides thoughtful guidelines for those who bear witness to Jesus; especially helpful is the explanation about the church's necessary involvement.

Nicholls, Bruce J. *Contextualization: A Theology of Gospel and Culture.* IVP, 1979. The gospel needs to be presented in forms that can be understood in the receiving culture; a clear, brief introduction.

Norman, Edward. *Christianity and the World Order.** OUP, 1979.

Peters, George W. *A Theology of Church Growth.* ZC, 1981. Provides a biblical and theological framework for "church growth" school; the message of evangelism is of the personal kind and the method, which shows insights into sophisticated communication models, lacks similar concern for love and service—a call for dialogue, though, that should be welcomed.

Ramseyer, Robert L. *Mission and the Peace Witness.** HP, 1979.

Scott, Waldron. *Bring Forth Justice.**† WBE, 1980.

————. *Karl Barth's Theology of Mission.* IVP, 1978. Works with Barth's theology in comparison with Glasser's "church growth" thinking; especially concerned with the slowness of indiginization.

Stott, John R. W. *Christian Mission in the Modern World.*† IVP, 1975. By defining key words (mission, evangelism, dialogue, salvation, conversion), provides a valuable introduction into current important issues; biblical insights and the urgency of the task are highlighted.

Stott, John R. W., and Robert Coote, eds. *Down to Earth: Studies in Christianity and Culture.* WBE, 1980. A collection of seventeen working papers that provide a valuable introduction to the ways in which cultural differences need to be understood as they relate to the Bible, evangelism, churches, and ethics; includes the Willowbank Report from the Lausanne Continuing Committee. The complete collection, with fewer explanations for laypeople, is edited by Stott—*Gospel and Culture*, WCL, 1979.

Tippett, Alan R. *Church Growth and the Word of God*. WBE, 1970. Biblical reflections on factors that help or hinder church growth; helpful.

Verkuyl, Johannes. *The Message of Liberation in Our Age*. WBE, 1975. Liberation issues in the Bible (justice, deliverance, mercy) are explained in light of today's need for personal and structural redemption; the church is to live and proclaim liberation.

Wagner, C. Peter. *Church Growth and the Whole Gospel*. HR, 1981. Summarizes the history of twenty-five years, including a discussion of ethical issues.

————. *Our Kind of People*. JKP, 1979. A study that defends "church growth" methods from various ethical challenges.

Walker, Alan. *A Ringing Call to Mission*. AP, 1966. Theological issues, critical current needs, and the role of the church are discussed, with special sensitivity to the city.

SEE ALSO What Christians Believe: The Kingdom of God.

World Evangelization

Rather than commenting on the many books by North Americans on world evangelization, this chapter will concentrate on what writers in other countries are saying about evangelism and missions. Missionary biographies, accounts from particular locations, church planting guides, and worldwide overviews are easily available. The insightful, often provocative, and much-needed comments from Christians outside North America require attentive response.

Orlando Costas has provided one of the best such works. Never failing to build on solid biblical, theological patterns, Costas's *The Church and Its Mission: A Shattering Critique from the Third World* evaluates both evangelical and ecumenical missionary efforts. His critiques offer both affirmation and challenge. Chapters 5 through 7 provide the most objective and thorough critique of church growth theory available. Other topics include missionary leadership styles, liberation theology, and North America's links with Latin America's churches. He criticizes theological misconceptions, explains the thinking of third world Christians, and offers practical suggestions for improvement. Costas is both a theologian and a pastor, so a reader's discomfort will be met with encouraging, biblical alternatives.

Similar concerns are introduced by Daniel Hess in *From the Other's Point of View*. Brief stories are effectively used to expose the reader to differences in values, economics, relationships, political structures, communication, emotions, and hopes. Hess wants the reader to understand Latins, believing that barriers can thus be lessened, since a cavalier approach to another person's culture makes effective communication impossible. Hess's very readable accounts will help dissolve those difficulties.

Pius Wakatama's *Independence for the Third World Church* is a reflection on recently heard calls for a missionary moratorium. After providing four differing views which all back such a halt in missionary activity, Wakatama sides with those calling for a selective withdrawal. As in the New Testament, there comes a time when local leadership is ready for independence. Continued paternalistic involvement by missionaries limits the development of leadership and hinders continued outreach to the local peoples. Denominations, mission boards and student activities receive special attention. Wakatama writes from the perspective of one converted through missionaries, educated in American institutions, and desiring to encourage the continued growth of the church in his native Zimbabwe.

Australian missiologist Rodger Bassham has authored *Mission Theology: 1945–75 (Years of Worldwide Creative Tension—Ecumenical, Evangelical, and Roman Catholic)*. Though not specifically evangelical, this technical reference work supplies an amazingly thorough, objective look at international missionary activity.

Anderson, Gerald H., ed. *Witnessing to the Kingdom: Melbourne and Beyond*. OB, 1982. Essays which enlighten current discussions in missiology.

Arias, Esther and Mortimer. *The Cry of My People*. Friendship Press, 1980. As a lucid, readable, human history of our neighbors to the south, this is hard to beat. Social, economic, and political issues are seen in relationship to biblical concerns for salvation and justice.

Bassham, Rodger. *Mission Theology: 1945–75 (Years of World-wide Creative Tension—Ecumenical, Evangelical, and Roman Catholic).* WCL, 1980.

Bryant, David. *In the Gap.* Inter-Varsity Missions, 1979. A challenging collection of biblical reflections, surveys of world missions, personal stories, suggested reading, missionary agencies, and resources; calls the reader to be a "world Christian," helping to bridge the gap between God and his world of people.

Costas, Orlando E. *The Church and Its Mission: A Shattering Critique from the Third World.* TH, 1974.

————. *From the Periphery: Missiology in Context.* OB, 1982. Expected soon; promises to be insightful and challenging.

————. *Theology of the Crossroads in Contemporary Latin America: Missiology in Mainline Protestantism: 1969–1974.* Amsterdam: Rodopi, 1976. An exceptionally perceptive look at the theology, missionary activities, church organizations, people, and nations which affected this era of Christian outreach in Latin America.

Dayton, Edward R., and David A. Fraser. *Planning Strategies for World Evangelization.* WBE, 1980. Resources in social sciences and management are helpfully appropriated in the quest to reach various people groups; focuses on the need to understand the meaning systems, needs, and behavior of the receiving group, with comments on planning and on evaluation.

Douglas, J. D., ed. *Let the Earth Hear His Voice.* World Wide Publications, 1975. Everything (addresses, study papers, seminars, statements) from the Lausanne Congress on World Evangelization (1974).

Hancock, Robert Lincoln. *The Ministry of Development in Evangelical Perspective.* WCL, 1979. Papers from a symposium convened by Carl Henry; approaches issues of spiritual and social witness, including biblical teachings, historical causes, strategy questions, and administrative needs.

Hess, Daniel J. *From the Other's Point of View.**† HP, 1980.

Hesselgrave, David John, ed. *Dynamic Religious Movements: Case Studies of Rapidly Growing Religious Movements Around the World.* BBH, 1978. Helpful analysis, from a "church growth" perspective of several especially active ministry areas.

_____. *Planting Churches Cross-Culturally.* BBH, 1980. Step-by-step explanation of how to start a new church; scriptural insights and helpful illustrations.

Hoekstra, Harvey T. *The World Council of Churches and the Demise of Evangelism.* TH, 1979. Evaluates the post-Edinburgh (1910) years, concluding that sociopolitical concerns displaced transcendent concerns; though accurate on some points, fails to understand the postcolonial era and the need for changes in classical missionary approaches.

Johnston, Arthur. *The Battle for World Evangelism.* TH, 1978. Laments the post-Lausanne emphasis among evangelicals on the integration of social action with proclamation; does not like the competition with "soul winning."

Mayers, Marvin K. *Christianity Confronts Culture.* ZC, 1974. The church is to bring changes as its mission continues, but not the imposition of one culture upon another; cross-cultural encounters are explored, and ethnocentric problems are confronted using tools of theology, psychology, sociology, anthropology, and education, with ample illustrations and case studies.

McCurry, Don M., ed. *The Gospel and Islam: A 1978 Compendium.* Missions Advanced Research and Communication Center (MARC), 1980. Collection of documents from a 1978 working conference (forty papers were required prereading!); valuable in all areas of theology, culture, methods, conversion, bibliographies, directories, world overview of Islam, new strategies.

Neill, Stephen. *Christian Missions.* Penguin, 1964. An international survey of activities with helpful evaluations; good bibliography.

_____. *Salvation Tomorrow.* AP, 1976. An insightful account of the modern ecumenical movement since 1910, including such modern congresses as Lausanne and Nairobi; deals with interreligious dialogue, the call by some for a moratorium, and revolution; sets forth proposals for theological education that challenge Western materialism and other injustices.

Nida, Eugene A. *Customs and Cultures*. WCL, 1975. Anthropology is not only required for missionaries but valuable for anyone seeking to understand the multitude of cultures, even on our own continent; includes comments on social norms, idioms, rituals, music, and religious beliefs.

————. *Message and Mission*. WCL, 1960. Reprint. 1979. Explores the use of symbols in cross-cultural communication, with insights into Scripture and many helpful illustrations from mission activities.

Paton, David M. *Breaking Barriers: Nairobi 1975*. WBE, 1975. Papers from the WCC meeting, including those by Yoder, Wallis, Hubbard, Sider, and Mooneyham.

Schlabach, Theron. *Gospel vs. Gospel: Mission and the Mennonite Church, 1863–1944*. HP, 1980. Internal debates can provide light for others, as here—a history and critique provides material for rethinking the interfacing of Christian missions, sociological concerns, evangelistic agendas, and so forth.

Shenk, Wilbert, ed. *Mission Focus: Current Issues*. HP, 1980. Collection of papers examining biblical reflections, including NT strategies, theological issues, historical evaluations, emerging directions; concerns in Africa, Asia, and Latin America are highlighted regarding evangelism, education, and politics.

Wakatama, Pius. *Independence for the Third World Church.**† IVP, 1976.

North American Evangelization

The commonly accepted designations for types of evangelism can be helpful here. Ralph Winter's categories range from E–0 for renewal work among nominal Christians to E–3 for evangelism that crosses cultural and language differences between the missionary and the recipient. The earlier section on Church Renewal would be defined as E–0. This section focuses on E–1 (outreach to people where there is no significant cultural separation) and E–2 (outreach across limited cultural differences, like Caucasian university students reaching out to Hispanic students, or a black church evangelizing among Asian-Americans). While some E–3 work takes place in North America, especially among recent immigrants, the previous section will be more applicable to that work.

Robert Henderson's *Joy to the World* calls people to understand, experience, and obey the joyous news of the Kingdom of God. Henderson paints a picture of the universal dark world in which evil is encountered in oneself, in interpersonal relationships, and in society's systems. As he warns against evangelism that selects limited segments of the Kingdom for its paradigms, Henderson counters the reductionism of many modern programs with a gospel that includes the Sermon on the Mount. The job of the evangelist can hardly be defined as including the need to create curiosity; Henderson more hopefully offers the rhetorical question, "How do you hide a revolution?" Biblical themes are used throughout as agenda-setters, and Henderson's insights into congregational life are invaluable.

Alfred Krass's *Five Lanterns at Sundown* is aptly subtitled "Evangelism in a Chastened Mood." Following a striking retelling of the Matthew 25 parable on the ten virgins who hoped to attend a wedding feast, Krass provides an exploration of the various ingredients of the story. Because the new order of God's eschatological activity is here, as both feast and judgment, Christians must act decisively. As the reader is carried through the exposition, it becomes apparent that Krass is not offering "how-to's." Rather, he is seeking a worldview shift. A person's concept of reality, including God's activity and the individual's significance in that reality, must be changed if evangelism is to take place. In fact, the task of evangelism is to invite others to participate in the reality demonstrated and proclaimed by Jesus. This one may require rereading, but it is worth the effort.

Master Plan of Evangelism, by Robert Coleman, is justly called a classic. Coleman, following Jesus' methods, sees that evangelism is primarily accomplished through intense, long-term relationships. The goal of evangelism is the producing of disciples. In turn, disciples will do evangelism. Each chapter explores a different ingredient of the relationship—selection, association, consecration, demonstration, delegation, supervision, reproduction—and practical, helpful comments about today's church conclude each chapter.

Though most Christians would agree that personal witnessing is important, fears and excuses seem to prevent many from such activity. Through her warm, personal stories, biblical reflections, and practical suggestions, Becky Manley Pippert can assist anyone in overcoming the stalemate. *Out of the Saltshaker and into the World* sees evangelism as a combination of lifestyle and words, encouraging the witness to honesty about one's own frailties, God's incredible offer, and the too seldom heard demands of discipleship. Also discussed is the need for a corporate witness of the local church. A sense of liveliness, faithfulness, and excitement for the task pervades this volume, making it especially helpful for church discussion groups.

Contemporary discussions require that theories find practical expression. Richard Mouw's *Political Evangelism* offers that benefit. Mouw understands evangelism to be the task of bringing the power of the gospel into confrontation with sin, whatever its form. He explains that a Christian's commitment to Jesus has political consequences which must be lived out as the church bears witness in a society. This is an excellent introduction to the practical implications of New Testament social ethics and today's practice of evangelism.

Finally, the cross-cultural perspective on evangelism requires comment. North America includes many diverse ethnic groups, and they most dramatically come together at universities and in urban settings. Those uninformed in cross-cultural matters perpetuate barriers through insensitivities to people and arrogance in one's own interpretation of the gospel. Thom Hopler's *A World of Difference* provides an easy-to-read exploration of these concerns. Based on studies of cross-cultural events in Scripture, his own experiences in Africa and urban America, and insights into relational issues and communication patterns, Hopler's tour through cross-cultural issues is without peer.

Armstrong, Richard Stoll. *Service Evangelism*. WP, 1979. A practical guide, focusing on personal "faith sharing" with emphasis on conversational modes and the witness as "ambassador"; includes a seminar outline for church use.

Borchert, Gerald L. *Dynamics of Evangelism*. WB, 1976. A brief overview of barriers to and guidelines for personal witnessing in the context of the local church.

Brown, Fred. *Secular Evangelism*. SCM, 1970. Appreciative of the needs of secular cultures, especially youth, to hear the gospel in a way that can be understood within their world view; provocative, helpful insights into Western culture.

Coleman, Robert E. *The Master Plan of Evangelism.**† FHR, 1963.

Ellison, Craig, ed. *The Urban Mission.* WBE, 1974. Thoughtful, practical essays on outreach in the city; includes Gish, Sider, Pannell.

Fackre, Gabriel. *Word in Deed: Theological Themes in Evangelism.* WBE, 1975. A refreshing interaction of social analysis, experiences in personal witnessing, the interrelationship between words and actions, and the concept of "theology in motion"; from the context of mainline churches.

Green, Bryan. *The Practice of Evangelism.* Scribners, 1951. Not as dated as one might think! Especially helpful chapter on "Dealing with Individual" concerning prayer and conversion.

Green, Michael. *First Things Last: Whatever Happened to Evangelism?* Discipleship Resources, 1979. A look at contemporary evangelism in light of the early church; includes discussions of motivation, methods, church life, the message, the role of the Holy Spirit; practical and encouraging.

Greenway, Roger. *Apostles to the City.* BBH, 1978. Studies urban ministries in the Bible, seeking ingredients that lead to renewal and reform; looks toward contemporary applications for Asia, Latin America, and the United States.

Greenway, Roger, ed. *Discipling the City.* BBH, 1979. Contributions by Conn and others on themes in urban ministries: Kingdom of God, salvation, contextualization, lay ministry, house churches, theological education; hopeful and informative.

Henderson, Robert T. *Joy to the World: An Introduction to Kingdom Evangelism.**† JKP, 1980.

Hopler, Thom. *A World of Difference: Following Christ Beyond Your Cultural Walls.**† IVP, 1981.

Jackson, Dave. *Dial 911.* HP, 1981. A Chicago-based ministry provides insights, practical suggestions, challenges for urban outreach.

Krass, Alfred C. *Evangelizing Neopagan North America.* HP, 1982. A theology of evangelism that approaches issues in hermeneutics—notably, accounts of Jesus' exorcisms; draws on missionary experiences to better understand contemporary "pagan" United States.

_____. *Five Lanterns at Sundown.** WBE, 1978.

Kraus, C. Norman, ed. *Missions, Evangelism, and Church Growth.* HP, 1980. A collection of essays which focuses on North American churches; examines lifestyles, worship, outreach, involvement in the world, with special attention to urban settings.

Little, Paul E. *How to Give Away Your Faith.* IVP, 1966. A lively, practical, biblical guide to personal evangelism; includes summaries of the message, answers to common questions, encouragement.

McElvaney, William K. *Good News Is Bad News Is Good News.* . . . OB, 1980. In light of the Third World's need for salvation (of all kinds), liberation theology has a relevant message for North Americans, mainly in reference to continued materialism, racism, and other sins from which we need to be liberated. The Good News, though often carrying painful messages, is still good.

Metzger, Will. *Tell the Truth.* IVP, 1981. Separates "human-centered" messages and methods from those which are "God-centered"; especially valuable for encouraging and guiding personal evangelism.

Mouw, Richard. *Political Evangelism.**† WBE, 1973.

Outler, Albert. *Evangelism in the Wesleyan Spirit.* Tidings, 1971. With a backdrop of John Wesley's style message, emphasizes the need for both nurture and outward authenticity; cautiously looks at the prospects of contemporary awakening.

Packer, J. I. *Evangelism and the Sovereignty of God.* IVP, 1961. Emphasis on effective outreach with helpful biblical and theological reflection.

Perkins, John. *Let Justice Roll Down.*† GL/R, 1976. The experiences of violence, injustice, hatred, and poverty can be met by the love and work of Jesus Christ; Christians must see the depth of the need and the sufficiency of the cross.

_____. *A Quiet Revolution.* WB, 1976. This is a story of Perkins and his Voice of Calvary ministries, and it needs to be heard and appropriated by churches throughout ministries that integrate economic and spiritual concerns; told with human warmth and Godly power.

Phillips, Keith W. *Everybody's Afraid of the Ghetto.* GL/R, 1975. Hope in the midst of despair, love penetrating hate and violence; Phillips and others offer realistic perspectives on urban ministry.

Pippert, Rebecca Manley. *Out of the Saltshaker and into the World.**† IVP, 1979.

Prior, Kenneth F. W. *The Gospel in a Pagan Society.* IVP, 1975. Paul's evangelism in Athens (Acts 17) is exposited as a model for modern, secular culture; very insightful and practical.

Schaeffer, Francis A. *Death in the City.* IVP, 1969. Working with Jeremiah and Lamentations, Schaeffer's evangelistic concerns are well presented.

Seamands, John T. *Tell It Well: Communicating the Gospel Across Cultures.* Beacon Hill, 1981. Verbal proclamation is seen as the priority while acts of love are seen only as supplemental expressions to substantiate the words; that dichotomy is regrettable, but the attention paid to issues in world religions is helpful.

Southard, Samuel. *Pastoral Evangelism.* Rev. JKP, 1981. Countering passive "client-centered" therapy approaches to pastoring, calls for evangelism that includes God's grace and holiness.

Watson, David. *I Believe in Evangelism.* WBE, 1976. People cannot share a life they do not have, so church life, worship, and the work of the Holy Spirit are seen as the necessary foundation for evangelism; helpful presentation of both the setting and the activities of renewal.

Wirt, Sherwood Eliot, ed. *Evangelism: The Next Ten Years.* WB, 1978. Essays honoring Billy Graham's sixtieth birthday; includes Leighton Ford on proclamation, Stanley Mooneyham on the relationship of evangelism to social action, Waldron Scott on the biblical theme of the Kingdom of God, and others.

SEE ALSO What Christians Believe: The Kingdom of God and the Christian Church: Church Renewal.

Apologetics

As Christians give witness to their Lord, they may benefit from a written, rational defense of their beliefs, an apologetic intended to support or substantiate evangelism or to help Christians become more assured of their own faith. At their worst, apologetics only cause arguments and create stubbornness—usually because love fails to surround the conversation. In their proper role, however, apologetics answer important questions, provide assurance that intellectual concerns are important, and offer well-reasoned challenges to those who critique Christian beliefs.

Anderson, J. N. D. *Christianity: The Witness of History*. TH, 1969. God's work in history provides evidence toward belief.

Carnell, E. J. *Christian Commitment: An Apologetic*. McP, 1957. A "spiritual proof" as opposed to a "rational proof" since simple observation and rational belief are insufficient; a "third method of knowing" is explained which works from ontological to presuppositional forms onto "truth as personal rectitude."

————. *A Philosophy of the Christian Religion*. Reprint. Baker, 1980. Argues that a rational, honest person must eventually adopt Christian beliefs since any value held will logically lead "up" to a Christian faith; critiques the lures of materialism, pleasure, and altruism, concluding that, since we must suffer, let us suffer for the right reason.

Chapman, Colin. *The Case for Christianity*. WBE, 1981. A seven-section approach to apologetics, beginning with basic human questions (meaning, values, truth, suffering), Christian answers, world-view issues, alternatives, and a focus on Jesus Christ; includes a plethora of quotations from others; use of pictures, graphics, and color to provide aesthetic quality, resulting in a very worthwhile textbook.

Henry, Carl F. H. *Remaking the Modern Mind*. WBE, 1948. Aptly defends the rationality of the Christian faith.

Holloway, Richard. *Beyond Belief*. WBE, 1981. In a society of observers, calls for an encounter with God rather than mere acceptance of rational data; the Jesus of the Sermon on the Mount can encounter people today.

Kreeft, Peter. *Between Heaven and Hell*. IVP, 1982. A creative, entertaining, yet sophisticated conversation "beyond death" among C. S. Lewis, John Kennedy, and Aldous Huxley concerning worldviews, eternal life, Jesus, and other issues in apologetics.

Lewis, C. S. *Mere Christianity*. McP, 1943. A classic apologetic for the Christian faith; describes and defends the essentials of belief and behavior.

————. *Miracles*. McP, 1947. Faces presuppositions and arguments concerning God's intervention in various ways in history.

Lewis, Gordon R. *Testing Christianity's Truth Claims: Approaches to Christian Apologetics*. MP, 1976. Looks at empiricism, rationalism, and mysticism, with an appreciative concentration on Carnell.

Morris, Thomas V. *Francis Schaeffer's Apologetics: A Critique*. MP, 1976. A needed examination of Schaeffer's weaknesses.

Pinnock, Clark H. *Reason Enough*.† IVP, 1980. Surveys three approaches to theism (pragmatic, experiential, cosmic) and two to particulars of the faith (history, community); concise, lucid.

Purtill, Richard. *C. S. Lewis's Case for the Christian Faith*. HR, 1981. Surveys and explains the arguments found in Lewis's works.

————. *Reason to Believe*. WBE, 1974. An introduction to the philosophy of religion that mainly answers those who challenge the reasonableness of monotheism and revelation.

————. *Thinking About Religion*. Prentice-Hall, 1978. An introductory textbook to help students learn how to think about religion; issues of reasons for belief, arguments for God, the problem of evil, miracles, the Bible, mysticism, and life after death are included.

Ramm, Bernard. *Protestant Christian Evidences*. MP, 1953. *Varieties of Christian Apologetics*. BBH, 1962. *The God Who Makes a Difference*. WB, 1972. Consistently clear, aware of the valuable contributions from others, avoids overstatement; accessible to the beginner yet worthwhile for the advanced.

Schaeffer, Francis A. *The God Who Is There*. IVP, 1968. *Escape from Reason*. IVP, 1968. *He Is There and He Is Not Silent*. TH, 1972. This trilogy is the foundation of Schaeffer's argument that we have lost rational roots and the possibility of knowing; surveys arts, philosophy, and other aspects of culture; often does not understand those whom he critiques yet there is value in his overall picture.

Sproul, R. C. *If There Is a God, Why Are There Atheists?*
Bethany, 1978. God is not merely a "projection"—he has
too many qualities believers would not wish were there;
valuable, brief challenge to the unbeliever.
Thielicke, Helmut. *The Faith Letters*. WB, 1978. For skeptics
and thoughtful believers, deals with a variety of issues (science, creation, history, suffering, world religions, prayer).
_____. *The Hidden Question of God*. WBE, 1977. Modern
questions raised by a secular society which sees religion as
archaic, humans as merely animals, the church as a failure,
truth as relative, and God as a human projection; these essays are theologically astute and pastoral.
_____. *How to Believe Again*. FP, 1972. Conversant with seri-
ous objections, shows that satisfying answers are available.
SEE ALSO The Christian in the World: Philosophy.

FAVORITE BOOKS

JACK ROGERS

Personal

Cry, the Beloved Country, by Alan Paton
Physics and Beyond, by Werner Heisenberg
Discussion and Debate, Tools of a Democracy, by Henry Lee
Ewbank and J. Jeffrey Auer
Modern Poetry, edited by Maynard Mack, Leonard Dean, and
William Frost
The Brothers Karamazov, by Fyodor Dostoyevsky

Professional

Reflections on the Psalms, by C. S. Lewis
The Church, by G. C. Berkouwer
Myths, Models, and Paradigms, by Ian G. Barbour
Christianity in Culture, by Charles H. Kraft
Institutes of the Christian Religion, by John Calvin

DAVID M. SCHOLER

Personal

Mere Christianity, by C. S. Lewis
Orthodoxy, by G. K. Chesterton

The Pursuit of God, by A. W. Tozer
The Case for Orthodox Theology, by E. J. Carnell
Redemption: Accomplished and Applied, by John Murray

Professional

Pagan and Christian in an Age of Anxiety, by E. R. Dodds
Evangelism in the Early Church, by Michael Green
The Interpretation of the New Testament, 1861–1961, by Stephen Neill
Martyrdom and Persecution in the Early Church, by W. H. C. Frend
The Bible and the Role of Women, by Krister Stendahl

LUCI SHAW

Personal

Flirting with the World, by John White
The Great Divorce, by C. S. Lewis
Pilgrim at Tinker Creek, by Annie Dillard
A Long Obedience in the Same Direction, by Eugene Peterson
Go, Make Learners, by Robert Brow

Professional

Walking on Water, by Madeleine L'Engle
The Habit of Being: Letters of Flannery O'Connor, edited by Sally Fitzgerald
The Mind of the Maker, by Dorothy L. Sayers
The Dynamics of Spiritual Life, by Richard Lovelace
Orthodoxy, by G. K. Chesterton
Triumphs of the Imagination, by Leland Ryken

DONALD W. SHRIVER

Personal

Letters and Papers from Prison, by Dietrich Bonhoeffer
Bonhoeffer: Exile and Martyr, by Eberhard Bethge
Diary of a Country Priest, by George Bernanos
Confessions of Saint Augustine
War and Peace, by Leo Tolstoy

Professional

Christ and Culture, by H. Richard Niebuhr
The Social Teaching of the Christian Churches, by Ernst
Troeltsch
Christianity and Classical Culture, by Charles Cochrane
Millhands and Preachers, by Liston Pope
Puritanism and Liberty, by A. S. P. Woodhouse

RONALD J. SIDER

Personal

Celebration of Discipline, by Richard J. Foster
The Autobiography of Malcolm X
Various works by Martin Luther
New Testament Documents: Are They Reliable? by F. F. Bruce
A New Way of Living, by Michael Harper

Professional

The Historian and the Believer, by Van A. Harvey
The Presence and the Future, by George E. Ladd
The Politics of Jesus, by John Howard Yoder
Miracles, by C. S. Lewis
Christ and Time, by Oscar Cullmann

HOWARD A. SNYDER

Personal

The Journals of John Wesley
Life and Letters of Frederick W. Robertson, edited by Stopford
A. Brooke
The Congregation in Mission, by George W. Webber
The Christian's Secret of a Happy Life, by Hannah Whitall
Smith
Wellsprings of Renewal, by Donald G. Bloesch

Professional

Sermons on Several Occasions, by John Wesley
The Technological Society, by Jacques Ellul
Entropy: A New World View, by Jeremy Rifkin
*The Believers' Church: The History and Character of Radical
Protestantism,* by Donald Durnbaugh

The Social Sources of Denominationalism, by H. Richard Niebuhr

Charles R. Taber

Personal

The Screwtape Letters, by C. S. Lewis
Five Lanterns at Sundown, by Alfred C. Krass
The Good Shepherd, by Leslie Newbigin
Rich Christians in an Age of Hunger, by Ronald J. Sider
Enough Is Enough, by John V. Taylor

Professional

Waterbuffalo Theology, by Kosuke Koyama
Christianity Rediscovered, by Vincent J. Donovan
The Flaming Center, by Carl E. Braaten
Message and Mission, by Eugene A. Nida
The Biblical Doctrine of the Church, by William Robinson

Dale Vree

Personal

The Way of a Pilgrim, translated by R. M. French
The Long Loneliness, by Dorothy Day
Murder in the Cathedral, by T. S. Eliot
Nine O'Clock in the Morning, by Dennis Bennett
Tales of Padre Pio, by John McCaffrey

Professional

Enthusiasm, by Ronald Knox
How to Serve God in a Marxist Land, by Karl Barth and Johannes Hamel
Laborem Exercens, by Pope John Paul II
False Presence of the Kingdom, by Jacques Ellul
The Cultural Contradictions of Capitalism, by Daniel Bell

THE CHRISTIAN IN THE WORLD

Introduction

In that the Christian life encompasses all of one's activities, vocational and educational pursuits are to be pursued in light of biblical values. A Christian's professional activities should reflect his or her beliefs concerning the sacredness of life, the value of God's creation, the importance of beauty, and biblical concerns for justice and love.

For example, a scientist should not only be concerned with careful stewardship of God's creation but should act in faithfulness to the Christian's call to be a peacemaker and to promote justice; this will affect what research can be pursued and the manner in which that work is done. The scientist seeks to be creative, certainly, but not without question. His or her work must be judged in light of Scripture, and thus many pursuits must be abandoned in favor of others that promote life, healing, justice, beauty, and stewardship.

Societies, periodicals, books, and co-workers can help provide resources and stimulation for Christians seeking to work out the implications of the Christian faith in their studies and careers. Each of the classifications below serves only as a broad introduction into such interdisciplinary questions. At the end of this section is a listing of professional organizations that can provide further information for specific needs.

PHILOSOPHY

Bloesch, Donald. *The Ground of Certainty*. WBE, 1971. Calls for the subordination of philosophy to revelation; mainly challenges theologians to interface with issues of world view and contemporary reality.

Clark, Gordon H. *A Christian View of Men and Things: An Introduction to Philosophy*. BBH, 1952. Tends toward rationalism.

Davis, Stephen T. *Faith, Skepticism, and Evidence: An Essay in Religious Epistemology*. Bucknell, 1978. The skeptic acts in many areas of partial knowledge, thus religious belief can be justified; helpful text on epistemology.

Evans, C. Stephen. *Subjectivity and Religious Belief*. WBE, 1978. Helpful introduction to subjective approaches to belief, with examples and comments on limitations; look for a new series, "Contours of Christian Philosophy", edited by Evans for IVP.

Geisler, Norman. *Philosophy of Religion*. ZC, 1974. Thomistic.

Holmer, Paul. *The Grammar of Faith*. HR, 1978. Values knowledge of God and fears loss of theology in approaches that emphasize subjective elements.

Holmes, Arthur F. *All Truth Is God's Truth*. WBE, 1977. An excellent historical survey on views of truth, primarily a text on the relationship between faith and reason.

————. *Christian Philosophy in the Twentieth Century*. Craig, 1969. Explains the limited role of reason and apologetics in a post-Kantian era.

————. *Philosophy: A Christian Perspective*.† IVP, 1975. Helpful, brief introduction.

Mavrodes, George. *Belief in God: A Study in the Epistemology of Religion*. Random House, 1970. Discussion of basic concepts concerning epistemology and experience.

Mitchell, Basil. *The Justification of Religious Belief*. Seabury, 1973. Helpful introductory discussion.

Plantinga, Alvin C. *God and Other Minds*. Cornell University Press, 1967. *God, Freedom, and Evil*. WBE, 1974. *The Nature of Necessity*. OUP, 1974. A leading U.S. philosopher; the second volume approaches both the problem of evil as well as an ontological argument for the existence of God.

Ramm, Bernard. *The Devil, Seven Wormwoods, and God*. WB, 1977. Explores the dangers and contributions of several "enemies" of the Christian faith.

Torrance, Thomas F. *Space, Time, and Incarnation*. OUP, 1978. Examines problems of spatial concepts in Nicene theology.

————. *Theological Science*. OUP, 1978. Valuable work in epistemology and metaphysics; this is science because it is a human endeavor to appreciate God, yet different than other sciences because God is not just part of the universe.

Trueblood, Elton. *Philosophy of Religion*. HR, 1957. A textbook that explains the need for philosophy, the place of rational issues in religion, possible defenses for them in evidence, and approaches to world religions and the problem of evil.

Wainwright, William. *Mysticism*. University of Wisconsin, 1982. Philosophical defense of religious experience; though not especially "evangelical," does not offer explanations that vary with orthodoxy.

Wolterstorff, Nicholas. *Reason Within the Bounds of Religion*. WBE, 1976. Suggests that readers use Christian "control beliefs" in developing individual philosophical perspective.

Yandell, Keith. *Basic Issues in Philosophy of Religion.* Allyn and Bacon, 1971. Thematic textbook.

————. *Christianity and Contemporary Philosophy.* WBE, forthcoming. New in the IFAX series on epistemology and ethics. Defends the cognitive status of Christianity.

HISTORY

Bebbington, D. W. *Patterns in History: A Christian View.* IVP, 1979. A helpful, nontechnical introduction to historiography and philosophy of history.

Cairns, Earle E. *God and Man in Time: A Christian Approach to Historiography.* BBH, 1979. History, both events and interpretation, is important to the Christian; history can be studied scientifically and with an interpretive world view that perceives God's activities.

Marsden, George, and Frank Roberts. *A Christian View of History.* WBE, 1975. The viewpoint of the student of history does make a difference—the approaches of Butterfield, Latourette, and Dooyeweerd are studied; history should not be divided between secular and church viewpoints.

Swanson, Roy. *History in the Making: An Introduction to the Study of the Past.*† IVP, 1978. A helpful introduction to the study and value of history.

SOCIAL SCIENCES

Bufford, Rodger K. *The Human Reflex: Behavioral Psychology in Biblical Perspective.* HR, 1981. Explores concepts and presuppositions of behavioral modification practice and possible applications in family development, Christian education, pastoring, and evangelism.

Cosgrove, Mark. *Psychology Gone Awry: An Analysis of Psychological World Views.* ZC, 1979. Naturalistic psychology cannot provide an adequate framework for studying human nature; Christian theism can.

Custance, Arthur C. *The Mysterious Matter of the Mind.* ZC, 1980. Examines various views on the mind/brain problem; understandable introduction, valuable for more advanced students and professionals.

DeSanto, Charles P., et al., eds. *A Reader in Sociology: Christian Perspectives.* HP, 1980. Forty essays on the nature of sociology, Christian views, issues of institutions, socialization, social change, and the questions of values, presuppositions, methods, and research; topics include male/female studies, aging, economics, race, power, family.

Ellul, Jacques. *The Betrayal of the West*. Seabury, 1978. Reflections of the arts, sciences, structures, and values of civilization; sees possibilities for self-correction in the West to overcome errors and evils.

————. *The New Demons*. Seabury, 1973. Though apparently secular, modern persons are very religious; our culture, a product of Christendom, now bows to myths of technology, advancement, wealth, power, science, paralleled with new signs of irrationalism.

Evans, C. Stephen. *Preserving the Person: A Look at the Human Sciences.*† IVP, 1977. A biblical view of humanness; critical of behavioral and Freudian psychology.

Jeeves, Malcolm. *Psychology and Christianity: The View Both Ways*. IVP, 1979. An informed introduction to integration including a look at methods, ends, values, conversion, guilt, ethical, and moral issues; evaluates contemporary trends in psychology.

MacKay, Donald. *Brains, Machines, and Persons*. WBE, 1980. *Human Science and Human Dignity*. IVP, 1979. Valuable defense of scientific studies, answering fears and misunderstandings of Christians; also indicates the limits of scientific inquiry.

Malony, H. Newton, ed. *Current Perspectives in the Psychology of Religion*. WBE, 1977. Essays on the history and trends of psychological studies of religion; discusses psychodynamics, religious experience, religious development.

Myers, David G. *The Human Puzzle: Psychological Research and Christian Belief*. HR, 1978. A valuable and thoughtful work of integration designed to illuminate the complexities of human nature.

EDUCATION AND WORLD VIEW

Guinness, Os. *The Dust of Death*. IVP, 1973. Discusses establishment and countercultural approaches to society; surveys various social critics (Marcuse, Ellul) and proposes a Christian "Third Way"; topics include technology, violence, Eastern religions, drugs, the occult. Though written before the era of the New Right, foresaw the backlash to the earlier New Left.

Malik, Charles. *Christian Critique of the University.* IVP, 1982. Expected soon; a prophetic critique of the role and future of university education.

McCarthy, Rockne, et al. *Society, State, and Schools: A Case for Structural and Confessional Pluralism.* WBE, 1981. From the Calvin Center for Christian Scholarship sessions on "Public Justice and Educational Equality"; defends pluralism and discusses various approaches for insuring genuine plurality.

Sire, James W. *The Universe Next Door: A Basic World View Catalog.*† IVP, 1976. Helpful guide to the various contemporary world views; start here for guidance on how others perceive themselves and their universe.

Stob, Henry. *Theological Reflections.* WBE, 1981. Twenty-nine essays on science, philosophy, revelation, the church, education, and many other topics.

Wilkes, Peter, ed. *Christianity Challenges the University.* IVP, 1981. Five University of Wisconsin professors deliver public lectures on Christian approaches to their disciplines; includes world views, botany, economics, the reliability of the OT, and medicine.

Wolterstorff, Nicholas P. *Educating for Responsible Action.* WBE, 1980. Helpful theories and strategies for moral education.

SEE ALSO The Christian Church: Christian Education.

THE ARTS

Rookmaaker, H. R. *Art . . . Needs No Justification.*† IVP, 1978. Art as thinking, praying, weeping, and working.

Ryken, Leland. *Triumphs of the Imagination.* IVP, 1979. Studies the form and content of literature with an appreciation for the Bible as a source for literary theory and as a guide for understanding literature from Shakespeare to Eliot, Milton, Tolkien, and others; helps make reading more enjoyable.

Ryken, Leland, ed. *The Christian Imagination: Essays on Literature and the Arts.* BBH, 1981. Gebelein, Thomas Howard, Lewis, Rookmaaker, and many others offer valuable and sometimes differing views on evangelical Christianity and the arts.

SEE ALSO The Christian Life: Miscellaneous Literature.

SCIENCE

Bube, Richard H. *The Human Quest: A New Look at Science and Christian Faith*. WB, 1971. Helpful look at the role of science and Christian misunderstandings; offers a helpful discussion of epistemology (the structures for establishing meaning) and relevant issues in the study of humanness, world view, creation, God's relationship to the world, and socio-ethical implications.

Custance, Arthur C. *The Doorway Papers*. ZC, 1975. A nine-volume attempt at a comprehensive view of Christianity and science with special attention given to issues in the origins of earth and humans; this massive undertaking, generally very dated, provides some insightful essays (well indexed) and many that are less convincing.

Henry, Carl F. H., ed. *Horizons of Science*. HR, 1978. Evangelical scientists speak on life, epistemology, evolution, environment, medical ethics, and psychology; provocative and sophisticated, yet readable for the layperson.

Jones, D. Garth. *Our Fragile Brains*. IVP, 1981. Brain research and implications for a theology of humanness.

Klaasen, Eugene. *Religious Origins of Modern Science*. WBE, 1977. Explains that the belief in an orderly creation forms the basis for science and theology.

MacKay, Donald M. *The Clockwork Image*. IVP, 1974. An exploration into the interface of science and Christianity, with emphasis on the meaning of humanness and on miracles; attempts to argue that determinism does not preclude human freedom.

———. *Science and the Quest for Meaning*. WBE, 1982. Anticipated to be a valuable integration of science and the Christian faith.

Ramm, Bernard. *The Christian View of Science and Scripture*. WBE, 1955. Works toward a philosophy of science that is compatible with Christianity and discovers eighteenth-century Christians who began such a move but got lost in the shuffle; provides helpful commentary on biblical texts and appreciates the full scope of modern sciences.

Utke, Allen R. *Bio-Babel: Can We Survive the New Biology?* JKP, 1978. A clear view of the future in sciences and technology brings out a challenge to the church to understand its environment and its biblical mandates.

WORLD RELIGIONS

Anderson, J. N. D. *Christianity and Comparative Religion.* IVP, 1971. A brief, valuable introductory text on the uniqueness of Christianity in relationship to other faiths.

Eerdmans Handbook to the World's Religions. WBE, 1982. Just released—a scholarly, attractive, readable textbook on past and current religions; illustrated and well indexed.

Neill, Stephen. *Christian Faith and Other Faiths.* OUP, 1970. Major religions receive attention, along with contemporary "primitive" religions and secularism; understands these faiths as if he were "inside" them yet without losing his own Christian viewpoint; an excellent textbook.

Yamamoto, J. Isamu. *Beyond Buddhism.* IVP, 1982. A brief, introductory presentation; accurate and helpful.

BUSINESS

Engstrom, Theodore, and Edward Dayton. *The Art of Management for Christian Leaders.* WB, 1975. *The Work Trap.* WB, 1980. Features many insightful essays on contemporary issues in management, vocations, goal setting, workaholism, training, and so forth.

———. *The Christian Executive.* WB, 1979. Topics covered are "You and Yourself" (time management, handling criticism, and approaches to leadership), "You and Others" (supervision, boards, your spouse, women leaders), and "You and the Organization" (planning, meetings, communication, conflicts).

———. *Strategy for Living.* GL/R, 1976. On the use of goals, setting priorities, planning, acting, evaluating; practical and encouraging.

Greenleaf, Robert. *Servant Leadership.* PP, 1977. A retired AT&T executive offers provocative comments on leadership which focus on serving those who are supervised; a leader can point the right direction, take risks, work with others, and evaluate himself or herself based on how the needs of others are met.

Kaye, Bruce, and Gordon Wenham, eds. *Law, Morality, and the Bible.* IVP, 1978. A symposium that dealt with absolutes and nonabsolutes in ethics; includes biblical themes of grace, freedom, law and order, practical concerns for Christian morality, and relevant issues for the role of law in society.

Kreider, Carl. *The Christian Entrepreneur.* HP, 1980. Ethical and business concerns about ownership, wages, profits, living standards, management, and production receive helpful introductory comments.

Sproul, R. C. *Stronger Than Steel: The Wayne Alderson Story.* HR, 1980. Values concerning the person in the work-place are discussed in light of labor negotiation in the steel industry; provides insightful, fresh ideas for Christian leadership.

Ward, Patricia, and Martha Stout. *Christian Women at Work.* ZC, 1981. A very helpful look at biblical values concerning work and vocation in exploring issues of creativity, finances, life cycles, recurrent difficulties, organizational problems, use of power, and helpful guidelines; men should read this one too, for ourselves and in order to be more sensitive as colleagues.

THE PROFESSIONAL CHRISTIAN SOCIETIES

Conference on Christianity and Literature
c/o Professor Roy Battenhouse, President
English Department
Indiana University
Bloomington, IN 47401
812-337-2133

American Scientific Affiliation
William Sisterson, Executive Secretary
5 Douglas Avenue, Dept. H
Suite 450
Elgin, IL 60120

Conference on Faith and History
  Professor Richard Pierard, Secretary
  Department of History
  Indiana State University
  Terre Haute, IN 47809
  812-232-6311 ext. 2305

Christian Association for Psychological Studies
  Dr. J. Harold Ellens, Executive Secretary
  The University Hills Christian Center
  2700 Farmington Rd.
  Farmington Hills, MI 48018

National Association of Christians in Social Work
  Dr. Peter Lauber, President
  Box 84
  Wheaton, IL 60187
  517-725-7193 (Owosso, MI)

Christians for Urban Justice
  598 Columbia Rd.
  Dorchester, MA 02125
  617-825-1613

Nurses Christian Fellowship
  233 Langdon Street
  Madison, WI 53703
  608-257-0263

Christian Medical Society
  1122 Westgate
  Oak Park, IL 60301
  312-848-9510

Christian Dental Society
  Everett Claus, Executive Secretary
  5235 Sky Trail
  Littleton, CO 80123
  303-794-2290

Missionary Dentists
  Dr. Vaughn Chapman
  1203 N. 200th
  Seattle, WA 98133
  206-546-4188

Christian Legal Society
  P.O. Box 2069
  Oak Park, IL 60303
  312-848-7735

The Lawyers' Christian Fellowship
  3931 E. Main Street
  Columbus, OH 43209
  614-231-6614

Association for the Advancement of Christian Scholarship
  229 College Street
  Toronto, Ontario M5T 1R4
  416-979-2331

National Educators Fellowship, Inc.
  E. A. Patchen, Executive Secretary
  1410 W. Colorado Blvd.
  Pasadena, CA 91105
  213-684-1881

FAVORITE BOOKS

C. Peter Wagner

Personal

The Case For Orthodox Theology, by Edward John Carnell
The Christian View of Science and Scriptures, by Bernard
  Ramm
Your Church Has Real Possibilities, by Robert H. Schuller
The Fourth Dimension, by Paul Y. Cho
American Cultural Patterns, by Edward Stewart

Professional

Understanding Church Growth, by Donald A. McGavran
Why Conservative Churches Are Growing, by Dean M. Kelly
Christianity in Culture, by Charles H. Kraft
Effective Church Planning, by Lyle E. Schaller
The Art of Readable Writing, by Rudolph Flesch

JAMES M. WALL

Personal

You Can't Go Home Again, by Thomas Wolfe
What Is Cinema? by Andre Bazin
Essays on Nature and Grace, by Joseph Sittler
Survey of the New Testament, by Albert Barnett
Roosevelt in Retrospect, by John Gunther

Professional

Systematic Theology, by Paul Tillich
Modern Literature and the Religious Frontier, by Nathan Scott
Pastoral Counseling, by Seward Hiltner
The New Shape of American Religion, by Martin E. Marty
Christ and Culture, by H. Richard Niebuhr

JIM WALLIS

Personal/Professional

The Long Loneliness, by Dorothy Day
Saint Francis of Assisi, by Abbe Omer Englebert
The Autobiography of Malcolm X
The Politics of Jesus, by John Howard Yoder
The Presence of the Kingdom, by Jacques Ellul

JOHN F. WALVOORD

Personal

He That Is Spiritual, by Lewis Sperry Chafer
The expository works of H. A. Ironside

Professional

Systematic Theology, by Lewis Sperry Chafer
Institutes of the Christian Religion, by John Calvin

Systematic Theology, by A. H. Strong
Dogmatic Theology, by William G. T. Shedd
Systematic Theology, by L. Berkhof
Systematic Theology, by Charles Hodge

ROBERT WEBBER

Personal

Beyond Fundamentalism, by Daniel Stevick
An Introduction to Christian Philosophy, by James Spier
The Imitation of Christ, by Thomas à Kempis
The Book of Common Prayer
For the Life of the World, by Alexander Schmemann

Professional

The Documents of Vatican II
The Institutes of the Christian Religion, by John Calvin
Early Christian Doctrines, by J. N. D. Kelly
Byzantine Theology, by John Meyendorff
Christ and Culture, by H. Richard Niebuhr

MIKE YACONELLI

Personal

The Presence of the Kingdom, by Jacques Ellul
The Technological Society, by Jacques Ellul
Tracks of a Fellow Struggler, by John Claypool
A Severe Mercy, by Sheldon Vanauken
Epistle to the Romans, by Karl Barth

Professional

Telling the Truth, by Frederick Buechner
Identity: Youth and Crisis, by Erik Erikson
Daily Study Bible, by William Barclay
The Preaching Event, by John Claypool

PHILIP YANCEY

Personal

Orthodoxy, by G. K. Chesterton
Telling the Truth, by Frederick Buechner

Anna Karenina, by Leo Tolstoy
Brother to a Dragonfly, by Will Campbell
The Problem of Pain, by C. S. Lewis

Professional

The Idiot, by Fyodor Dostoyevsky
The Gulag Archipelago, by Aleksandr Solzhenitsyn
Symbolism and Belief, by Edwyn Bevan
Pilgrim at Tinker Creek, by Annie Dillard
Natural Law in the Spiritual World, by Henry Drummond

Index

O

O'Collins, Gerald S. J., 107
O'Connor, Elizabeth, 2, 5, 7, 10, 82, 95, 141, 147–148, 151
O'Connor, Flannery, 19, 20, 96
Oden, Thomas C., 103, 158
Ogilvie, Lloyd, 141–142
Ohsberg, N. O., 158
Oraker, James R., 13
Orr, James Edwin, 83, 88, 94, 144
Ortiz, Juan Carlos, 5
Osborne, Grant R., 51, 53, 121, 159–160
Osterhaven, M. Eugene, 91
Outka, Gene, 125
Outler, Albert C., 93, 142, 176
Owen, John, 126

P

Packer, James I., 2–3, 5, 31, 35, 41, 103, 105, 116, 134, 176
Padavano, Anthony, 25
Padilla, Rene C., 35, 84, 163
Palmer, Earl, 142
Palmer, H., 55
Palmer, Phoebe, 83
Pannell, William E., 31, 139–140, 163, 175
Pannenberg, Wolfhart, 24, 93, 103, 107, 120
Pascal, Blaise, 23, 93, 123, 142, 143
Paton, Alan, 126, 180
Paton, David M., 172
Patterson, Ben, 143
Pattison, E. Mansell, 151
Paul, Cecil R., 154
Paulus, Trina, 22
Paxson, Ruth, 24
Payne, David F., 62, 77
Payne, J. Barton, 54
Peck, Scott, 96
Pelikan, Jaroslav, 89–90, 91
Penner, Clifford, 11, 13
Penner, Joyce, 11, 13
Percy, Walker, 18
Perkins, John, 176
Perkins, Pheme, 48, 58
Peters, George W., 167
Peters, Ted, 120
Peterson, Eugene H., 10, 156, 158, 181

Peterson, Lorraine, 21
Phillips, J. B., 25
Phillips, Keith W., 177
Phypers, David, 109
Piepkorn, Arthur C., 88
Pierard, Richard, V., 132, 134, 135
Pink, Arthur, 96
Pinnock, Clark H., 32, 108, 116, 121, 122, 143, 179
Pippert, Rebecca Manley, 5, 96, 155, 174, 177
Plantinga, Alvin C., 185
Plantinga, Theodore, 5
Plato, 94
Pope, Liston, 182
Powell, John, 25
Prior, Kenneth F. W., 177
Progoff, Ira, 141
Purkiser, W. T., 70, 74
Purtill, Richard, 179

Q

Quebedeaux, Richard, 30–31, 35, 143–144

R

Rainford, Marcus, 82
Ramm, Bernard L., 32, 51, 53, 88, 105, 110, 116, 130, 179, 185, 189–190, 193
Ramsey, A., 111
Ramseyer, Robert L., 164–165, 167
Rasmussen, Larry L., 128–129, 138
Rauschenbusch, Walter, 124, 125
Rayburn, Robert, 151
Reeve, Pamela, 22–23
Reicke, Bo, 48
Renwick, A. M., 85, 88
Restak, Richard, 26
Richards, Lawrence O., 6, 151, 159, 160, 162
Richardson, Alan, 78
Richardson, Peter, 130
Ridderbos, Herman N., 55, 74, 81, 116, 120
Rifkin, Jeremy, 182
Rinker, Rosalind, 10
Roberts, Frank, 186
Roberts, Robert C., 93
Robertson, O. Palmer, 75
Robertson, Pat, 144
Robinson, Haddon W., 154
Robinson, J. Armitage, 68

Stringfellow, William, 24, 127, 130, 131–132, 135
Strong, A. H., 195
Sturzo, Luigi, 124
Suenens, Leon Joseph, 105
Swanson, Roy, 186
Sweet, J. P., 70
Swindoll, Charles R., 6, 22

T
Taber, Charles R., 183
Tasker, R. V. G., 25, 57
Taylor, John B., 64
Taylor, John V., 139, 183
Taylor, Ken, 21, 22
Taylor, Richard S., 70, 74, 136
Taylor, Willard S., 70, 74
Teilhard de Chardin, Pierre, 93
Temple, William, 142
ten Boom, Corrie, 14, 15
Tenney, Merrill C., 41–42, 48, 79
Terrien, Samuel, 76
Tetlon, Elizabeth M., 80, 156
Thielicke, Helmut, 10, 59, 61, 95, 98, 102, 103, 106, 107, 111–112, 113, 126, 127–128, 130, 143, 146, 147, 152–153, 154, 158, 180
Thiselton, Anthony, 33, 37, 55, 56, 84
Thomas à Kempis, 96, 123, 195
Thompson, John A., 46, 61, 64, 107
Thompson, W. Ralph, 58
Tillich, Paul, 92, 194
Tippett, Alan R., 168
Tolkien, J. R. R., 16, 17, 18, 96, 189
Tollers, Vincent L., 53
Tolstoy, Leo, 126, 181, 196
Toon, Peter, 89, 91, 108, 120, 147
Topel, L. John, 103
Torrance, Thomas F., 105, 141–142, 146, 152, 185
Torrey, R. A., 82, 96
Tournier, Paul, 83, 95, 112, 113, 123, 125, 157, 158
Tozer, A. W., 6–7, 82, 84, 94, 181
Traina, Robert, 144
Travis, Stephen, 41
Trobisch, Walter, 13
Trocmé, Andre, 45, 50
Troeltsch, Ernst, 125, 182
Trotti, John, 37

Trueblood, Elton, 50, 124, 152, 162, 185
Tupper, E. Frank, 93
Turner, George A., 91
Tuttle, Gary, 53
Tuttle, Robert G., Jr., 93, 111
Tweedie, Donald, 158

U
Ugolino (Brother), 82
Underhill, Evelyn, 83
Updike, John, 18
Urban, Wilbur M., 96
Utke, Allen R., 190

V
Vanauken, Sheldon, 14, 15, 195
van den Loos, H., 50
van Ruler, Arnold A., 42
Van Til, Henry, 125
Venning, Ralph, 96
Verduin, Leonard, 114, 135
Verkuyl, Johannes, 140, 168
Virkler, Henry, 53
von Rad, Gerhard, 61, 63
Vree, Dale, 183

W
Wagner, C. Peter, 168, 193–194
Wainwright, Geoffrey, 100, 103
Wainwright, William, 185–186
Wakatama, Pius, 169, 172
Walker, Alan, 168
Walker, G. S. M., 89
Wall, James M., 194
Wallace, Ronald S., 64
Wallechinsky, David, 25
Wallis, Jim, 81, 161, 162, 163, 172, 194
Walter, J. A., 130–131
Waltke, Bruce, 41, 53
Walvoord, John F., 64, 120, 194–195
Wangerin, Walter, 18–19, 20
Ward, Patricia, 191
Warfield, B. B., 81, 115, 126, 143
Watson, David, 177
Watson, Thomas, 96
Watts, John D. W., 58, 65
Webber, George W., 182
Webber, Robert E., 2, 6, 32, 36, 131, 135, 195

DATE DUE

GAYLORD			PRINTED IN U.S.A.